and the works that have immortalized both. What will make this book a pleasure to read and reread is the grace and ease . . . with which this gifted author weaves the various strands of his story into a narrative that is at once complex, allusive, and engagingly accessible. . . . I can't think of a more charming, informative guide to Shakespeare and his world . . . and I don't know of any introduction to the plays that can match this one for the elegance with which it evokes the atmosphere of the theater's golden moment.''

—John F. Andrews, Editor,
The Shakespeare Guild

S. SCHOENBAUM is Distinguished Professor of Renaissance Literature at the University of Maryland and the Director of the Center for Renaissance and Baroque Studies. He is the author of nine books, including *Shakespeare's Lives* and *William Shakespeare: The Globe and the World.* He lives in Washington, D.C.

Shakespeare

His Life, His English, His Theater

S. Schoenbaum

A SIGNET CLASSIC

SIGNET CLASSIC
Published by the Penguin Group
Penguin Books USA Inc., 375 Hudson Street,
New York, New York 10014, U.S.A.
Penguin Books Ltd, 27 Wrights Lane, London W8 5TZ, England
Penguin Books Australia Ltd, Ringwood, Victoria, Australia
Penguin Books Canada Ltd, 2801 John Street,
Markham, Ontario, Canada L3R 1B4
Penguin Books (N.Z.) Ltd, 182–190 Wairau Road, Auckland 10, New Zealand

Penguin Books Ltd, Registered Offices: Harmondsworth, Middlesex, England

Published by Signet Classic, an imprint of New American Library, a division
of Penguin Books USA Inc.

First Signet Classic Printing, August, 1990
10 9 8 7 6 5 4 3 2 1

For Marilyn again

Contents

Preface

Scholarship, as I am fond of saying, is process. The planning of this long-meditated book moved appreciably closer to a final consummation during a fortnight in May 1988 in—where else?—Sofia, Bulgaria. So I should like, before all else, to say an appreciative word about the Bulgarian connection. My room at the Grand Sofia Hotel overlooked the handsome shell-shaped square with its imposing equestrian statue of Czar Alexander II, who in 1878 liberated Bulgaria from captivity to the Ottoman Empire; in the background, the National Assembly, and beyond that the Alexander Nevsky Cathedral, both resplendent with their golden cupolas.

I had come with my wife, Marilyn, to Sofia to give lectures at the University of Sofia on Shakespearean biography, which for some years had been at the forefront of my scholarly activities, and on *Macbeth* and *Antony and Cleopatra*, and to conduct a seminar on Shakespeare's sonnets. For idle moments I had taken along with me a copy of the penultimate draft of *Shakespeare: His Life, His English, His Theater*. In an atmosphere of happy collegiality I conversed with a number of members of the Sofia faculty: Professor Janna Molkova, the head of the English Department, Professor Alexander Shurbanov, and Professor Vladimir Phillipov. Above all, I would like to express grateful appreciation to Ms. Boika Sokolova-Lozarnova, who brightened my days in Sofia and has since brightened them with her correspondence. Nor should I fail to mention the spouses, Vladimir Lazarov and Daniela Shurbanov, or the engaging postgraduate students who ministered to our

9

needs, Irena Nikolova and Plaumen Batembergsky. Derek Roper was also on hand from the University of Sheffield in England. He had come to give a Byron lecture—shades of *Fortunes of War!*—Byron being something of a national hero in those parts. Mr. Roper and I met by chance at the airport after our plane touched down. As a result of subsequent talks with these worthies, I introduced a number of small emendations into my text, and began to map out a substantial section that was yet to be composed.

To paraphrase someone who knew whereof he spoke, the person who spent all his/her time reading what had been written about Shakespeare wouldn't have time to read anything else—including Shakespeare. And that individual would no more than scratch the surface. Out of compassion for the ordinary reader I have resisted the temptation to document the pages that follow, but I have included as an appendix a list of a number of items that struck me as being both useful and accessible.

To these I should here like to add *The Oxford Shakespeare*, with which I have myself been honored to have some association. The text of *The Complete Works* in that edition (1986), of which Stanley Wells and Gary Taylor were the general editors, is of course what incomparably counts the most, but students will consult with profit—as I myself do almost every day—the prefatory notes to individual items contained therein, as well as the editors' *Textual Companion* (1987), compiled with the assistance of John Jowett and William Montgomery. Acknowledgment is due also to *The World and I*, which published my article, "Shakespearean Themes" (April 1989), containing a small portion of the matter incorporated in the pages that follow.

Diane Clark, a word-processor whiz who has been working with me for a decade, managed to unscramble an incongruous mix of handwritten and typescript copy to produce print-out that my editor and the printers could cope with after the sharp eye of Barbara Eaton had a go at it.

I am obliged to Professor Richard Hosley for his careful perusal of the section on playhouses (pages 40–62) and for suggestions that saved me from error.

Quotations from Shakespeare derive from individual editions of plays in the Signet Classic Shakespeare, of which Sylvan Barnet is the General Editor. Michelle Green had a final helpful look at the typescript before it went to the printers. At Penguin Books USA Inc., Ms. Rosemary Ahern and Ms. Connie Lofton were patient and sympathetically helpful editors.

I would also like to thank John Andrews and Sylvan Barnet for taking the time to read my typescript, despite all their other pressing obligations. Needless to say, any errors, limitations, and oversights are strictly my own responsibility. Should this book be translated into Bulgarian, as I hope may come to pass, I will be back at the Grand Sofia Hotel to raise a glass to the health of all my well-wishers.

—S.S.
September 1989

1

Origins, Education,
and Embarkations

Displayed until recently in Holy Trinity Church, hard
by the river Avon's bank at the southern edge of the Old
Town district of Stratford-upon-Avon, the town's parish
registers memorialize the most notable events in the life
of any community: birth, marriage, and death. The bap-
tismal register records the christening of William, son
of John Shakespeare, on April 26, 1564. Posterity has
chosen to celebrate the advent of the national poet on
the 23rd, the day set aside for the feast of St. George,
the patron saint of England. Birth certificates, as we
know them, did not then yet exist, but a three-day interval between birth and baptism does not strain cre-
dulity. Of the date of Shakespeare's death we have more
certainty, for his monument in Stratford Church tells us
that the poet died on April 23, 1616, when he was in
his fifty-third year. The burial register lists his intern-
ment on April 26. On the slab covering Shakespeare's
grave in the church chancel, these words are carved:

> Good friend for Jesus' sake forbear
> To dig the dust enclosed here.
> Blessed be the man that spares these stones,
> And cursed be he that moves these bones.

Whether written by Shakespeare or another, this celebrated malediction has effectively accomplished its purpose, for no church official—sexton or clerk—has ever
sought to move Shakespeare's bones, although mis-

guided enthusiasts have sometimes come armed with
shovels and pails.

For the student of Shakespeare's writings, what illumination may be gleaned from the record of what happened to him between christening and burial, that record
which centuries of scholarly diligence has brought to
light? Very little, according to an oft repeated cultural
commonplace. Writing in the eighteenth century, the
learned Shakespearian editor George Steevens summed
up knowledge in a single memorable sentence: "All
that is known with any degree of certainty concerning
Shakespeare is that he was born at Stratford-upon-Avon,
married and had children there, went to London, where
he commenced acting and wrote poems and plays, re-
\rned to Stratford, made his will, died, and was buried." More recently, George Bernard Shaw has allowed,
"Everything we know about Shakespear can be put into
a half-hour sketch"; in the upshot, Shaw required not
a half hour but only a paragraph for his sketch.

As often the case, conventional wisdom is not entirely misguided. From the pen of Shakespeare's colleague—and most formidable playwriting rival—Ben
Jonson, we have prefaces and prologues, tributary verses
in Latin and English to esteemed personages, a commonplace book *(Timber, or Discoveries)* encapsulating
some of his literary principles and prejudices, an English grammar, and a translation of Horace's *Art of Poetry.* In 1616 Jonson brought together his own plays and
saw them through the press in a grand folio volume,
thus providing a precedent for the 1623 Shakespeare
Folio—the collected edition brought together by Shakespeare's longtime theatrical associates. Jonson's conversation, rich in opinions and personal anecdotes, was
jotted down by the Scottish litterateur William Drum-
mond, who, for a couple of weeks in 1618, welcomed
Jonson as his house guest at Hawthornden. Jonson's ag-
gressively assertive personality ensured notice. For
Shakespeare we have no such memorabilia expressive
of authorial personality: no letters, no conversations; it
goes without saying, no diaries. Those records we do

have mostly betoken formal, often legal, occasions:
register entries, deeds of purchase, court notices, a last
will and testament, and the like. Yet for Shakespeare
more records have survived than for most Elizabethan
dramatists, and these are not without interest or significance. The essential facts may be expeditiously
summed up.

The Shakespeares came of sturdy Midlands yeoman
stock. The poet's paternal grandfather, Richard, a hus-
bandman, tilled the soil and pastured his livestock in
the environs of Snitterfield, a village some three miles
northeast of Stratford. He performed jury service, appraised the inventories of deceased locals—the office of
friends and good neighbors—and paid his fines for failing to yoke or ring his swine, or to attend the manor
court at castled Warwick, six miles distant. His lands
he rented from a prosperous local squire, Robert Arden.

Richard Shakespeare had at least two sons. One, John
(William's father), married the squire's youngest daughter, Mary, who had lately (following her father's death)
inherited the Asbyes estate of fifty acres. By then John
had migrated to Stratford, where he set himself up as a
glover and "whittawer," or curer and whitener of skins,
a profession requiring a seven-year apprenticeship. John
prospered. He had subsidiary dealings in wool, bought
lands and houses, including the double house in Henley
Street identified by tradition as the birthplace of William Shakespeare.

The Shakespeares had eight children, four sons and
four daughters. One, Edmund, followed in his elder
brother's footsteps by becoming an actor in London, for
which troupe is not known. He died young. John Shakespeare was apparently illiterate—Snitterfield had no
school—and signed documents with his mark, a pair of
glover's compasses or a cross. (His wife too could not
sign her name, as was the case with as many as eighty-
nine percent of women in this period.) Notwithstanding, civic recognition came to him. At first appointed
to minor offices, such as inspector of ale and bread, he

rose to become, in 1568, the bailiff of Stratford—mayor,
we would say. After election to the highest office his
town had to offer, Master Shakespeare considered ap-
plying to the Heralds' College for a coat of arms. But
nothing came of the request, although John received
from the college a "pattern," or sketch, of his arms.
Years later, when his son William, now the famous poet
and playwright, applied (as it seems) in his behalf, the
herald noted, "And the man was a magistrate in
Stratford-upon-Avon. A justice of peace, he married a
daughter and heir of Arden, and was of good substance
and habilité."

An anecdote set down in the next century recalls John
Shakespeare as a "merry-cheeked old man in his
shop." But hard times overtook him, as economic re-
cession gripped the Midlands. After 1575 John purchased no properties; three years later the aldermen
excused him from paying his weekly tax for poor relief;
in 1572 he appeared in a list, twice drawn up, of nine
persons who stayed away from divine services "for fear
of process for debt," arrests by sheriff's officers then
being permitted on Sundays. In fact, recusancy—the refusal to attend Church of England services because of
a continuing adherence to the Catholic faith—is the
more likely explanation for John's nonattendance. Fortunately, the education of his children did not put John
out of pocket. According to an early biographer, Nicholas Rowe, still in touch with local tradition, the dramatist's father bred him "for some time at a free
school." Although pupil enrollments at the King's New
School of Stratford-upon-Avon in the sixteenth century
have unsurprisingly failed to survive, there is no reason
to doubt Rowe.

The school was a superior institution of its kind, the
masters holding bachelor's and master's degrees from
Oxford University and drawing better stipends than most
of their provincial counterparts. Here, after acquiring
the rudiments of reading and writing at an attached *petty*
school (not the grammar school proper; at the petty
school the children—aged four or five—would be taught

the basics by an usher or *abecedarius*). A child would spend long hours memorizing by rote his Latin grammar, an experience perhaps recalled with rueful amusement in *The Merry Wives of Windsor,* in which the bumbling Welsh parson-pedagogue Sir Hugh Evans puts little William through a model interrogation for the benefit of his disgruntled mother:

Evans. Show me now, William, some declensions of your pronouns.
William. Forsooth, I have forgot.
Evans. It is *qui, quae, quod.* If you forget your *qui's,* your *quae's,* and your *quod's,* you must be preeches [i.e., flogged]. (IV.i.71–76)

Having survived Lily's *Grammatica Latina,* scholars proceeded to their Latin axioms and phrases, then to *Aesop's Fables,* and the bucolic eclogues of Baptista Spagnuoli, called Mantuanus ("Old Mantuan, old Mantuan!" rapturously declared Holofernes, the schoolmaster in *Love's Labor's Lost,* "Who understandeth thee not, loves thee not."). Terence too joined the curriculum, and Plautus's plays were read, although less often. In some schools the children acted a scene from either as a weekly exercise.

Other literary classics included the poetry of Virgil, maybe Horace, and certainly Ovid, who would remain for Shakespeare a lifelong favorite. In the early *Titus Andronicus,* Ovid's *Metamorphoses* is brought onstage as an essential property when the raped and mutilated Lavinia turns the book's leaves with her handless stumps; "Lucius, what book is that she tosseth so?" Titus demands of his grandson; and the boy: "Grandsire, 'Tis Ovid's Metamorphoses; / My mother gave it me" (IV.i.41–43). Near the end of his career, in *The Tempest,* Shakespeare returned to Ovid for his most poignant echo, when Prospero renounces his magic and prepares to drown his book (V.i.50–57).

The grammar-school course of study would have also

featured rhetoric and moral philosophy (Cicero) and history, limited to Roman classics: Caesar or Sallust, the latter noted for his terse, epigrammatic style. In the upper school the students encountered Greek, with the Greek New Testament their source for constructions. Thus would Shakespeare have acquired the small Latin and less Greek with which Jonson credits him, although by present-day standards the Latin, at least, was far from negligible.

How long Shakespeare attended the Stratford free school we can only guess; Rowe reports that the father was forced, because of "the narrowness of his circumstances, and the want of assistance at home . . . to withdraw him from thence." Shakespeare never proceeded to university, a consideration that has prompted anti-Stratfordian fantasies respecting the authorship of the canon, as has the fact that blue blood did not course in his veins. Snobbery has perhaps played its part in such movements, having as their candidate the Earl of Oxford or another noble lord, or Francis Bacon, Baron Verulam: learned counsel, statesman, philosopher, and essayist. Perhaps even a syndicate wrote the plays. After all, how could a Stratford glover's son have written all those works upon which the world has set so inestimable a value? But then, how could anyone have written them? In the last resort, supreme creation has its incomprehensible aspect. A university career, moreover, would not necessarily have better equipped a young man for a career in letters: we do well not to confuse a modern liberal arts curriculum with the altogether narrower course of study, inherited from the Middle Ages, of an English university in the sixteenth century. The formidably learned Jonson never went to university either, and other literary eminences, past and present, have endured similar privations. Like some of these, Shakespeare must have early on acquired a taste for reading, a quick and retentive memory, and an abiding fascination with people and ideas. His own genius and the bookstalls of Paul's Churchyard—center of London's book trade—would furnish the rest.

Very early on, Shakespeare married and had children. On November 28, 1582, the Bishop of Worcester, in whose diocese Stratford lay, issued a bond authorizing the marriage of "William Shakespere" and "Ann Hathwey of Stratford" after one asking of the banns rather than the customary three. Pronouncement of the banns in church allowed members to come forward if they knew of any hindrance to matrimony. The Hathaways in fact dwelt in Shottery, a settlement of farmhouses in Stratford parish. Anne's interests were safeguarded by two sureties, Fulke Sandells and John Richardson, who undertook to pay the bishop or his officers £40 should any action be brought against them for issuance of the license. (Much confusion—and some romance—has surrounded another entry, made the previous day in the bishop's register. It names Anne Whateley of Temple Grafton as the bride. The other Anne appears here once and nowhere else. She seems never to have existed, the entry clerk having made a careless slip—he had lately had dealings with a Whateley in a different context.) Shakespeare's wife was probably the eldest daughter of Richard Hathaway, a substantial Warwickshire yeoman; his spacious thatched farmhouse, visited by pilgrims as Anne Hathaway's Cottage, still stands. In his will, dated September 1, 1581, and drawn up shortly before his death, Hathaway specifies no daughter Anne, but the names Anne and Agnes were used interchangeably, and the latter was bequeathed ten marks (£6.13s.4d.) to be forthcoming on her wedding day. Anne was seven or eight years her husband's senior and pregnant; hence the need to hasten matrimony. The Stratford register records the baptism, on May 26, 1583, of Susanna, daughter to William Shakespeare. Two years later his twins, Hamnet and Judith, were christened in the Holy Trinity font. They were named after lifelong family friends, Hamnet and Judith Sadler. Long afterward Hamnet Sadler witnessed the dramatist's will and was remembered in it with a bequest for a memorial ring. Hamnet Shakespeare was already dead; buried, at the age of eleven, on August 11, 1596.

Between the birth of the twins and the first reference to Shakespeare in London, seven years elapsed. For this interval, known to biography as the Lost Years, only a single reference to the name survives, this in litigation pressed by John Shakespeare over a sum of money in 1588: concern with mundane affairs did not cease during the year of the Armada. The period is not, however, bereft of legend, which flourishes in such voids. The most sensational concerns Shakespeare as poacher. Not too long after the dramatist's death, an obscure Gloucestershire clergyman, Richard Davies, noted that Shakespeare was "much given to all unluckiness in stealing venison and rabbits, particularly from Sir _____ Lucy"—the knight's Christian name, Thomas, escapes Davies—"who had him oft whipped and sometimes imprisoned and at last made him fly his native country to his great advancement." In the next century Rowe, who would not have had access to his predecessor's jottings, gave the story in his *Life*, and included the full name:

He had, by a misfortune common enough to young fellows, fallen into ill company; and, amongst them, some that made a frequent practice of deer-stealing engaged him with them more than once in robbing a park that belonged to Sir Thomas Lucy of Cherlecot, near Stratford. For this he was prosecuted by that gentleman, as he thought, somewhat too severely; and in order to revenge that ill usage, he made a ballad upon him. And though this, probably the first essay of his poetry, be lost, yet it is said to have been so very bitter, that it redoubled the prosecution against him to that degree that he was obliged to leave his business and family in Warwickshire for some time, and shelter himself in London.

(In *The Merry Wives of Windsor*, I.i.31, Falstaff has "committed disparagements" upon Shallow, a Gloucestershire justice of the peace. "Knight," he upbraids the fat roisterer, "you have beaten my men, killed my deer, and broke open my lodge.") For long accepted without demur by most biographers, the deer-poaching tradition has certain inherent improbabilities: Lucy, for example, did not then have a park at Charlecote to lure clandestine hunters. The episode is now consigned to the Shakespeare mythos, although some responsible scholars are willing to allow it a possible grain of truth.

The mythos has yielded other intriguing tidbits. Half a century after the dramatist's death, John Aubrey, setting down notes for the disordered manuscripts of his *Brief Lives,* said of Shakespeare, "Though as Benjamin Jonson says of him, that he had but little Latin and less Greek, he understood Latin pretty well, for he had been in his younger years a schoolmaster in the country"— intelligence Aubrey credits (in a marginal note) to "Mr. Beeston": presumably William Beeston, the son of Shakespeare's one-time acting colleague Christopher. Elsewhere in his *Life* Aubrey writes that Shakespeare, "being inclined naturally to poetry and acting, came to London, I guess, about eighteen, and was an actor at one of the playhouses and did act exceedingly well." These reports may appear to be mutually contradictory, and perhaps they are; but it is also worth noting that in this period schoolmasters often had an early start—for example, the astrologer-physician Simon Forman, who saw Shakespeare's plays performed at the Globe during their author's lifetime, was teaching as an unlicensed usher (as assistant masters were until the last century termed in England) while still in his teens.

In the absence of verifiable data, speculation flourishes, biography (like nature) abhorring a vacuum. Could our William Shakespeare be the William Shakshafte cited in the 1581 will of Alexander Houghton of Lea Hall, near Preston in Lancashire? To his half brother Thomas this Houghton bequeathed "all his musical instruments and play-clothes," and if Thomas was not inclined to keep players, then it is the testator's wish that Sir Thomas Hesketh (his friend and second wife's relation) keep the instruments and play-clothes: "And

I most heartily require the said Sir Thomas to be friendly unto Fulk Gillom and William Shakeshafte now dwelling with me, and either to take them into his service or else to help them to some good master." Variant spellings of surnames were by no means uncommon at this time: the dramatist Shakespeare is (for example) listed in one record as "Shaxberd."

The Houghtons were enormously wealthy landholders who clung tenaciously to the old faith in a district where Catholics, treated with toleration, were numerous. Still, one had to be careful. Was the young Shakespeare similarly persuaded, and engaged by the Houghtons as a schoolmaster or (more likely) assistant schoolmaster? Once engaged, his aptitudes would lead him to take part in interludes and "musics" in the Houghtons' magnificent Banquetting Hall. Lancashire is a far way from Stratford, and the Warwickshire Shakespeares had no Lancashire connections. But William's schoolmaster John Cottom, himself Catholic, hailed from those parts, and close at hand to the Hoghtons; eventually he returned to Lancashire. Cottom might have provided his pupil with the Lancashire connection. Shakespeare could then, by an easy transition, have passed into Lord Strange's men: the Stanleys, powerful aristocrats, had houses in Lancashire, and the company's patron, Ferdinando, Lord Strange, was a Stanley. The first troupe of which we know Shakespeare definitely to have been a member evolved out of a nucleus of actors previously with Strange's men. Many Shakeshaftes, however, including some named William, dwelt in Lancashire and neighboring Cheshire. In the end, the arguments for identification are no more than circumstantial, and have been available for some time; but their recent reassertion, vigorously and learnedly argued by E. A. J. Honigmann in *Shakespeare: The "Lost Years"* (1985) deservedly has attracted much notice.

Others have suggested that Shakespeare spent the Lost Years as a conveyancer's clerk occupying a desk in the office of a prosperous country lawyer (a view which since the eighteenth century has appealed to generations of attorneys, including the Victorian Chief Justice, Lord Campbell). Or perhaps Shakespeare found employment, like Thomas Kyd's father, as a scrivener, or served as a foot soldier in the campaigns in the Low Countries. Or maybe he visited Italy, the scene of so many of his plays, but of course Shakespeare may have picked up his happy familiarity with things Italian from interchanges with any of the many Italians then residing in, or visiting, London. Whether the youthful Shakespeare pursued any of these—or any other—occupations, or merely tended his father's shop, he did not do so for very long. Possibly he joined one of the touring companies—Leicester's, the Queen's, or another—that touched down in Stratford in the late eighties to perform at the Guild Hall and the inn yards of Bridge Street. Whatever indeed happened, we know for a fact that by 1592 Shakespeare had established himself in the metropolitan theatrical world as actor and playwright, for in that year another dramatist, dying in misery and squalor, in his last outpourings, in *Greene's Groatsworth of Wit, bought with a million of Repentance*, subjected Shakespeare to a venomous attack.

2

Shakespeare's English

The headmaster of London's Merchant Taylors' School, Richard Mulcaster, might in 1581 laud English as "a tongue of itself both deep in conceit and frank in delivery," no language being better able "to utter all arguments, either with more pith or greater plainness, than our English tongue is, if the English utterer be as skilful in the matter, which he is to utter, as the foreign utterer is." The Stratford grammar-school curriculum, however, included no instruction in the mechanisms of Shakespeare's own language, except for what analogies with Latin grammar might provide. Treatises existed: for example, Thomas Smith's *Dialogue concerning the Correct and Emended Writing of the English Language*, published in Latin in 1568, which superfluously increased the alphabet to thirty-four letters, or John Hart's *Method or Comfortable Beginning for All Unlearned, Whereby They May Be Taught to Read English* (1570), which, using special characters for *ch, sh,* and other consonantal combinations, proved uncomfortable. Prescriptive school grammars, now themselves by and large antiques, came into existence only in the eighteenth century. Shakespeare and his schoolmates managed very well without such rigors.

The language in which they communicated linguists term Early Modern English. Although Modern—or Elizabethan—English differs in some fundamental respects from the English of today, modern readers have no difficulty in understanding the essentials of the language as it was used four centuries ago. In theaters, directors may abridge or transpose scenes, or here and here alter words that have changed meaning or dropped out of everyday currency altogether, but the plays that Shakespeare created almost four hundred years ago still move and entertain spectators who have never studied them, in more or less the form in which he wrote them (archaisms are often updated), despite changes in the minutiae—if not the fundamentals—of expression. Such divergences may be illustrated by the small change of language, such as the choice of a preposition: "But thou wilt be avenged *on* my misdeeds" *(Richard III,* I.iv.70); "He came *of* an errand to me" *(The Merry Wives of Windsor,* I.iv.75); "And what delight shall she have to look *on* the devil" *(Othello,* II.i.224–25); and ". . . we are such stuff / As dreams are made *on*" *(The Tempest,* IV,i.156–57)—where today we would use, respectively, *for, on, at,* and *of.*

Linguistically, Shakespeare's formative experience was much more similar to our own than it was to that of Chaucer, just two hundred years earlier. In such matters—as in others—a century can make a big difference. Shortly after Chaucer's death in 1400 (he was the exact contemporary of the Richard II whose tragedy Shakespeare dramatized), the so-called Great Vowel Shift had begun to manifest itself. All the long vowels that could be—in phonetic terms—raised (this refers to the tongue in relation to the roof of the mouth), gradually came to be elevated in their articulation, and those that could not (phonetically *i = u =*) became diphthongs *(ai, au).* Thus did English vowels attain their approximate modern pronunciation; Middle English *wi = f* became Modern English *wife, shoure* became *shower.* By the sixteenth century the process of discarding the ancient inflectional endings had pretty well run its course. Nouns now generally added *s* to signal their plural, but a few old weak plurals ending in *n* survived (e.g., the modern *oxen);* so in Shakespeare we find, in addition to the modern form, *eyen (eyes)* and *shoon (shoes.) Kine* turns up once (in *1 Henry IV), cows* not at all.

Among the verbs, *hath* and *doth* coexisted with *has* and *does,* with the older forms—especially in the case of *hath*—predominating; they would remain in use until the eighteenth century. The auxiliary verb *do* was increasingly associated with asking questions or negating sentences, or for emphasis. Thus, in *3 Henry VI* (V.vi.71–75), after young Prince Edward has been stabbed to death on Tewkesbury plain, his mother, Queen Margaret, begs his murderers to slay her too:

> *Queen Margaret.* What? Wilt thou not? Then, Clarence *do* it thou.
> *Clarence.* By Heaven, I will not *do* thee so much ease.
> *Queen Margaret.* Good Clarence, *do;* sweet Clarence, *do* thou *do* it.
> *Clarence.* Didst thou not hear me swear I would not *do* it?

Chaucer's fellow Londoners used the *-eth* ending for the third person singular of the present tense: "he liveth" and "he walketh." By Shakespeare's time the common colloquial form ended in *-s*, or *-es* where pronunciation required a syllable, e.g., *watch, watches.* But one was free to use either old or new, the former generally being shown some preference for dignified literary purposes or to meet the metrical requirements of the verse line. In *The Merchant of Venice* Portia pleads,

> The quality of mercy is not strained;
> It drop*peth* as a gentle rain from heaven
> Upon the place beneath. It is twice blessed;
> It bless*eth* him that give*s* and him that take*s*.
> 'Tis mightiest in the mightiest; it become*s*
> The thronèd monarch better than his crown.
> (IV.i.183–88)

In the trial scene as a whole, the *-s* termination outnumbers *-eth* by two to one. "But look," Horatio points out

the sentries at Elsinore as the first scene of *Hamlet*
draws to a close,

the morn in russet mantle clad
Walks o'er the dew of yon high eastward hill.
(I.i.166–67)

Walks as a verb occurs seventeen times in Shakespeare,
walketh not at all. The verb *lives* appears 129 times,
liveth three times. "Heaven is here," Romeo protests
to Friar Laurence, "where Juliet *lives*," but Falstaff,
rising up after playing dead on Shrewsbury field in *1
Henry IV*, offers as his apologia that "to counterfeit
dying when a man thereby *liveth*, is to be no counterfeit." As Shakespeare's career proceeded, he used the
eth ending less frequently.

Working without the rigidities espoused by the ped-
agogues of a later age, and without the now taken-
for-granted handy adjunct of a desk dictionary, Shakespeare is untrammeled by modern anxieties about
correctness—or, rather, what we now judge to be correct. (The earliest dictionaries were bilingual vocabularies
prepared by schoolmasters for those studying Latin or
one of the Romance tongues [Italian, French, Spanish]
or compilations of "hard words," such as Robert Caw-
drey's *Table Alphabetical, containing and teaching the
true writing and understanding of hard usual words
borrowed from the Hebrew, Greek, Latin, or French,
&c.* [1604], the first of its kind.) Double negatives he
takes in stride. "You may *deny* that you were *not* the
mean," Richard upbraids Edward's queen in *Richard III*.
Shakespeare can say *no* where today's educated speaker
feels obligated to say *"any."* In *The Comedy of Errors*,
Luciana, having mistaken one of the twin Antipholuses
for the other, reports to her sister, "First he denied in
him you had no right." Double comparatives, superla-
tives, and prepositions, being the norm, surface unself-
consciously: "more nearer" in *Hamlet*, "more older"
in *The Merchant of Venice*. In *Julius Caesar* Cassius

expects to grace Brutus's heels "with the most boldest and best hearts of Rome," and Antony in the Forum pointing to the wound left in Caesar by Brutus's dagger inveighs against this "most unkindest cut of all." Such constructions—merely emphatic—in time came to be regarded as redundant and hence not good English. The poet Alexander Pope, preparing the text for his 1723 edition of Shakespeare, altered lines to conform with his age's prescriptive standard; the timely addition of a superfluous *this* replaced Antony's superfluous (as Pope deemed) *most:* "This, this was the unkindest cut of all." Elsewhere Pope replaced *more corrupter* with *far corrupter, more fitter* with *more fitting*. As such doublings are common in Shakespeare, Pope had his work cut out for him.

Where the verb is at some remove from the applicable preposition, Shakespeare may insure clarity by repeating the preposition without worrying about the resultant redundancy. *"In* what enormity is Marcius poor *in* that you have not in abundance?" is the unflattering question put by Menenius to the tribunes of the people in *Coriolanus*. Reminiscing about Bertram's "good father" in *All's Well That Ends Well*, the king recalls that *"on* us both did haggish age steal *on."* *Whom* may be used where today's strict grammatical constructionist would choose *who:* "Of Arthur, *whom* they say *is killed* tonight" *(King John,* IV.ii.165); "Young Ferdinand *whom* they suppose *is drowned"* *(The Tempest,* III.iii.92).

Other anomalies (by present-day standards) abound, and they do not as a rule merely characterize the speech of Shakespeare's more lowly personages. In *As You Like It,* the witty Rosalind says "have *swam"* (IV.i.35), Edgar in *King Lear* tells the blinded Gloucester "thou hast perpendicularly *fell"* (IV.vi.54), and in *Antony and Cleopatra* the wounded Scarus assures his emperor that had his men fought so at first, "we had *droven* them home" (IV.vii.5). For *shake,* literate modern usage forms the preterite and the past participle of the "strong" verb by changing the root vowel *(shook, shaken*), but in Shakespeare the form of the verb made by adding a dental suffix, *shaked*, coexists with the traditional forms. We also find *beated* (Sonnet 62), *becomed* (*Antony and Cleopatra*, III.vi.i.26), and *blowed* (*Othello*, III.iii.186), along with—more frequently—*beat*, *became*, and *blew*. In the last scene of *The Comedy of Errors*, Antipholus of Ephesus explains how "these errors are *arose*," and in *Twelfth Night* the Countess Olivia tells the duke's ambassador of love that "He might have *took* his answer long ago."

Familiarity accustoms the modern reader to the variations in word order with which Elizabethan English disports itself. We have "dear my lord" for "my dear lord" (*Julius Caesar*, II.i.255), "sweet my mother" for "my sweet mother" (*Romeo and Juliet*, III.v.200). Shakespeare speaks of "too hard a keeping oath" (*Love's Labor's Lost*, I.i.65) and "poor a thousand crowns" (*As You Like It*, I.i.2); Othello will not "scar that whiter skin of hers than snow" of the sleeping Desdemona he is about to murder (V.ii.4). "Tongue-tied our Queen, speak you," Leontes bids Hermione as Polixenes prepares to depart in *The Winter's Tale* (I.ii.270)—whereas we would say, "Our tongue-tied [i.e., silent] Queen." Sometimes a simple accusative is elliptically employed where we would require both personal and relative pronouns: "*Him*"—that is, he whom—"I accuse / The city ports by this hath entered" (*Coriolanus*, V.vi.5–6).

To modern eyes and ears, verbs do not always agree in number with their subjects, but Shakespeare may here be drawing upon northern forms in which a plural subject could take a verb with an inflection ending in *s*. In *Richard II* Northumberland complains, "These high wild hills and rough uneven ways / *Draws* out our miles and *makes* them wearisome" (II.iii.4–5), and Aumerle asks, "*Is* Bushy, Bagot, and the Earl of Wiltshire dead?" (III.ii.141). Sometimes confusion is caused by the proximity of an intervening noun: ". . . the *voice* of all the *gods* / *Make* heaven drowsy (*Love's Labor's Lost*, IV.iii.343–44), "The *venom* of such *looks*, we

fairly hope, / *Have* lost their quality" *(Henry V,*
V.ii.18–19). These—and other instances of "bad English"—are entirely characteristic of Shakespeare's age.
In the study they may make us pause before moving on;
in the theater they give no difficulty. Correctness can be
relative.

A simple, basic monosyllable may expressively illus-
trate the processes of linguistic change. In Chaucer's
English, the third-person singular neuter pronoun was
declined *hit, his, hit.* In unstressed positions, *hit* weak-
ened to *it* for both subject and object early in the modern period, but *his* remained in use for the neuter
possessive until the middle of the seventeenth century.
By then gender had become sex-linked rather than a
purely grammatical category, and *his* had come to seem
odd as a genitive neuter because of its coincidence with
the masculine genitive, a coincidence sometimes
avoided (as early as the fifteenth century) by the use of
thereof or *of it.* Not until John Florio's copious Italian-
English dictionary of 1598, *A World of Words,* does possessive *its* turn up in print. Florio went on to use the new
pronoun frequently in his greatest work, the translation
of Montaigne's *Essays,* published in 1603. The King
James Bible of 1611 manages without *its.* The form occurs only a dozen times in the Shakespeare canon, and
none of these in works published during his lifetime.
Sometimes Shakespeare uses *it,* a provincial variant for
the possessive. "It lifted up *it* head," Horatio says of the
Ghost in *Hamlet,* and Ophelia's corpse is described by
the Gravedigger as of one that "did with desperate hand
/ Fordo *it* own life." And the Fool in *King Lear* offers
his own sample of the wisdom of natural lore:

The hedge-sparrow fed the cuckoo so long
That it's had *it* head bit off by *it* young.
(I.iv.221–22)

The second person pronouns present more complex
issues. The older declension—*thou, thy, thee* for the

singular; *ye, your, you* for the plural—were giving way to *you* and *your* irrespective of number, but subtle distinctions continued to be made. These Shakespeare's works exemplify. Generally, *you* is what linguists refer to as an unmarked form, somewhere between the polarities of formality and informality, politeness and impoliteness, leaving *thou* free to occupy a wide spectrum of contrasting uses. *Thou* signified different things, according to the people who used it and to whom they were speaking. *Thou* was the pronoun of elevated poetic purpose and solemn religious discourse. "*Thou*, Nature, art my goddess," is the bastard Edmund's invocation in *King Lear* (I.ii.1ff.); "to thy law / My services are bound." The ruling classes also generally addressed servants and other inferiors as *thou*. In his prison cell in the Tower, the wretched Clarence calls, "Where art *thou*, keeper? Give me a cup of wine." But it is the Second Murderer who replies, "*You* shall have wine enough, my lord, anon." Later, when the murderers reproach Clarence for his delinquencies, they slip into the *thou* form of address *(Richard III* (I.iv)). When *sir* is included, especially in anger, *thou* may be replaced by *you*. "But tell me," Valentine asks his servant, Speed, in *The Two Gentlemen of Verona*, "dost *thou* know my lady Sylvia?", but, in the same scene (II.i): "Go to, sir: tell me, do *you* know madam Sylvia?" In *Julius Caesar* (I.i), Flavius, the tribune of the people, asks a carpenter in a Roman street, "Speak, what trade art *thou?*" and—addressing a cobbler;—"*You*, sir, what trade art *thou?*" In *Twelfth Night* Sir Toby goads on Sir Andrew Aguecheek to draft a challenge to his rival, "Taunt him with the license of ink; if *thou thou*'st him some thrice, it shall not be amiss" (III.ii.45–47). Yet, in the same passage, Sir Toby himself uses the same equivocal *thou* for Sir Andrew. In bidding farewell to his countrymen before taking his own life at the end of *Julius Caesar,* Brutus appropriately distinguishes between *thou* and *you:*

> Farewell to *you;* and *you;* and *you,* Volumnius;
> Farewell to *thee,* too, Strato.   (V.v.30–31)

Volumnius was Brutus's schoolfellow; Strato, his servant.

Brutus and Portia, a married couple, use *you* with each other. Another wife, Lady Percy in *1 Henry IV,* mostly addresses her Hotspur as *you,* but for her emotional appeal to the husband who has banished her from his bed, she switches (after one *thou*) to *you,* and later in the scene twits her "mad-headed ape" with *thy* and *thou*—"In faith, I'll break *thy* little finger, Harry, / An if *thou* will not tell me all things true"—before reverting, with underlying seriousness, to *you:* "Do *you* not love me? Do *you* not indeed?" In the first scene of *King Lear,* Kent, Edmund, Gloucester, and Lear all with appropriate decorum use *you,* as do the three daughters in addressing their father. He, also appropriately, uses *thou,* but for Cordelia, "our joy," he switches to *you;* until, that is, her refusal to take part in an emotional auction shocks and enrages him. He then uses *thou,* not the customary *thou* of father to daughter, but the *thou* of anger: "*Thy* truth, then, be *thy* dower!" The force of the pronoun here resides in its contrast with the expected usage. So too does Kent, in his unmannerly anger, address his king as *thou:*

> Revoke *thy* gift,
> Or, whilst I can vent clamor from my throat,
> I'll tell *thee* thou dost evil.   (I.i.167–68)

So much force can the choice of pronoun have.

"I marvel that thy master hath not eaten thee for a word," banters the clown Costard with Don Adriano de Armado's diminutive page, Mote, in *Love's Labor's Lost,* "for thou art not so long by the head as *honorificabilitudinitatibus*" (V.i.44)—a word that, since the eighteenth century, has often been cited as the longest in English. Be that as it may, it is certainly the longest word in Shakespeare, and, unsurprisingly, occurs just once in the canon. Merely to pronounce the word confers upon the speaker incantatory gratification; he has no need to define the meaning, which is (more or less) "worthiness." Deriving from Latin *honorifica,* the word appears in the writings of Petrus of Pisa, Charlemagne's tutor, in the eighth century, in a treatise by Dante (c. 1300), and in continental dictionaries beginning in 1200.

This was long before the advent of printing encouraged, via translations, the extension of vocabulary. In England printing from movable type had existed for less than a century when Shakespeare was born. William Caxton—a retired cloth trader and diplomat who mastered the new craft in Cologne before setting up shop in London—in 1474 issued the first printed book in the English language, *The Recueil* [i.e., compilation] *of the Histories of Troy.* Translations, treatises, and textbooks were soon pouring from English presses. Explorers described their expeditions through the untracked wildernesses of the New World. Ptolemy gave way to Copernicus, as astronomers on this little dark planet whereon we live charted the heavens. With the once universal church wracked by schism, theological controversy and sectarian polemics flourished. Books retailed the findings. Translators Englished the early and late historical and literary classics of Greek and Roman antiquity; Thucydides and Plutarch, Aristotle and Vergil found new audiences becoming acquainted (in Sir Thomas Elyot's phrase) with "the knowledge which maketh a wise man." Nor were medieval and contemporary spokesmen neglected; Saint Augustine, Boethius, Erasmus, and Martin Luther found English readers in the English tongue. Even zealous Protestants might have catholic tastes: Arthur Golding, a Londoner and a Puritan, translated both Calvin and Ovid, and from the latter's pagan *Metamorphoses* managed to draw a Christian moral. Shakespeare knew the *Metamorphoses* in the original and also in Golding's rendition.

New concepts required new words, and Englishmen

found their own language wanting. In his *Brief Discourse of War* (1590), Sir Roger Williams promiscuously incorporated neologisms for current fortifications, and succinctly justified his use of "strange names" by lamenting, "I know no other names than are given by the strangers [foreigners], because there are few or none at all in our language." Translators from the Latin often made do with barely altered Latin equivalents. Many of the new words came from Romance sources—French, Italian, Spanish, and Portuguese—but Greek was also levied upon. "I intended to augment our English tongue, whereby men should as well express more abundantly the thing that they conceived in their hearts . . . ," wrote Elyot, "having words apt for the purpose, as also interpret out of Greek, Latin, or any other tongue into English, as sufficiently out of any one of the said tongues into another." Why not? The endeavor was not ignoble. In *The Governour* (1531), Elyot insisted that he always declared plainly the meanings of his coinages so that nothing was hard to understand. His Latinate augmentations included *maturity,* in the now obsolete sense of "due promptness." Shakespeare incorporated *maturity*—with the more modern meaning—in his own vocabulary, using the word twice, in *Troilus and Cressida* (I.iii.317) and Sonnet 60: "Nativity, once in the main of light, / Crawls to *maturity.* " Such polysyllabic accretions, more literary than conversational, and smelling of the lamp, came to be known as "ink-horn" words, alternatively, "hard words." They received a mixed press. In his *New World of English Words* (1658), Edward Phillips—John Milton's nephew—wryly observed that "some people, if they see but a hard word are as much amazed as if they met with a hobgoblin." His uncle was not intimidated by such hobgoblins.

Nor was Shakespeare. He might good-naturedly mock linguistic affectation. Don Adriano in *Love's Labor's Lost* dallies preposterously with his *excrement;* that is, as here used, "that which grows out or forth" (i.e., his *excrescence, hair*), an ink-horn usage first encountered in the 1590s. (In modern productions Don Adriano's *excrement* always draws a laugh.) The schoolmaster Holofernes, in the same comedy, may think ill of those who, like Don Adriano, fail to pronounce *b* in *doubt* and *debt*, or the *l* in *calf* and *half;* to leave out the *h* from *abhominable* smacks to him of *insanie.* The spelling *abhominable* was common enough in Shakespeare's time, deriving from its reputed—but mistaken—Latin origin in *ab* plus *homine*, taken to mean "away from man, inhuman, beastly," rather than—correctly—from Latin *abominabilis* (French *abominable*), i.e., detestable. In Justice Shallow's house in provincial Gloucestershire in *2 Henry IV*, Falstaff's crony Corporal Bardolph sees a soldier as "better *accommodated* than with a wife"—an expression, common enough in military jargon, which immediately makes a hit with the Justice:

It is well said, in faith, sir, and it is well said indeed, too. "Better accommodated"! It is good, yea indeed is it; good phrases are surely, and ever were, very commendable. "Accommodated"—it comes of "*accommodo.*" Very good, a good phrase.   (III.ii.71–75)

In his *Discoveries* Ben Jonson cites *accommodation* as one of "the perfumed terms of the time." Despite his frolics with perfumed terms, Shakespeare by his practice allies himself with the innovators rather than detractors; as another poet and dramatist, John Dryden, avowed in the next age, he traded both with the living and the dead for the enrichment of his native tongue.

Many of the words that constitute Shakespeare's astonishingly rich vocabulary—estimated at some twenty thousand words, not counting inflected forms as distinct words—were of recent origin. Some, now at home in the language, are first recorded only a year or two before Shakespeare uses them; Latinate words such as *allurement, critical, demonstrate, hereditary, imper-*

tinency, jovial, pathetical, and *prodigious,* and Romance words, *barricade, cavalier, mutiny,* and *renegade.* These words are all no earlier than the latter decades of Elizabeth's reign. Others are not recorded before their appearance in the dramatist's writings; among these are *apostrophe, assassination, dislocate, indistinguishable, premeditated, reliance,* and *submerged. Assassination,* which occurs once (in *Macbeth,* I.vii.2), recalls "Assasincs, a company of most desperate and dangerous men among the Mohammedans" as used in Richard Knolles's *General History of the Turks* (1603), which Shakespeare promptly drew upon for information about Venetian-Turkish conflicts when he wrote *Othello.* There is no recorded appearance of *assassination* before Macbeth's soliloquy. The ubiquity of terrorism has made this word frequent enough, but some of Shakespeare's ink-hornisms never really took root. *Troilus and Cressida* is in this respect especially bountiful, the experimental polysyllables including *abruption, appertainments, embrasures, unplausive,* and *persistive.* Other, now more commonplace, words first encountered in Shakespeare include *barefaced, countless, dwindle,* and *laughable.*

Old and new ways with words come together strikingly in *Macbeth.* After the murder of Duncan, as the knocking at the gate is heard, Macbeth looks at his bloodstained hand and asks, appalled,

> Will all great Neptune's ocean wash this blood
> Clean from my hand? No, this my hand will rather
> The multitudinous seas incarnadine,
> Making the green one red.   (II.ii.57–60)

Considered only as statement, the last two lines make essentially the same hyperbolic point. In doing so, they set in opposition to each other Latinate polysyllabic diction and Anglo-Saxon terseness. The words *multitudinous* and *incarnadine* (as a verb), so far as is known, here appear for the first time.

On a simpler level, dialect forms redolent of his Warwickshire heritage left their imprint on the poet of the
London stage. The Midland dialect is reflected in *blood-
bolter'd* (*Macbeth*, IV.i.123), "having the hair matted
with blood"; *potch* (*Coriolanus*, I.x.15), "thrust"; and
gallow (*King Lear*, III.ii.45), "fright." The First Player
in *Hamlet*, enacting Hamlet's favorite speech, Aeneas's
tale of woe to Dido, with its account of Priam's slaughter, uses the word *mobled* (II.ii.513), an epithet queried
by Hamlet ("The mobled queen?") but applauded by
Polonius ("That's good; 'mobled queen' is good"). Not
of Latin origin, *mobled* (i.e., "muffled") probably derived from Warwickshire, where it is found until the
nineteenth century.

Omissions or infrequent usages may hold an interest
of their own. The nature of Shakespeare's religious per-
suasion has stirred a sufficiency of discussion, but the
doctrinal controversies that so agitated his contemporaries left little in the way of a self-evident imprint on
his writings. So the vocabulary of faith in the canon
testifies. It may be noted, however, that the word
Puritan occurs seven times, thrice in *Twelfth Night*.

Ink-horn terms, even if they be "hard words," present fewer problems for audiences today than conversational words that have undergone changes in meaning
since Shakespeare's time. In this category belong *acci-
dent* (occurrence), *advertise* (inform), *appeal* (accuse),
brave (splendid, showy), *competitor* (associate), *doom*
(judgment), *libertine* (one who follows his own incli-
nations), *lust* (pleasure, desire), *presently* (instantly
[usually]), *silly* (innocent), and numerous others. In *The
Winter's Tale* the Shepherd who discovers an abandoned
infant on the Bohemian shore exclaims, "What have we
here? Mercy on's, a barne, a very pretty barne; a boy
or a child, I wonder?" (III.iii.68–69). *Child* here means
girl-child. In Shakespeare "my child" always signifies
a daughter. *Girl* used to be applied to a young person
of either sex, but had begun to be narrowed in meaning,
and to replace the exclusively feminine gender meaning
of *child*. (The word *barne*, from Old English *bearn*, for

a child of either sex was apparently already restricted to northern dialect.) For Elizabethans a banquet was a light repast of sweetmeats, fruit, and wine; such, presumably, constituted the "most delicious banquet" the Lord in *The Taming of the Shrew* (Induction, 39) orders to be set before Sly when he awakens from his drunken stupor, or the "trifling foolish banquet" that Capulet's guests leave without sampling in *Romeo and Juliet* (I.v.124). *Deer* has never lost its Old English unchanged plural *(deor)*, but specialization, a well-documented semantic process, has affected meaning. A deer once could be any wild creature. So it is in Shakespeare; in *King Lear* ". . . mice, and rats, and such small *deer* / Have been Tom's food for seven long year" (III.iv.141–42). *Tonight* may mean "last night," as when Shylock confesses to Jessica that he "did dream of money-bags *tonight*" (*The Merchant of Venice*, II.v.18). In Shakespeare, adverbial *still* normally signifies "always"; *along* may mean "at full length." Complete about-faces of meaning are not out of the question. "By heaven," Hamlet cries as the Ghost beckons him to follow, "I'll make a ghost of him that *lets* me." *Lets* here signifies *prevents* (e.g., in lawn tennis a let ball is an obstructed ball). The human tendency to procrastinate is exemplified by what has happened to *presently*. It is used often by Shakespeare to mean "immediately, instantly, directly," rather than in the present-day sense of "after a little while," although the modern meaning may be implied when Mrs. Page in *The Merry Wives of Windsor* cautions Mrs. Ford that Falstaff will be arriving *presently* (IV.ii.92). The dramatist uses *owe* to mean *own:* Prospero upbraids the newly arrived Ferdinand, "Thou dost here usurp / The name thou *ow'st* not" (I.ii.454–55). Yet *owe* also appears in its modern sense, as when the Officer in *The Comedy of Errors* insists that ". . . if I let him go, / The debt he *owes* will be required of me."

Sometimes Shakespeare employs words closer to their etymological sense. *Communicate* (used three times) may now mean "to impart, transmit," but in *The Com-*

edy of Errors Adriana sees her husband as an elm and herself a vine "whose weakness married to thy stronger state / Makes me with thy strength to *communicate*"; that is, "share," a sense not elsewhere encountered in Shakespeare. *Expect* kept its Latin meaning, "to await": "My father at the road [i.e., anchorage]," Valentine bids Proteus adieu in *The Two Gentlemen of Verona*, "*Expects* my coming." In *Troilus and Cressida* we find *expecter*, "one who waits." (Shakespeare can happily noun it with a verb or verb it with a noun—Cleopatra dreads the possibility of seeing some squeaking Cleopatra *boy* her greatness, Petruchio is *Kated* in *The Taming of the Shrew*, and "Lord Angelo *dukes* it well in *Measure for Measure.)* *Atone*, a sixteenth-century augmentation, means in Shakespeare "agree, be reconciled," not the modern "make amends for wrongdoing." Thus, in the last scene of *As You Like It*, Hymen, the god of marriage in classical mythology, descends to solemnize a quartet of pairings:

> Then is there mirth in heaven
> When earthly things made even
> *Atone* together.   (V.iv.180–81)

Few notes at parting contribute so much to a play's thematic orchestration.

3

London's Playhouses

When Shakespeare was born, England did not yet have a theater built expressly for the performance of plays. Until recently it was thought that the first English custom-built playhouse was the one called— appropriately enough—the Theater, put up in 1576. But the Theater in fact was preceded by almost a decade: the Red Lion, in the parish of Stepney in London's eastern suburbs, erected by John Brayne—by occupation a well-to-do grocer and the brother-in-law of James Burbage. In 1567 it was in place, complete with scaffold, or stage, trapdoor, and turret probably with some sort of tiring house for the actors to change costumes. Within a decade other playhouses began to appear. Shakespeare was twelve when the same Brayne with Burbage erected the Theater, which (unlike the Red Lion) became justly famous. The Theater was located in the Liberty (i.e., district controlled by the city, although situated outside its boundary) of Halliwell (or Holywell), St. Leonard's, Shoreditch, to the north of the medieval walled city, some distance outside the Bishopsgate entrance. Their plot of land, formerly the site of a priory of Benedictine nuns with a Holy Well (hence the place name), thus lay outside the jurisdiction of the city authorities, who, being by disposition Puritan, did not take kindly to amusements such as stage plays. These were the first custom-built public playhouses in Europe in more than a millenium; indeed, since Roman times.

Then in his mid-forties, Burbage was, according to a contemporary report, "by occupation a joiner, and reaping but a small living by the same, [he] gave it over

and became a common player of plays." He threw in
his lot with Leicester's men, and continued as a "fellow" of that or another troupe for a year or two after
his Theater had opened its doors. Being then of small
credit—not worth above a hundred marks (a mark was
valued at 13s.4d.)—he turned to his brother-in-law for
the necessary capital, which came in the end to about
£650. As a joiner—that is, one who made house fittings,
furniture, and the "joints" that held structural timbers
together—Burbage was naturally drawn to wood as his
building material rather than the newer Renaissance
preference for brick and plaster. His Theater was a
"public" playhouse, in the sense that it catered to the
heterogeneous spectators (although these chiefly represented the upper levels of the social order) who pressed
around the stage, while patrons who could afford better
places sat comfortably in the "twopenny rooms" and
"gentlemen's rooms" of the several galleries, or, splendidly secluded, in the "boxes of the Lords' room." (In
Every Man out of His Humour [1599], Jonson alludes
to the taking of tobacco by gallants "over the stage i'
the Lords' room" [II.iii.193]).

During its twenty-year history the Theater was occupied by various acting companies: Leicester's (1576–
78), Warwick-Oxford's (1579–82), occasionally by the
Queen's (1583–89) and the Admiral's Men (1590–91),
but principally by Shakespeare's troupe, the Lord
Chamberlain's Men, formed in 1594. In time, Burbage
quarreled with his brother-in-law, and the dispute led to
blows, then, after Brayne's death, to suits and counter-
suits by the widow. The building of the Theater was a
speculative venture: Burbage dreamt of the "continued
great profit and commodity through plays that should be
used there every week." By his shrewd, if sometimes
unscrupulous, dealings, he prospered, and some time
before he died in 1596 Burbage had acquired the Blackfriars priory, the great hall of which would ultimately
contain the Blackfriars theater, the winter house of
Shakespeare's company. Burbage's son Cuthbert would
later hail his father as "the first builder of playhouses"

(a commendation that perhaps owes more to filial devotion than to strict adherence to fact); and Richard, his younger son, would become the foremost tragedian of the age and the first to give stage life to the roles of Hamlet, Othello, and Lear.

England had professional theater before it had the Theater. As early as 1469 we begin to encounter notices of players wearing the "badge" or livery of some noble patron: the earls of Oxford, Derby, or some other aristocrat, or even King Henry VII or his son Prince Arthur. The Duke of Gloucester had his men too; the same Gloucester, Shakespeare's "lump of foul deformity," who would become King Richard III. The actors received an allowance of cloth so that they could wear the colors of the sponsoring house, and so avoid the penalties to which "rogues, vagabonds, and sturdy beggars" were subject, as a 1572 statute (not the first to deal with the problem) proclaimed. (Boys played female parts and continued to do so until the Restoration.) When the players performed before their masters in elegant houses or palaces, they received meals and lodgings and a cash reward, but generally their connection with the patron was nominal. These troupes were enlisted for other acting dates. For example, in the Induction, scene ii, to *The Taming of the Shrew*, trumpets announce the arrival of players to offer their services to the lord of the manor. They are given friendly welcome in the buttery before being called upon to present their play before Sly the tinker. And Prince Hamlet (II.ii) welcomes the players to Elsinore, noting how the boy who played young women's parts has grown since last he saw him: "What, my young lady and mistress! By'r lady, your ladyship is nearer to heaven than when I saw you last by the altitude of a chopine" (a lady's thick-soled overshoe). In marketplaces the actors—troupes of four, five, or six men, with a boy apprentice—set up their cloth-covered playing booths on small rectangular platforms mounted on trestles or barrels. Over the booth front were hung curtains, behind which the actors changed costume. The troupes performed in open street squares, in schoolhouses, before the mayor and corporation in guild halls, in animal-baiting rings when the bears or bulls were not being tormented by dogs, even, on occasion, in local churches. They pitched their booths on village greens. In open situations without control of access, one of their number would usually pass through the throng for donations. They acted in enclosed inn yards, setting up their stage against a wall at one side of the yard, with the standing audience surrounding the stage on three sides, or occasionally viewing the performance, while seated, from windows and galleries overlooking the yard. Sometimes a lump payment may have been made by the innkeeper who sold the ale. In halls (private or public) they performed on the floor or upon a dais set up against the hall screen, which was normally equipped with doorways and—to prevent drafts—covered with hangings. Between engagements the players strolled from town to town with playing packs strapped to their backs. The luckier ones had horses; some even had wagons. These unpretentious strollers were the professional progenitors of the Shakespearean acting company that was called upon to perform before monarch and court.

Long after the London amphitheaters had become the talk of the Continent, itinerant companies traversed the provincial circuit. At Shakespeare's Stratford the first professional troupe known to have performed came in 1569; John Shakespeare was then bailiff and accordingly approved the actors' remuneration—nine shillings for the Queen's Men, twelvepence for the Earl of Worcester's Men when they performed at the guild hall. During the five years from 1579 to 1584 seven different acting companies visited Stratford. At Knowsley Hall, Lancashire, one Thursday in 1587, the Earl of Leicester's Men played, and again on Friday, "and on Saturday they departed away, and Mr. Sorrowcold, a preacher, came." The formidable Ben Jonson himself was in 1601 reminded by a rival dramatist of how he had once ambled by a play-wagon in the highway in his leather pilch—or outer garment—and taken mad

Hieronimo's part in Thomas Kyd's *Spanish Tragedy*, one of the great and long-lived early war-horses of the Elizabethan repertory. But some grew wealthy. In the same year, 1601, in *The Return from Parnassus*, an anonymous comedy acted by the students of St. John's College, Cambridge, the poor scholar Studioso enviously evoked the actor's life while a consort of fiddlers tuned:

> England affords those glorious vagabonds,
> That carried erst their fardels on their backs,
> Coursers to ride on through the gazing streets,
> Sweeping it in their glaring satin suits,
> And pages to attend their masterships;
> With mouthing words that better wits have framed,
> They purchase lands, and now esquires are made.

Yet even during the glory days, with *King Lear* recently added to their offerings, the King's Men came to Maidstone, in Kent, and the mayor disbursed only a modest £2.5s. to the company, inclusive of the trumpeters who heralded the performance.

Playhouses sprouted up to both the north and south of the city walls. It is fitting that such amenities should grace a newly prominent capital city, the latest wonder of the Western world, for London had grown at a phenomenal rate. When Henry VII, the first Tudor monarch died in 1509, London had little more than fifty thousand inhabitants residing within the ancient walled city and its liberties. Within a century the urban sprawl—mainly to the east and west—had boosted the population to nearly two hundred thousand, as thousands of migrants picked up stakes to move to the metropolis each year. The Theater stood about a mile north of the capital's eastern limit; the Curtain, the next playhouse to be built, a few hundred yards closer in; then the Fortune, closer still to the center, just about a mile north of St. Paul's; and the Red Bull, adapted from former inn buildings, at the upper end of St. John's Street, easily accessible, with the sign of the bull displayed before its door. South of the river lay the open-air amphitheaters of Bankside: the Globe, Bear Garden, Rose, and Swan.

(In February 1989 announcement of the discovery of remains of the Rose playhouse during building works close to the south end of Southwark Bridge created a stir. The first playhouse to be put up south of the Thames, the Rose—an open-air, irregularly polygonal amphitheater—represented the investment of the theatrical magnate Philip Henslowe in partnership with one John Cholmley; the builder was John Griggs, by occupation a carpenter. The Rose sponsored plays by Marlowe, Kyd, Greene, and others. In 1606 it is alluded to as "the late playhouse," but for a time it gave the Theater and the Globe a run for their money, and the discovery of remains—almost four centuries after the event—holds the promise of unexpected new information for theatrical historians: scholarship, it cannot be repeated too often, is process.)

Opposite busy jetties or "stairs," these were reached by boatmen who plied the Thames like Venetian gondoliers. Pleasure seekers flocked to the playhouses, to the consternation of Puritan divines. "Will not a filthy play, with the blast of a trumpet, sooner call thither a thousand than an hour's tolling of a bell bring to the sermon a hundred?" thundered the preacher at Paul's Cross one Sunday in 1578. "If you resort to the Theater, the Curtain, and other places of plays in the city, you shall on the Lord's day have these places, with many other that I cannot reckon, so full as possibly they can throng." Reasonable admission prices encouraged custom. At the Theater, or "some other painted stage," Gabriel Harvey—barrister and controversialist—wrote in 1579 to his friend Edmund Spenser, a theatergoer and his companions could "laugh their bellies full for pence or two-pence apiece." Twenty years later, inflation still had not taken its toll, as in later ages it would. In 1599 a visiting Swiss physician, Thomas Platter from Basel, saw a play one afternoon at the Curtain, and afterward noted of his experience:

> . . . whoever cares to stand below only pays one English penny, but if he wishes to sit he enters by another door, and pays another penny, while if he desires to sit in the most comfortable seats which are cushioned, where he not only sees everything well, but can also be seen, then he pays yet another English penny at another door. And during the performance food and drink are carried round the audience, so that for what one cares to pay one may also have refreshment.

What did the public playhouses of Shakespeare's age look like? And how do we know? They are featured on maps and panoramas. In his bird's-eye view of London from Bankside, c. 1616, the Dutch engraver J. C. Visscher prominently featured the playhouses in conventional eight-sided representations that are now generally discredited; it is not certain that Visscher had ever set foot in the city. Wenzel Hollar was to do so, and represented them more reliably in his 1647 "Long View," for which a pen-and-ink sketch showing the Second Globe (the first had long since been destroyed by fire) and the Hope playhouse also survives. There are other panoramas, engraved, or painted, mostly deriving from Visscher. No architectural plans have come down to us, but we do have builders' contracts for the Fortune and the Hope. Although the Fortune was, unlike the other named playhouses, square (perhaps influenced by the rectangular shape of inn yards) rather than round or polygonal, the master carpenter, Peter Street, had previously supervised the erection of Shakespeare's Globe, and modelled the new playhouse on it. The Hope, a dual-purpose theater and animal-baiting house built in 1614 on the site of the old Bear Garden, was to be of "such large compass, form, wideness, and height as the playhouse called the Swan," built a generation earlier. A visiting university student from Leyden, Johannes de Witt, in 1596 sketched the interior of the Swan. His drawing does not survive, but a copy of it by De Witt's friend and fellow student, Arend van Buchell, does, and remains, although difficult to interpret, the only authentic representation of the interior of an Elizabethan playhouse. Records of litigation sometimes furnish factual details. The play texts themselves enable us, of course, to make inferences about likely production techniques and stage structure, and some of the early editions have title-page illustrations—for example, the anonymous *Swetnam the Woman-Hater Arraigned by Women*, produced at the Red Bull by Queen Anne's company (c. 1618)—which the theater historian at his peril ignores, although, one or two excepted, these are probably unreliable.

Tourists and locals took in performances and sometimes commented on what they observed. Thus, the German merchant Samuel Kiechel recorded in 1594 that "there are some peculiar houses, which are so made as sometimes to have three galleries over one another, inasmuch as a great number of people always enters to see such an entertainment. It may well be that they take as much as from 50 to 60 dollars [$10 to $12] at once, especially when they act anything new, which has not been given before, and double prices are charged. This goes on nearly every day in the week; even though performances are forbidden on Friday and Saturday, it is not observed." Two years later, a native, the antiquary William Lambarde, remarked in the revised edition of his *Perambulation of Kent* on "such as go to Paris Garden [where the Swan was situated], the Bel Savage [an inn used as a playhouse], or Theater, to behold bearbaiting, interludes, or fence play, can account of any pleasant spectacle, [if] they first pay one penny at the gate, another at the entry of the scaffold, and the third for a quiet standing."

It is a clear assumption that, however much they differed in particular details, the outdoor amphitheaters shared certain generic features. According to contemporary report and modern computation, these houses could accommodate three thousand. Built with a timber frame on brick and pile foundations, the round three-story structure—the Globe had a diameter of one hundred feet—had three levels of encircling galleries reached by enclosed exterior staircases. As the galleries were vertically above one another, no spectator sat far from the stage. The "yard," unsurfaced in the animal-baiting houses, was probably paved with brick or stone, making possible a drainage system to carry off rainwater falling into the yard. Extending into the middle of the yard was the large rectangular stage platform—some forty-three feet wide and twenty-seven and one-half feet deep or, rounded off, twenty-eight feet—sometimes rimmed with a low railing.

In *Antony and Cleopatra* (IV.iii) music plays under the stage as the god Hercules, from whom Antony claimed descent, abandons him. Other plays call for "music" within or "above." Green rushes were strewn on the stage floor. At the rear of the yard, set into the frame of the playhouse, was a "tiring-house," where the actors changed costume. Two or (more usually) three massive, round-headed, double-hung doors, opening onto the stage on both sides—with hangings within, or in front of, the open doorways—facilitated entries and exits. In the second story, above the doors, were the openings of the Lords' rooms—six in the Swan drawing, probably five in other playhouses—which were partitioned off from the galleries of the frame; these rooms might serve as boxes for the affluent (the admission here was probably sixpence, a day's wage for a workman), as a supplementary playing area for action above, or as a music room. In Thomas Middleton's *A Chaste Maid in Cheapside* (1609)—the only play known definitely to have been performed at the Swan, although it may have been composed with another house in mind—a stage direction calls for recorders (vertical English flutes) to play dolefully while coffins are carried in; then, while "all the company seems to weep and mourn, there is a sad song in the music-room" (V.iv). In Beaumont and

Fletcher's *The Captain,* acted at around the same time
by Shakespeare's company, Celia commands,

> Give me my veil, and bid the boy go sing
> That song above I gave him; the sad song.
>   (III.iv)

The stage superstructure included two large columns,
in the Corinthian style in the Swan drawing, rising from
the stage and the yard below to support a "cover" or
"heavens" thrusting out from the tiring-house façade
and protecting the rear of the stage from the elements.
Customers merely paying the basic admission were thus
not sheltered. Painted zodiacal signs, and the sun,
moon, and stars, adorned the underside of the heavens;
"this most excellent canopy the air, look you," Hamlet
says to Rosencrantz and Guildenstern, "this brave o'er-
hanging firmament, this majestical roof fretted with
golden fire" (II.ii.307–10). The Globe stage, where
Richard Burbage performed as Hamlet, indeed had a
majestical roof, or, more technically, a stage ceiling.
Immediately above the stage cover, on a fourth story,
stood the "hut" housing the suspension-gear for flying
effects. Within the hut stagehands prepared the machin-
ery for descents, and produced (when called upon)
thunder and lightning. Thatch or tile covered the roof
hut. Alongside the hut, a small platform accommodated
the stagehand who sent up the flag that flew during performance. Thus Jupiter could fly down, seated upon his
eagle and throwing thunderbolts, while lightning played
and Posthumus slept *(Cymbeline,* V.iv). In the middle
of the stage, a large trapdoor permitted the gravedigger
in *Hamlet* to turn up Yorick's skull (V.i), and the Ap-
paritions to rise, accompanied by thunder, in the
Witches' cave in *Macbeth* (IV.i); it served too for the
pit into which Titus's sons fall in *Titus Andronicus*
(II.iii). The Globe was put up at a cost of £700, twice
that—an extraordinary sum—when rebuilt in 1614 after
being destroyed by fire. At the Fortune, and perhaps at

other playhouses too, the elaborately painted woodwork imitated the look of marble. Such were the "sumptuous" and "gorgeous" playhouses, temptations to sin, described by the Puritan preachers.

From late 1608 onward, Shakespeare's company, known since 1603 (when the old queen died) as the King's Men, had a second venue in the disused monastery hall that the elder Burbage had obtained years earlier with conversion in mind. The "private" Blackfriars theater stood in the heart of London, less than three hundred yards southwest of St. Paul's Cathedral. It had been converted from the so-called Parliament chamber, a hundred feet in length (internal measure), of the Upper Frater (or dining hall) of the old priory. In its mid-sixteenth-century state, subdivided into apartments, it was described as consisting of

> all those seven great upper rooms as they are now divided, being all upon one floor and sometime being one great and entire room with the roof over the same covered with lead . . . and also all that great pair of winding stairs with the staircase thereunto belonging which leadeth up unto the same seven great upper rooms out of the great yard.

The rectangular auditorium occupied only two thirds of the available space: at most forty-six feet by sixty-six feet—considerably smaller than the outside dimensions of the public playhouses (the Fortune measured eighty feet square, and the diameter of the round playhouses was one hundred feet). It could seat around seven hundred; this was a more intimate house. Galleries—probably three—ran around the theater on three sides. At one end was the stage, occupying the approximately thirty-foot width of the space lying between the side stage boxes of the gentlemen's rooms. The theater entrance and stairway were to the back of the auditorium. At the rear of the stage the tiring-house—also running the entire width of the hall—was modeled on the screen installations of a Tudor domestic hall, with three doorways in the façade. The tiring-house's second-story gallery provided boxes, one of which served as a music room. Because the building was not open to the sky, candles, hung in branches over the stage, furnished illumination. The basic admission price was sixpence, which allowed entry to the galleries. An additional shilling provided a bench in the paved pit. Those wishing to be seen as well as see could, for two shillings, pass through the tiring-house and sit on the stage on a hired stool. The best seats, the boxes over the stage, went for half a crown (2s.6d.).

At the Blackfriars, in a glittering and hushed atmosphere, the King's Men catered to a socially privileged clientele of gentry, courtiers, and hangers-on, ladies with their masks and fans, merchants, prosperous citizens, professional types, and intelligentsia; a more uniformly elite audience than that which stood watching for a penny, or sat for twopence, on Bankside. Shakespeare's plays continued to be performed at the Globe as well as the Blackfriars, and intimate effects—such as the snuffing out of Desdemona's life on her bridal-sheeted bed in *Othello*—were certainly possible at either house, but for some scenes the Blackfriars provided an ideal setting. In II,ii of *Cymbeline* Iachimo stealthily creeps out of the chest in Imogen's bedchamber, lit by a single flickering taper; he makes notes of the surroundings—the window, the adornment of the bed, the painted arras—and, more especially, of the sleeping woman with the mole on her left breast; then he slips off her bracelet and tiptoes back into the chest, closing the lid over his head. It is easier to conjure up such a scene in the enclosed, candlelit private house in Blackfriars than in the open-air vastness of the Globe amphitheater—but the scene could be (and doubtlessly was) staged effectively at the Globe.

The leading adult troupes of Shakespeare's day consisted of from eight to twelve ''sharers,'' who, having a direct financial stake in the enterprise, divided up expenses—properties, costumes, rents, and the like—and profits. Apparel outlays loomed large. In 1602 Worcester's men laid out £6.13s. for the gown worn by Mrs. Frankford, the heroine of Thomas Heywood's *A Woman Killed with Kindness*, a minor theatrical masterpiece— thirteen shillings more than they paid Heywood for the tragedy. Thomas Giles in 1572 complained about the hiring-out of court costumes to common players, "by reason of which common usage, the gloss and beauty of the same garments is lost and cannot so well serve to be often altered and to be showed before her Highness as otherwise it might and hath been used; for it taketh more harm by once wearing into the city or country where it is often used than by many times wearing in the Court, by the great press of people and foulness both of the way and weather, and soil of the wearers who for the most part be the meanest sort of men." The impresario Philip Henslowe in 1601 recorded paying 6s.7d. to mend a tawny coat "which was eaten with the rats"; this at a time when a journeyman earned one shilling for a day's labor. In addition, there were the outlays for the "hirelings," who were paid a weekly wage for performing with the company. Most Elizabethan plays called for a total of at least sixteen players. The company also had to look after the expense of supplementary personnel: the gatherers, gatekeepers, musicians, and the "tiremen" to assist with costume changes. By late in the Jacobean period, after Shakespeare had departed the scene, the more prestigious troupes had a total work force of perhaps forty or more.

In 1590, at the Theater and possibly also at the Curtain, the Admiral's Men—originally under the patronage of Charles Lord Howard, first earl of Nottingham and Lord High Admiral—joined forces with Strange's Men, sponsored by the Earl of Derby. The next year the amalgamated company quarreled with James Burbage and moved to the Rose, Philip Henslowe's Bankside playhouse. The alliance disintegrated in 1594, Strange's Men returning to the Theater and forming the nucleus of a new troupe, the Lord Chamberlain's Men. They would become, with Shakespeare as their "ordinary poet"—their regular playwright—the age's preeminent troupe. The Admiral's Men, remaining at the Rose, were their most formidable rival; Elizabethan show business was nothing if not competitive. Henslowe's stepdaughter Joan had married Edward Alleyn, universally admired for his acting prowess. "Not Roscius nor Aesop, those admired tragedians that have lived ever since before Christ was born," enthused Thomas Nashe in 1592 in *Pierce Penniless, his Supplication to the Devil,* "could ever perform more in action than famous Ned Alleyn."

He was celebrated for his impersonation of the title roles in Marlowe's *Tamburlaine* and *Doctor Faustus;* he was Barabas, Marlowe's Jew of Malta. *Doctor Faustus* became the subject of a curious and oft retold myth. During one performance, runs a version,

As a certain number of devils kept every one his circle there, and as Faustus was busy in his magical invocations, on a sudden they were all dashed, everyone harkening other in the ear, for they were all persuaded, there was one devil too many amongst them; and so, after a little pause, desired the people, to pardon them, they could go no further with this matter. The people, also understanding the thing as it was, every man hastened to be first out of doors. The players (as I heard it), contrary to their custom of spending the night in reading and in prayer, got them out of the town the next morning.

The episode was reputed to have caused Alleyn's early retirement from the stage; such is the power, even for actors, of theatrical illusion. Alleyn, notwithstanding, returned to the stage in 1600 at the Fortune, which he and his father-in-law had erected as a new home for the Admiral's Men. The local citizenry predictably disapproved of the imminent appearance of a playhouse in their midst, until a letter from the Privy Council to the

Middlesex justices of the peace laid special stress on the queen's desire that Alleyn take up once again his career as a player, "whereof, of late, he hath made discontinuance." He resumed. At the coronation procession for James I in 1604, Alleyn appeared as the Genius of the City and delivered a "gratulatory speech" to the new monarch "with excellent action and a well tuned, audible voice." Show business was good to Alleyn. He amassed a great fortune, and in later years—after his final retirement from the stage—devoted himself to philanthropy, founding the College of God's Gift at Dulwich, which remains to this day the repository of the Henslowe papers.

For the rare super-production, such as Heywood's five *Ages* plays—dramatizing the whole history of classical myth and legend from the birth of Jove to the siege of Troy—rival companies might temporarily amalgamate; in his preface to *The Iron Age,* Heywood, looking backward in 1632, boasts, "These were the plays often (and not with the least applause) publicly acted by two companies, upon one stage at once, and at one time have thronged three several theaters with numerous and mighty auditories." Although doubling of parts, then as now, was the rule, the company hirelings still had their work cut out for them.

The Silver Age calls for forty-one speaking parts, exclusive of "servicemen, swains, Theban ladies, the seven planets and the Furies." Some of Shakespeare's plays make comparable demands. *Antony and Cleopatra* has thirty-four name parts, apart from officers, soldiers, messengers, and attendants; *Richard III* offers thirty-seven roles, besides guards, halberdiers, gentlemen, lords, citizens, attendants, soldiers, two murderers, the Keeper of the Tower, the Lord Mayor of London, messengers, a priest, a scrivener, two bishops, a page, the sheriff of Wiltshire, the ghosts of Henry VI, Edward, Prince of Wales, and Richard's other victims.

In an age of drama, performance was not the prerogative of the elite adult companies. Schoolboys not only did scenes from Plautus and Terence in the classroom, ut also acted in their masters' plays. At an academy pened in a disused Carmelite monastery at Hitchen in Iertfordshire, Ralph Radcliffe converted the refectory nto a theater, and in mid-century regaled the local pop-lation with plays on Biblical and Chaucerian themes Job's sufferings, Patient Griselda, etc.). In college halls t Oxford and Cambridge, university students frolicked luring term with original plays, usually in Latin, on lassical themes.

In London, professionalized children's troupes lent iquance to the theatrical bill of fare. The boys of the Aerchant Taylors' School acted before paying audi-nces until, because of "the tumultuous disordered per-ons repairing thither to see such plays as by our scholars vere here lately played" so the masters of the com-any decreed in March 1574—"henceforth there shall e no more any plays suffered to be played in this our ommon hall, any use or custom heretofore to the con-rary in any wise notwithstanding." A theatrical indus-ry, based upon child actors, evolved out of the chapels ttached to (or closely associated with) the court: the welve boys of the Chapel Royal, serving the monarch t Whitehall and during royal progresses; the Windsor 3oys six at first, finally ten—of the Chapel Royal of Vindsor; and the "singing school" of St. Paul's Cathe-Iral, consisting of ten boys. All had masters who nur-ured, for financial reward, the new juvenile rofessionalism; promoters invested in these enterprises s speculations.

Although no more than two children's companies lourished at any given time, they gave the adults a run for their money. Edward Pearce set up the new company of Paul's Boys in 1599, and the next year Henry Evans—y profession a scrivener—rented, for use by child ictors, the Blackfriars theater constructed by James Bur-page shortly before his death, but left vacant because of protests by the precinct's well-heeled householders, inenamored of the prospect of a commercial playhouse in their midst. The children offered concerts before per-formances and between the acts. When on September 18, 1602, Philipp Julius, Duke of Stettin-Pomerania, visited the Blackfriars theater, for an hour—*eine ganze Stunde*—he enjoyed a program of music by lutes, mandolins, and bandores (guitar-like instruments), violins, and flutes, while a boy sang in a tremulous voice, *cum voca tremulo*. With this overture concluded, the play began. The children's companies were noted for their accomplished musicianship. In John Marston's *The Malcontent* (1604), a Blackfriars tragicomedy appropriated by Shakespeare's company, an Induction especially written by John Webster for the purloined prize speaks of "the not received custom of music in our theater." Presumably the company lacked a consort of strings and woodwinds, although to be sure they had trumpets, drums, flutes, and fiddles for stage music when this was required for a call to arms, a banquet entry, a magical effect, or a serenade. A jig—a humorous skit consisting of songs and dances, so called because of the *gigue,* a stringed instrument used for accompaniment—followed tragedies as an afterpiece to dispel any lingering tragic gloom. The word *jig* occurs more than once in Shakespeare. "Prithee, say on," Hamlet urges the First Player after Polonius's interruption, "he's for a jig or tale of bawdry" (II.ii.511). Presumably a jig was performed after *Hamlet* at the Globe. Will Kempe, who played Peter in *Romeo and Juliet,* was celebrated as a jig-maker as well as clown for the Lord Chamberlain's Men, but he had left the company shortly before *Hamlet* was composed. Comedies ended with a dance, not infrequently a wedding dance. (In due course more elaborate musical effects became commonplace at the public amphitheaters too. "Play fiddlers, anything," bids Arthur much later in Brome and Heywood's *Late Lancashire Witches* [1634] at the rebuilt Globe, and *"Musicians show themselves above"* [apparently in a curtained alcove]. Thus was the music room pressed into service.)

The Children of the Chapel performed at the private house Burbage had built until, with the death of the old queen and extinction of the Tudor line, they became in 1604 the Children of the Queen's Revels, under the patronage of Queen Anne, James's consort. The other leading adult troupe, the Admiral's Men, was transformed two years later into Prince Henry's Men, the company of the heir apparent. Shakespeare's troupe—as previously noted—had the preceding year received, in recognition of their preeminence, a royal patent certifying them as the King's Men.

The children naughtily played with fire. Satirical comedy was their forte, and in Ben Jonson, George Chapman, John Marston, and Thomas Middleton they secured the services of leading avant-garde spirits for their repertories, although some playwrights—most notably Jonson and Middleton—wrote for both the boys and the men. When in 1604 Jonson, Chapman, and Marston pooled their talents on *Eastward Ho!* for the Queen's Revels children, they had the audacity to mock the new monarch's Scottish entourage, and for their pains Jonson and Chapman landed in prison, in danger of having their ears and noses slit, while Marston prudently decamped. (This was a censored drama, although the stringency of the control exercised varied. Plays had to be licensed for performance by the Master of the Revels. Sir Edmund Tilney was appointed to this post in 1579 and held it until his death thirty years later. He was succeeded by his nephew, Sir George Buc, an historian and poet, who served until he went mad in 1622 and was removed from office. The censor's hand fell heavily on *Sir Thomas More*, in the revised manuscript of which Shakespeare probably had a hand. *Sir Thomas More* never received the Revels Office's imprimatur. The politically sensitive abdication scene of *Richard II* was omitted from the first three quartos, and not printed until 1608—five years after Queen Elizabeth's death—with a title-page advertisement of "new additions of the Parliament scene, and the deposing of King Richard, as it hath been lately acted by the King's Majesty's servants at the Globe." The scene was, however, probably performed earlier. In his sixty-sixth sonnet Shakespeare chafes at "art made tongue-tied by authority.'') Four years later, Chapman offended again with his ten-act drama, *The Conspiracy and Tragedy of Charles, Duke of Byron,* acted by the same company. The play grated on French sensibilities. As acted at the Blackfriars theater, it included a scene in which the French queen boxed the ear of the reigning king's mistress. The ambassador protested, and the performance ground abruptly to a halt. Not only did the play portray scandalous goings-on at a contemporary court, but—according to Antoine de la Boderie, the ambassador—it also ridiculed the English king, ''his Scottish mien, and all his favorites astonishingly; for after having made him curse heaven because of the flight of a bird, and having had him strike a gentleman for having beaten his dogs, they depicted him drunk at least once a day.''

The augmentation of the theatrical scene did not go unnoticed at the Globe. ''There is, sir,'' Rosencrantz, newly arrived at Elsinore, informs Prince Hamlet (not without comic exaggeration), ''an eyrie of children, little eyases [young hawks] that cry out on top of question, and are most tyrannically clapp'd for't. These are now the fashion, and so berattle the common stages— so they call them—that many wearing rapiers are afraid of goose-quills and scarce come thither.'' In answer to Hamlet's query, Rosencrantz reports that the boys carry it away, ''Hercules and his load too'' (II.ii.369–70). Thus, for fear of ridicule, did timorous, rapier-adorned gallants hesitate to patronize the common stages; the pen was proving—literally—mightier than the sword. (Hercules's load was the world, which the god was frequently represented as carrying on his shoulders: probably an emblem of the Globe playhouse.)

This was a Globe that commanded little in the way of stage scenery to present the pictorial aspect of theatrical illusion. A pair of opened double doors disclosed a curtained alcove where characters could be revealed, or ''discovered,'' in shop, study, bridal chamber, monastic or prison cell, closet, or whatever enclosed space the script called for. Within this aperture in the stage façade the players at Elsinore may have enacted the murder of Gonzago, while center stage King Claudius and Queen Gertrude viewed the performance from their "state"—the canopied throne on a dais at the front—and, from one side, Hamlet and Ophelia watched the royal couple and the springing of the mousetrap. Later, in the Closet Scene, the curtains or hangings of the discovery space served as the arras behind which Polonius concealed himself to eavesdrop, and through which Hamlet made his fatal pass with his sword. Here Prospero had his cell with books in *The Tempest,* and in the last scene of the play Ferdinand and Miranda were discovered, *"playing at chess."* (In Barnabe Barnes's *The Devil's Charter,* performed in 1607 by the King's Men at the Globe, the two sons of Katherine, presumed dead, are discovered *"at cards,"* and one of the principals enters *"out of his study"* only to exit *"into his study."*)

Tents might be pitched on stage, recalling the booths used earlier by itinerant players. "Up with the tent," orders Richard III on the eve of the Battle of Bosworth. While he speaks, his tent is pitched (V.iii) and furnished. Supers put up Richmond's tent on the other side of the stage. When the five lords withdraw into the king's tent (V.iii.47 *s.d.),* the attendant soldiers presumably exit through a door, the stage tent being unlikely to accommodate so many. Guarded by a couple of men-at-arms, Richard lies down on his straw bed, or mattress, and sleeps his troubled sleep. The ghosts of victims past make their entrance upon the stage, bid Richard to despair and die, and wish Richmond peaceful slumber, before King Richard starts up out of his dream and Richmond awakes refreshed at four to begin his day. *Antony and Cleopatra* required a monument large enough to contain the dying Antony and several women on top, but not too high for the soldiers to lift him up (IV.xv). "O come, come, come," Cleopatra begs from above, and *"They heave Antony aloft to Cleopatra."*

The troupes were well provided with the portable

properties their plays required. Beds were thrust upon
the stage. The flourishing of swords evoked armies
clashing on the battlefield—often enough in Shakespeare's early *Henry VI* plays to prompt a sneer from
Jonson when, years later, he came to revise his *Every
Man in His Humour,* a play that had originally featured
Shakespeare in its cast. Jonson, as he boasts in his Prologue, was unwilling to purchase audience delight by
having his actors

                                  with three rusty swords
And help of some few foot-and-half-foot words,
Fight over York and Lancaster's long jars;
And in the tiring house bring wounds to scars.

In *Julius Caesar* Brutus and Marc Antony deliver their
funeral orations for assassinated Caesar from an improvised rostrum or "pulpit" (III.ii)—but the stage's upper
level could have easily sufficed. Hirelings brought out
the stocks ordered to humiliate Kent in *King Lear* (II.ii).
Chambers—cannons used for ceremonial purposes—
were discharged during performances of *Henry VIII,*
with fateful effect one afternoon in 1613, when fire con-
sumed the Globe.* Taking inventory of the property stock
of the rival Admiral's Men at the Rose in 1598, Henslowe
listed Cupid's bow and quiver, two lion heads, a "great
horse with his legs," a tree of golden apples, three imperial crowns and a single plain one, and (among other
items) a wooden hatchet and golden fleece.

Costumes represented a larger company investment
than apples or fleece, even if golden. In *A Quip for an
Upstart Courtier* (1592) Greene satirically tells of the
player in his murrey—mulberry, i.e., purple-red—gown
covered with rabbit fur "and laid thick on the sleeves
with lace, which he quaintly bare up to show his white
taffeta hose and black silk stockings; a huge ruff about
his neck wrapped in his great head like a wicker cage,

*See page 206–07

a little hat with brims like the wings of a doublet, wherein he wore a jewel of glass, as broad as a chancery seal." For some actors such ostentation was purchased on the cheap; "it is the English usage," Thomas Platter remarked, "for eminent lords and knights at their decease to bequeath and leave almost the best of their clothes to their serving men, which it is unseemly for the latter to wear, so that they offer them for a small sum to the actors." But the actors also paid extravagant sums for individual costumes; we know from Henslowe's *Diary* and Alleyn's accounts. The players were gorgeously appareled in the formal processions, funerals, and other scenes of stately occasion. For the coronation of Henry VIII's new queen a stage direction in the Folio text *(Henry VIII, IV.i)* reads:

THE ORDER OF THE CORONATION

1. *A lively flourish of trumpets.*
2. *Then two judges.*
3. *Lord Chancellor, with purse and mace before him.*
4. *Chorister, singing.   Music.*
5. *Mayor of London, bearing the mace. Then Garter, in his coat of arms, and on his head he wore a gilt copper crown.*
6. *Marquess Dorset, bearing a scepter of gold, on his head a demicoronal [i.e., small coronet] of gold. With him, the Earl of Surrey, bearing the rod of silver with the dove, crowned with an earl's coronet. Collars of S's.*
7. *Duke of Suffolk, in his robe of estate, his coronet on his head, bearing a long white wand, as High Steward. With him, the Duke of Norfolk, with the rod of marshalship, a coronet on his head. Collars of S's.*
8. *A canopy borne by four of the Cinque-ports; under it, the Queen in her robe, in her hair, richly adorned with pearl, crowned. On each side her, the Bishops of London and Winchester.*

9. *The old Duchess of Norfolk, in a coronal of gold, wrought with flowers, bearing the Queen's train.*

10. *Certain Ladies or Countesses, with plain circlets of gold without flowers.*

Exeunt, first passing over the stage in order and state, and then a great flourish of trumpets.

Yet the beloved clown Tarlton—flat nosed and squint of eye—could entrance spectators in his plain country coarsely textured homespun, "his suit of russet, his buttoned cap," foul shirt, wide-puffed breeches, short ankle-strapped boots, and belt with leather purse attached, as he came on stage beating his tabor or drum. Elizabeth's favorite clown, he died in 1588, the year of the Armada. Clowns are different: another, Will Kempe, was one of the original Chamberlain's Men, but dropped out of the company in 1600 to dance the morris, for a wager, from London to Norwich, some hundred and fifty miles, as the crow flies—a feat which took him a month. "I have danced myself out of the world," he said afterward, perhaps alluding to his leavetaking of the Globe.

4

Plays and Playwrights

Mysteries

Long before playhouses first opened their doors in England, there was abundant—and diverse—theatrical fare to entice multitudes of spectators of all classes. The *Regularis Concordia* ("harmony of the rule") of Eth elwold, Bishop of Winchester in the last quarter of the tenth century, prescribes the representation of a chanted trope, or interpolation, during the Easter service. Dressed in a white linen robe, with a palm in his hand, a monk representing an angel approached the sepulcher—a permanent or temporary stone structure in which a crucifix had been solemnly deposited—and chanted, *"Quem quaeritis in sepulchro, O Christicolae?"*: "Whom do you seek in the tomb, O followers of Christ?" He was joined by three other brethren who stood for the three women come with spices to anoint the body of the Savior (the three Maries of the gospels of Matthew and Mark). These responded in unison, *"Jesum Nazarenum crucifixum, O caelicolae"*: "Jesus of Nazareth who was crucified, O dwellers in heaven." From such modest beginnings developed the corpus of English liturgical drama, one of the glories of the later Middle Ages.

By the fourteenth century some cathedral towns—among them York, Coventry, and Chester—boasted their own cycles of Mystery plays, thus called because they were sponsored by the local "mystery," or craft, guilds, and acted in the vernacular by mimes belonging to the companies. The cycles dramatized sacred history and prophecy from the fall of Satan until the Judgment Day. The actor playing God the Father wore a white coat and (until the harmful effects of such cosmetics were realized) gilded his face. Demons were appropriately hideous. Among the Old Testament events staged were Adam's temptation by the serpent and his exclusion, with Eve, from Paradise; Cain's slaying of Abel; the anguished colloquy between Abraham and Isaac, the young son he was called upon to offer up in sacrifice in the land of Moriah; and Noah's flood. New Testament themes followed, as the angel Gabriel announced the Incarnation to Mary. The shepherds and Magi offered homage to the infant Jesus in the manger, Christ withstood temptation in the wilderness, and Lazarus miraculously rose from the dead. The entry into Jerusalem, Christ's sufferings on the cross, and his burial and resurrection were reenacted. Antichrist made his appearance, and Doomsday concluded the sequence.

Sometimes a guild's choice of subject exhibited a nice propriety: the shipwrights might take on ''The Building of the Ark''; the goldsmiths, ''The Magi''; and the butchers, ''The Crucifixion.'' In late May or early June, when the rigors of winter were past and days had lengthened, on the Thursday following Trinity Sunday—Corpus Christi Day, the festival honoring the sacrament of the Last Supper—the Host was borne through the narrow medieval streets while the mayor and corporation and guild worthies followed in solemn procession. Pageants—movable scaffolds, a couple of stories high, on wheels—stopped at fixed locales for performance of their plays before throngs of waiting townspeople. Then the pageant wagons rolled on to the next stop and another showing. Or the cast may have merely displayed their theme in *tableaux vivants* on the scaffold, and reserved actual performance to the marketplace or a town green. Indeed, the Mystery cycles did not invariably call for pageants to facilitate production, nor were all sponsored by the craft guilds. Strolling players apparently acted the *Ludus Coventriae*, the lengthy Prologue to which ends with this announcement:

> A' Sunday next, if that we may,
> At six of the bell, we 'gin our play
> In N————town.

Which town is N town? Any at which the strollers paid a call; so the blank space (*N* apparently signifies *nomen* [name]) in the manuscript signifies.

The repertories of the actors—amateur or professional—were ample. The Towneley plays, probably acted at Wakefield, numbered thirty-two. Forty-eight plays and a fragment have come down for York. It was a long day's entertainment, more likely (in some cases) two days'. The great sometimes deigned to attend; in 1484, while on a royal progress, Richard III—the abortive hedgehog of Shakespeare's history—stopped in Coventry to view the pageants on Corpus Christi Day.

As the liturgical drama evolved, ceremonious observances (*officia*) gave way to shows (*spectacula*). For its play of the Last Judgment the Coventry drapers' company was—the records indicate—equipped with an earthquake and "a barrel for the same." Violence had its innings. In "The Trial before Annas and Caiaphas" from the *Ludus Coventriae*, Christ's tormentors "beat Jesus about the head and the body and spitten on his face and pullen him down and setten him on a stool and casten a cloth over his face." Homely realism and buffoonery, sometimes ribald, also entered in. Barely mentioned in the Bible, Noah's wife is a scold who fearfully refuses to join her family on the ark until finally, as the waters rise, she has no choice but to rush on board. Noah strikes her, and she strikes him. Both address the spectators, Mrs. Noah noting that the wives in the audience wish their husbands dead, and Noah urging the husbands, "if ye love your lives," to chastise their wives' tongues. In "The Second Shepherds' Play," by an anonymous playwright known to dramatic historians as the Wakefield Master, shepherds in the temperate Holy Land complain about the bleak northern winter and their marital perturbations or worry about their flocks. While the shepherds snore, Mak the sheep stealer comes along, helps himself to a fat lamb, and brings it home to his wife, Gill; all this before an angel enters to sing "Gloria in excelsis." The shepherds kneel before their newborn Savior, the lamb of God, lying in the very cradle where a few moments earlier Mak's purloined lamb had been secreted.

The Mysteries left their traces on Shakespeare's art. All four extant cycles—the York, Wakefield, Chester, and N-town plays—include "The Harrowing of Hell." Not present in Scripture, the event became by early tradition part of the Passion, and came to be used ceremonially for the dedication of churches. This tradition held that Jesus' first act after His crucifixion and burial was to rescue from hell the souls of the virtuous refused heaven because of Adam's transgression; Jesus "descended into hell, and rose the third day"—so the Apostle's Creed instructs the faithful, and the twenty-fourth Psalm exhorts, "Lift up your heads, O ye gates; and be ye lift up, ye everlasting doors; and the King of glory shall come in." Those everlasting doors enter into *Macbeth* when the knocking on the gate is heard at Inverness after Duncan's murder, and the drunken Porter imagines himself to be the porter of hell-gate. In "The Shearmen and Tailors' Pageant" at Coventry, a stage direction declares, "Here Herod rages in the pageant and in the street also." Herod's rages were remembered and became a byword for bombastic actorial excess. Shakespeare alludes twice to Herod thus. "What a Herod of Jewry is this!" exclaims Mrs. Page, outraged by one of Falstaff's excesses in *The Merry Wives of Windsor*. And Hamlet, counseling restraint to the First Player, speaks of a performance that "out-Herods Herod." True, we associate the Mystery plays with their heyday in an earlier period, but Shakespeare as a youth of fifteen might conceivably have seen one of the last performances of the guild plays at nearby Coventry.

Moralities

If the Bible, Old Testament and New, furnished a
matchless—and inexhaustible—repository of events to
engage the dramaturgical imagination of Shakespeare's
predecessors, other options were available to them. Allegorical modes beckoned; personified abstractions
contested the soul's pilgrimage in the Morality plays.
The two earliest surviving examples belong to the beginning of the fifteenth century. In *The Pride of Life*,
performed outdoors on a stationary stage with fixed
properties, the King of Life, seconded by his retainers
Might and Health, glories in his invincibility and possessions. But neither knight, nor Caesar, nor King, can
escape "dreary death's" summons; only deeds of char-
ity can ensure eternal life. So the Bishop, fetched to the
King of Life's tent by his messenger, Solace, preaches
in a long sermon. Undaunted, the King dispatches Solace in his behalf to challenge Death to a duel. Here the
manuscript breaks off, but the Prologue has predicted
that in the duel Death will triumph and that only the
intercession of the Blessed Virgin will save the King of
Life from the fiends. For *The Castle of Perseverance* a
sketch in the early manuscript depicts the castle itself,
surrounded by a ditch. Spectators, some at least, sat on
the piled-up excavated earth. Vexillatores—banner bear-
ers announced performance "on the green" at undern
(9:00 A.M.). Scaffolds were provided for the principals.
The Morality follows Mankind's life from his birth, naked and helpless, to old age. Good and Bad Angels
contend for his soul. The Bad Angel tempts Mankind
with the World, the Flesh, and the Devil. Covetousness,
Envy, Wrath, Gluttony, Sloth, Lechery, and (chief of
all) Pride—the Seven Deadly Sins—lure him. The Good
Angel sends the reinforcements of Conscience, Confession, Penance, and the seven cardinal virtues. Shrift
and Penitence lead the hero into the Castle of Perseverance, or steadfastness, which is stronger than any castle
in France. "Mankind's bed"—so the manuscript dia-
gram records—"shall be under the Castle, and there

shall the soul lie under the bed till he shall rise and play.'' Eventually Mankind is granted absolution. In the end the Father, seated on His throne, renders Judgment:

> My mercy, Mankind, give I thee.
> Come and sit at my right hand.

A *Te Deum* hymn of thanksgiving brings *The Castle of Perseverance* to a close. Thus did the anonymous playwright give dramatic form to the *Psychomachia*—the battle for the soul of man—as embodied in the epic poem by the early Christian poet Prudentius (348– c.405), who had depicted the struggle of Christendom as one between pagan vices and Christian virtues.

The best-loved example of this genre is also the simplest and most compelling. ''Here beginneth a treatise how the high Father of Heaven sendeth Death to summon every creature to come and give account of their lives in this world, and is in manner of a moral play''— so reads the title page of the anonymous *Everyman* (c. 1495). Representative man beseeches Fellowship, Kindred, and Goods to accompany him on his last journey, but all refuse. However, Good Deeds, lying cold on the ground, asks her sister Knowledge to help Everyman to make his dreadful reckoning. She assents:

> Everyman, I will go with thee and be thy guide,
> In thy most need to go by thy side.

Brought to Confession, he does penance for his sins. The end is near; Beauty, Strength, Discretion, and Five Wits now all in turn forsake Everyman. But Good Deeds stays until soul parts from body and an Angel welcomes Everyman into the heavenly kingdom. A Doctor has the last word, warning young and old alike to beware of the deadliest sin of the seven, Pride. No psychomachia complicates an elemental drama that never digresses from its somber devotional theme. The play evidently made an impression when it first was printed in the early fifteenth century, for four specimens—out of a total of perhaps ten—survive. In modern times the theme has continued to exercise its hold—witness the great Swedish director Ingmar Bergman's celebrated 1956 film, *The Seventh Seal*, in which Death comes to claim a knight returning from the Crusades to a fourteenth-century Sweden magically translated into the medieval present.

No evidence of contemporary performance of *Everyman* has come down. More in the mainstream of popular dramatic entertainment is *Mankind* (c. 1471), performed by a troupe of half a dozen strolling players on an improvised platform stage in provincial inn yards. The dialogue refers to the host—"the good man of this house"—and to the groundlings that stand and "ye sovereigns that sit." Mercy piously exhorts Mankind, a simple young farmer, to virtuous living; Mischief and his cohorts—New Guise, Nowadays, and Nought—seek to tempt him to depravity. Midway through the play, offstage shouts and an explosion of powder herald the imminent arrival of the chief Vice Titivillus, diabolically costumed, with his legs under him, and clutching a net for sinners. The cast now proceeds to take up a collection—"Else there shall no man him see."

He loveth no groats, nor pence, nor twopence;
Give us red royals if ye will see his abominable
    presence.

A "royal"—a coin worth about ten shillings—might have discouraged even those most eager to see the Devil himself, so the auditors are assured that "ye that may not pay the one, pay the other": that is, groats, pence, or twopence. Titivillus then proceeds to net Mankind: He places a board under the earth the hero is tilling; snatches away his sack of corn, and walks off with his spade. Seduced, Mankind adjourns to the alehouse with New Guise, Nowadays, and Nought, now his boon companions. Eventually he succumbs to despair until Mercy saves him from the familiar triumvirate of enemies: the World, the Flesh, and the Devil. The last word of *Mankind* is "amen," but before that the "worshipful sovereigns," sitting or standing, have been regaled with song, instrumental music, and dance, and cheerful off-color merriment about bodily functions; above all with the "abominable presence" of Titivillus.

As a genre, the Morality continued to flourish into the middle decades of the sixteenth century. The Vice remained the chief attraction as he practiced his diabolical—and entertaining—wiles against a succession of Mankind heroes. However, the term "Vice" itself, to denote this theatrical personage, first appears not in a Morality play, but in the list of characters prefixed to interludes by John Heywood. As a young man Heywood performed at court as a singer and player of the virginals. His allegiance was to the humanist circle around Sir Thomas More, to whom he was by matrimony related. Heywood's interludes, performed at court and by the boy choristers of St. Paul's Cathedral, evoke another world than *Mankind.* Merry Report, the Vice of *The Play of the Weather,* is the omnipotent god Jupiter's representative, a lightly bantering joker and prankster; No-lover-nor-loves in *The Play of Love,* on the other hand, is a playfully vexatious practical joker. Both seem to owe more to the traditions of the court fool or domestic jester than to any inn-yard Vice.

The Moralities themselves evolved into hybrid forms. In the 1560s Leicester's Men acted at court, in London, and on tour Thomas Preston's *Cambyses,* "a lamentable tragedy mixed full of pleasant mirth" (as the early title page has it). A cast of eight managed the thirty-eight speaking roles in a play featuring as its protagonist Cambyses, the wicked King of Persia, who when accused of drunkenness shoots an arrow through the heart of a child to prove the steadiness of his hand. But the great audience pleaser was the Vice Ambidexter, who is (as his name implies) a double dealer. In *Cambyses* the classical history of Herodotus and the personified abstractions of the Morality drama intermingle, but in time Preston's play became a byword for ludicrous and old-fashioned rant. It held the stage long enough for Shakespeare to have possibly seen it; certainly he knew of its existence. "Give me a cup of sack to make my eyes look red," Falstaff asks of Prince Hal at the Boar's Head in *1 Henry IV,* "that it may be thought I have wept, for I must speak in passion, and I will do it in King Cambyses' vein" (II.iv.384–87).

Of the Morality play the memory in Shakespeare's day was yet green. He assumes an easy familiarity with the Vice and that anarchic personage's bravura delight in deploying the instrumentalities of language to serve his mischievous ends. In *Richard III* the Duke of Gloucester sizes up the precocity of young Prince Edward, a mere child, and mutters in a stage whisper, "So wise so young, they say, do never live long." Overhearing, the prince asks, "What say you, uncle?" and Richard, playing with the sounds of words, replies, "I say, without character fame lives long"; then, in another aside, congratulates himself on his own wit:

> Thus, like the formal Vice Iniquity,
> I moralize two meanings in one word.
> (III.i.79–83)

Here, "formal" seems to mean "conventional" or "regular," while "moralize" (to interpret morally or symbolically) plays upon the audience's awareness of the moral interlude and the Vice's role in it. A Vice named Iniquity had indeed figured in two popular polemical mid-century Moralities, anti-Catholic in flavor, *Nice Wanton* and *King Darius,* published respectively in 1560 and 1565. In *The Two Gentlemen of Verona,* Speed's comment to the clown Launce, "Well, your old vice still; mistake the word" (III.i.282) itself plays upon *vice/Vice.* At the Boar's Head in Eastcheap, Prince Hal taunts Falstaff as "that reverend vice, that grey iniquity." And another clown, Feste, goes off singing from the disconsolate Malvolio, imprisoned in a dark room:

> I am gone, sir, and anon, sir,
>   I'll be with you again,
> In a trice, like the old Vice,
>   Your need to sustain;
> Who, with dagger of lath, in his rage and his wrath,
>   Cries, "Ah, ha!" to the devil:
> Like a mad lad, "Pare thy nails, dad.
>   Adieu, goodman devil!"
>
> *(Twelfth Night,* IV.ii.123–31)

The Vice sometimes carried a dagger of wood or lath (a thin strip of sawn or split timber). On the battlefield of Agincourt in *Henry V,* the Boy describes that huffer Pistol as "this roaring devil i' th' old play, that everyone may pare his nails with a wooden dagger" (IV.iv.74–75). If no extant Morality depicts the Vice actually paring the Devil's nails, or talons—figuratively the phrase meant "to dress down"—the young Shakespeare may nonetheless have seen a troupe representing such an action, or perhaps he merely imagined it. In his *Declaration of Egregious Popish Impostures,* an attack on exorcism as practiced by the Jesuits, the prelate Samuel Harsnett recalls old plays in which "the nimble Vice would skip up nimbly like a jackanapes onto the devil's neck, and ride the devil a course and belabour him with his wooden dagger, till he made him roar, whereat the people would laugh." Shakespeare knew the *Declaration,* published in 1603, for he used it as a source in *King Lear* and other plays.

Now and then his own market town offered opportunities for amateur theatricals. At Pentecost, the disguised Julia recalls in *The Two Gentlemen of Verona,*

> When all our pageants of delight were played,
> Our youth got me to play the woman's part,
> And I was trimmed in Madam Julia's gown,
> Which served me as fit, by all men's judgments,
> As if the garment had been made for me.
>
> (IV.iv.159–63)

On one occasion the Stratford corporation laid out money for a Pentecost entertainment. In 1583 they disbursed 13s. 4d. "to Davy Jones and his company for his pastime at Whitsuntide." This Jones had been married to Elizabeth, the daughter of Adrian Quiney, John Shakespeare's Henley Street neighbor and the father of the poet's friend Richard Quiney. After Elizabeth's death in 1579 Jones took as his wife a Frances Hathaway. Was Shakespeare one of the young men who trimmed themselves for this Whitsun pastime?

Gorboduc

More ambitious pastimes beguiled viewers at the ancient universities of Oxford and Cambridge and, in London, at the Inns of Court, where students trained for the bar. For the Christmas revels of 1561–62 the gentlemen of the Inner Temple performed *Gorboduc, or The Tragedy of Ferrex and Porrex,* by Thomas Norton and Thomas Sackville. Still in their twenties, they had already distinguished themselves in letters: Norton, a zealous Protestant reformer, with his translation of Calvin's *Institutes;* Sackville, with his contributions to the celebrated collection of verse complaints, *A Mirror for Magistrates,* which Shakespeare knew and drew upon when he came to write *Richard II.* Norton and Sackville were members of Queen Elizabeth's first Parliament and pursued successful careers in the law. Norton became a wealthy courtier and political power, and died Earl of Dorset.

Other writings, not all of them for the stage, were designated "tragedies," but *Gorboduc* qualifies as the first regular tragedy in English, and the first play in blank verse [unrhymed iambic pentameter]: the "strange metre"—so the publisher described it—first used a few years earlier by the Earl of Surrey for his translation of two books of Virgil's *Aeneid.* Like Seneca's classical tragedies, *Gorboduc* is divided into five acts; unlike them, it features dumb shows that perhaps owe something to the visual symbolism of English pageants and masques. Shakespeare would include dumb shows in *Cymbeline* and *The Tempest;* and, in *Hamlet,* the visiting players at Elsinore, acting before King Claudius's court, precede their play with a dumb show representing the murder of Gonzago. The royal family of Gorboduc—like King Lear and his family—belongs not to English history but to pseudo-history, which could purportedly be traced back to Brute, the great-grandson of Aeneas, the founder of the Roman empire. Like *King Lear, Gorboduc* dramatizes the fatal consequences attendant upon the division of the kingdom during the sovereign's lifetime. Wars, rape, and rebellion ensue; as he sleeps, Prince Porrex is murdered by his own mother. But if much happens in *Gorboduc,* it is also true that little happens, at least on stage. It is left for a messenger (the Nuntius) or one of the queen's waiting women to convey word of the atrocities. Most of the dialogue consists of perorations or of consultations between the princes and their advisers good or bad, an inheritance from the Morality tradition; not all late medieval–early Renaissance plays delighted multitudes with a nimble Vice.

An immediate success, *Gorboduc* was chosen for royal performance at Whitehall Palace on January 18, 1562—the only play known to have been acted at Elizabeth's court between Twelfth Night (January 6) and Candlemas (February 2)—and was printed three years later. Sir Philip Sidney was among those who saw *Gorboduc* performed. In his *Apology for Poetry,* the age's most dazzling courtier and most versatile man of letters took note of the experience. Finding the tragedy "full of stately speeches and well-sounding phrases, climbing to the height of Seneca his style," he nevertheless thought *Gorboduc* defective in its observance of Aristotle's unities:

But if it be so in *Gorboduc,* how much more in all the rest? Where you shall have Asia of the one side, and Afric of the other, and so many other under kingdoms, that the player, when he comes in, must ever begin with telling where he is, or else the tale will not be conceived. Now shall you have three ladies walk to gather flowers, and then we must believe the stage to be a garden. By and by, we hear news of shipwreck in the same place, then we are to blame if we accept it not for a rock. Upon the back of that comes out a hideous monster with fire and smoke, and then the miserable beholders are bound to take it for a cave; while, in the meantime, two armies fly in, represented with four swords and bucklers, and then what hard heart will not receive it for a pitched field?

Now of time they are much more liberal; for ordinary it is, that two young princes fall in love; after many traverses she is got with child, delivered of a fair boy, he is lost, groweth a man, falleth in love, and is ready to get another child; and all this in two hours' space; which, how absurd it is in sense, even sense may imagine; and art hath taught, and all ancient examples justified, and at this day the ordinary players in Italy will not err in.

But the only unity required by Aristotle in his *Poetics* is that of action; the so-called Aristotelian unities of time and place were foisted upon him by Italian Renaissance critics.

Unities

Thus arose the neoclassical doctrine of the unities to which Sidney subscribes. He was not alone in doing so. In 1578, in the Epistle Dedicatory to his two-part play *Promos and Cassandra,* the adventurer and miscellanist George Whetstone faulted the English playwright for grounding his work on impossibilities: "Then in three hours runs he through the world, marries, gets children, makes children men, men to conquer kingdoms, murder monsters, and bringeth gods from heaven and fetcheth devils from hell. . . . Many times (to make mirth) they make a clown companion with a king." Shakespeare read Whetstone: he would use *Promos and Cassandra* as a principal source for *Measure for Measure*, and would go on, in *King Lear*, to make his Fool companion to a king. Had he lived, how would Sidney, his age's embodiment of the aristocratic ideal, have responded to the dramatic art of the glover's son from Stratford? We can only guess, but no doubt Shakespeare's happy indifference to such constraints would not have gone unnoticed by Sidney. In *Antony and Cleopatra,* Alexandria and Rome and other outposts of the empire share the same stage, and in *The Winter's Tale* "after many traverses" a child is lost, grows to maturity, falls in love, and is herself ready to bear children. Yet—early and late in his career—in *The Comedy of Errors* and *The Tempest,* Shakespeare strictly—and happily—observed more unities than Aristotle dreamt of.

University Wits

Playhouses had existed no more than a decade when, in 1586, Sidney died of a wound received while campaigning in the Low Countries. Shakespeare, then twenty-two, possibly had made his debut as a man of the theater; if not, he would do so very shortly. In *Hamlet,* written around the turn of the century, the lord chamberlain of King Claudius's court furnishes the prince with an appreciative inventory of the offerings that the players have brought to Elsinore:

The best actors in the world, either for tragedy, comedy, history, pastoral, pastoral-comical, historical-pastoral, tragical-comical-historical-pastoral; scene indivisable, or poem unlimited. Seneca cannot be too heavy, nor Plautus too light.   (II.ii.405–10)

Polonius knows whereof he speaks, for in his youth he had himself acted Julius Caesar in a university play, and been killed by Brutus in the Capitol. All the genres enumerated by Polonius, and other types (often, as his catalogue suggests, in mixed forms) already were part of the repertory when Shakespeare took up his pen. The impact of the University Wits—graduates of Oxford and Cambridge who earned their precarious livelihood by writing for the common stage—was being felt.

John Lyly

The youngest of the University Wits was John Lyly (1554?–1606), who had previously, in 1578, caused a fashionable sensation with his prose novel, *Euphues, The Anatomy of Wit*, and its sequel, *Euphues and His England*, published two years later. Lyly's dazzling artificial style with its amalgam of literary devices— rhetorical questions, metaphor and simile, elaborate alliterative patterning, fictitious natural history and the affectation of abstruse learning, and balanced and antithetical clauses—took the town by storm. The euphuistic style was carried over into the romantic comedies on mythological and allegorical themes that Lyly wrote for the boy actors of the Chapel Royal and St. Paul's School. Queen Elizabeth on a number of occasions viewed them at court. In 1632, not long before the nonexistent curtain came down on the drama of an age, the stationer Edward Blount in his Preface to the readers of Lyly's *Six Court Comedies*, which he took upon himself to reprint, proudly claims, "Our nation are in his debt for a new English which he taught them. *Euphues and His England* began first that language. All our ladies were then his scholars, and that beauty in Court which would not parley Euphuism was as little regarded as she which now there speaks not French." Shakespeare would pay euphuism the tribute of parody with Don Armado's amorous epistle in *Love's Labor's Lost* (IV.i) and Falstaff's wise saws to Prince Hal at the Boar's Head Tavern in *1 Henry IV* ("For though the camomile, the more it is trodden upon the faster it grows, yet youth, the more it is wasted the sooner it wears. . . ." (II.iv)). Shakespeare lampoons, but the witty raillery of his lovers and the flip rejoinders of his pages, the contrapuntal courtships of the comedies (generally) and the blend of fantasy and realism in *A Midsummer Night's Dream* owe something, perhaps a good deal, to Lyly's precedence. So too the fairies of the last act of *The Merry Wives of Windsor*.

Christopher Marlowe

Lyly scatters songs through his comedies, but otherwise prose is his vehicle; blank verse, introduced so early in Elizabeth's reign, had to be rediscovered for the commercial stage. No one knows for certain just when that took place, but blank verse still retained its freshness when in 1587 the Prologue to *Tamburlaine the Great* strode forth and, speaking for the playwright, delivered a defiant manifesto:

> From jigging veins of rhyming mother wits,
> And such conceits as clownage keeps in pay,
> We'll lead you to the stately tent of war,
> Where you shall hear the Scythian Tamburlaine
> Threatening the world with high astounding
>   terms. . . .

Thus did the Master of Arts from Cambridge University heap scorn on the rough rhyming verse of the untutored "mother-wits" of contemporary theater land. Marlowe goes on to equate inarticulateness with political impotence; in the first lines of *Tamburlaine* the witless King of Persia confesses his inadequacy. "Brother Cosroe, I find myself aggrieved," he laments,

Yet insufficient to express the same,
For it requires a great and thund'ring speech.

Tamburlaine suffers from no such impediment as he embarks upon the heroical progress that the title page of the early edition sums up: "Tamburlaine the Great, who, from a Scythian shepherd, by his rare and wonderful conquests became a most puissant and mighty monarch; and, for his tyranny and terror in war, was termed the Scourge of God." Tamburlaine's career epitomizes the limitlessness of human aspiration for which the Renaissance would become a byword; he is one of literature's magnificent (in Harry Levin's term) overreachers.

The most meager stage equipment summons up grandiose effects; costume and a few stage properties are all that Marlowe requires to supplement the mighty line to which Jonson in time would pay tribute. Crowns, the tangible symbols of power, are bandied about; at his siege of Damascus, Tamburlaine proves himself a master of psychological warfare, shifting his colors—as day succeeds day—from white to red to black to terrify the citizenry. In the sequel play, *The Bloody Conquests of Mighty Tamburlaine,* called forth by the immense success of the first installment, two captive kings with bits in their mouths draw the conqueror's chariot as he scourges them with whips, shouting:

Holla, ye pampered jades of Asia!
What, can ye draw but twenty miles a day?

These lines would resonate in the popular imagination for years. In an Eastcheap tavern in *2 Henry IV* (II.iv), Shakespeare's Pistol—a hollow vessel that makes a great sound—massacres Marlowe's lines while mimicking them:

                     Shall pack-horses
And hollow pampered jades of Asia,
Which cannot go but thirty mile a day. . . .

But the world conqueror is at length himself conquered when death cuts off the progress of his pomp. Tamburlaine had in the First Part recognized that poetry cannot express the inexpressible. In the Second, his beloved Zenocrate falls sick and dies, leaving her distraught husband to rave and temporarily go mad, and carry with him her corpse

> Embalmed with cassia, ambergrise, and myrrh,
> Not lapped in lead, but in a sheet of gold.

Tamburlaine has the Governor of Babylon hanged in chains from Damascus's walls and shot by his viceroys; he orders all the citizens—men, women, and children—drowned, and in open defiance of Mahomet has all the "superstitious books," the Korans, placed in a heap and burned. Earlier, Tamburlaine had boasted that sickness and death could never conquer him, but to that inevitability Renaissance individuality could vouchsafe no answer. A six-foot plot of earth awaited the Scythian conqueror, as it does all folk.

Although chronology is uncertain, *The Jew of Malta* may have come next. Certainly, with Alleyn in the starring role, it enthralled spectators as much, if not more, if we may judge from the records of performance left by Henslowe, the manager of Strange's Men. Barabas the Jew is a Tamburlaine of the countinghouse, into which the wealth of the world flows: heaps of gold, bags of precious stones—"infinite riches in a little room." Machiavelli—as Elizabethans understood him—introduces the play. "I count religion but a childish toy," he declares, "And hold there is no sin but ignorance." The hero-villain Barabas is the first of many stage Machiavels. When the state extorts his fortune, he sets about gathering another. He contrives to have his daughter's two Christian suitors kill each other, poisons her and a whole nunnery, strangles a friar, and even-

tually becomes Governor of Malta before meeting his
end, like the devil he is, by being boiled in a caldron.
His excesses, abetted by his purchased Turkish slave,
Ithamore, have their own brand of cruel hilarity. Barabas is no Shylock, but *The Jew of Malta*, revived around
the same time, was not far from Shakespeare's mind
when he turned to *The Merchant of Venice*. The same
was the case with Marlowe's *Edward II* when Shakespeare came to write *Richard II*. Edward is homosexual
as Richard is not, but in both plays anointed monarchs
make a comparable descent from absolute authority to
vulnerable powerlessness.

The Chorus of the play for which Marlowe is today
best remembered, *The Tragical History of Doctor Faustus*, alludes to previous triumphs: to *Tamburlaine*
("the pomp of proud audacious deeds") and *Edward II*
(" sporting in the dalliance of love / In Courts of
kings, where state is overturned"). For Faustus the will
to power has intellectual curiosity as its activating prin-
ciple. An alumnus, like Hamlet, of Wittenberg University, he dismisses, in turn, Aristotle's logic, medicine,
the law, and divinity; only necromantic books, the re-
positories of forbidden knowledge, hold what he seeks.
So he makes his pact with the Devil: Mephistopheles
will serve him while Faustus lives. Good and Bad Angels contend for his soul; Pride, deadliest of the seven
sins, spurs him on. The Morality plays of the preceding
age provide a dramatic antecedent for this Mankind hero
envisaged as Renaissance intellectual, but classical mythology furnished the emblematic image for Faustus's
tragedy in the tale of Icarus, who had tried to fly too
high:

>   swollen with cunning, of a self-conceit,
>   His waxen wings did mount above his reach,
>   And melting, heavens conspired his overthrow.

The power for which Faustus has sold his soul is, in the
comical and farcical central scenes of the play, trivially

expended. At his bidding, he is granted his vision of the face that launched a thousand ships, but this Helen of Troy has no more substance than a shade; in such compacts the petitioner always loses. In the last scene the clock strikes twelve; Faustus's twenty-four years have expired. As thunder crashes and the devils come in to claim his soul, he cries, too late, "I'll burn my books!": the ultimate sacrifice for one who venerated learning. The Chorus points the moral:

> Regard his hellish fall
> Whose fiendful fortune may exhort the wise
> Only to wonder at unlawful things
> Whose deepness doth entice such forward wits
> To practice more than heavenly power permits.

No secular play is more suffused with religious feeling than *Doctor Faustus*, yet scandalous contemporary reports spoke of Marlowe as a blasphemer and atheist. Shakespeare alludes to the play, a perennial stage favorite, in *The Merry Wives of Windsor*, when Bardolph excitedly reports encountering "three German devils, three Doctor Faustuses" (IV.v.123–69).

Born in the same year as Shakespeare, Marlowe came of similar provincial middle-class stock, the son of a shoemaker in Canterbury. By the time he reached twenty-nine he had had at least seven plays performed— among them a tragedy on a Vergilian theme for the boy actors, *Dido, Queen of Carthage,* and a topical tragedy on the St. Bartholomew's Day Massacre of thousands of French Protestants in 1572, *The Massacre at Paris,* which survives in a fragmentary and disordered text— as well as an accomplished translation of Ovid's elegies and a glittering, long erotic narrative poem, *Hero and Leander.* Marlowe was reputed hot-tempered as well as free-thinking, and before he was thirty he had been slain (so the inquest postmortem concluded) in a brawl over the reckoning at a house of public refreshment in Deptford, "a little village about three miles distant from London." Shakespeare, who may have seen *Hero and Leander* in manuscript, would pay his fellow poet the compliment of quotation, for Marlowe is the dead shepherd to whom Phebe, speaking in pastoral character, alludes in *As You Like It*:

> Dead Shepherd, now I find thy saw of might,
> "Who ever loved that loved not at first sight?"
> (III.v.81–82)

Shakespeare is not known anywhere else in the corpus of his writings to have referred directly to a contemporary English poet.

Thomas Kyd

Unlike Marlowe, Thomas Kyd never went to a university. The son of a London scrivener, he was educated at Merchant Tailors' School, which in Richard Mulcaster had an outstanding Elizabethan humanist as headmaster. All the same, the paths of the two playwrights crossed. For a time Kyd shared lodgings with Marlowe, whose "atheistical" writings surfaced during a house search by government agents. Kyd was imprisoned and tortured; he would die young, a broken man. His fame rests on a single play. *The Spanish Tragedy* introduced, to sensational effect, revenge tragedy to the Elizabethan stage. Published anonymously in 1592, the play had by 1633 gone through ten printed editions; updated with additions (some by Jonson), it continued to lure spectators. Its plot is as elaborately patterned as its rhetorical blank verse. The Ghost of Don Andrea, slain in the wars with Portugal, and Revenge serve as Induction and constant stage presences: *The Spanish Tragedy* revels in play-within-the-play structures and motifs. It offers dumb shows (organic rather than merely ornamental), a wedding masque with the torches extinguished in blood, and—harbinger of *Hamlet*—a final inset play

mounted by the protagonist and presented before royalty; the play thus performed, *Soliman and Perseda,*
recapitulates themes of the surrounding drama and furnishes an appropriately bloody conclusion in which the
principals kill in earnest, not sport. The main action is
supplemented by a thematically integrated underplot
having to do with malfeasance in Portugal: multiple
plots, of which *King Lear* is the supreme instance,
would characterize much of Elizabethan dramaturgy,
comic as well as tragic. But *The Spanish Tragedy* offered playgoers a new theatrical excitement that was not
merely technical. In the pleasant arbor of Hieronimo,
Marshal of Spain, his son Horatio makes love one night
in secret—so he thinks—to Bel-Imperia, a woman above
him in station. Suddenly a forewarned rival suitor and
his cutthroat followers burst upon the lovers. Horatio is
hanged from a tree in the garden and stabbed to death
before the horrified young woman. Her mouth plugged
up to stop her screams, Bel-Imperia is abducted. For
moments the stage remains bare except for Horatio's
dangling corpse. Then old Hieronimo enters in his
nightshirt. "What outcries pluck me from my naked
bed," he exclaims,

And chill my throbbing heart with trembling fear,
Which never danger yet could daunt before?

(The passage is echoed comically by Shakespeare in *A
Midsummer Night's Dream* when Titania, awaking to
behold Bottom, exclaims, "What angel wakes me from
my flow'ry bed?" (III.i.130)). Hieronimo's own outcry,
"Who calls Hieronimo?" would become a great tag
line of the Elizabethan stage. As a dramatist, Kyd had
discovered electricity.

  In the scenes that follow, Hieronimo, frustrated in his
quest for justice by higher-ups, hovers between madness
and sanity. "The heavens are just," his wife, Isabella,
had comforted him, "murder cannot be hid." Yet it *is*
hid until a letter written in blood flutters down from the

casement of the room where Bel-Imperia is concealed, and reveals to Hieronimo the identities of the murderers. Responsible as marshal for justice in Spain, he becomes a private avenger. In his essay on revenge, Shakespeare's contemporary Francis Bacon had written, "Revenge is a kind of wild justice." Such is the vengeance taken by Hieronimo in *The Spanish Tragedy*. At one point Hieronimo recites in soliloquy a pastiche of verses from Virgil, Lucretius, Horace, and other Latin poets resisting any temptation to suicide. At another, he reads from the book in his hand, *"Vindicta mihi,"* vengeance for me. His text is the *Octavius* of Seneca, whose ghost hangs over *The Spanish Tragedy* every bit as noticeably as that of Don Andrea. Not for Hieronimo the St. Paul of Romans: "Vengeance is mine, I will repay, saith the Lord." In the end, Hieronimo bites out his own tongue rather than reveal what he has contrived; the rest is blood and silence. The guilty, the less guilty, and the innocent have perished, all caught up in the operation of (in G. K. Hunter's phrase) the "justice machine"; a machine indifferent to human happiness, which requires its sacrifices in order for its mandate to be fulfilled. The impact of Kyd's *Spanish Tragedy* is to be encountered in Shakespeare's *Titus Andronicus*. Without it we would also be without the greatest of all revenge plays, *Hamlet*, at least in the form in which we know it.

Other wits—some university, most not—enhanced the rich experimental mix of Elizabethan drama in the first years of the commercial playhouses. Journeyman dramatists, mostly anonymous, fashioned plays from the reigns of English monarchs as they found them recounted in Raphael Holinshed's *Chronicles of England, Scotland and Ireland* (1577, 1578) and other Elizabethan chronicles that constitute the earliest attempts at a continuous account of the whole of English history. The anonymous *Reign of King Edward III* (c. 1590–95) is sufficiently distinguished for some authorities (beginning with Capell in the eighteenth century) to have thought it likely that Shakespeare had a hand in it. There were at least three Henry V plays—all of them anonymous and two lost—before Shakespeare's. Thomas Nashe in 1592 exclaimed, "What a glorious thing it is to have Henry the Fifth represented on the stage, leading the French King prisoner, and forcing both him and the Dauphin to swear fealty." Three years later the Admiral's Men were drawing throngs for a new play that the company's manager Henslowe called "Harey the V"; meanwhile the rival Queen's Men were performing *The Famous Victories of Henry V, containing the honourable battle of Agincourt*, although this history was not printed until 1598, the year before Shakespeare's own version was completed.

George Peele

Another University Wit, George Peele gained his B.A. and M.A. at Oxford before immersing himself in the London theatrical milieu. He lived riotously (so report held), and a decade after his death in 1596 his madcap escapades and witticisms (most no doubt apocryphal) were memorialized in a pamphlet, *The Jests of George Peele*. Peele composed pageants and described tilts, but mainly he turned out plays—all sorts of plays: English history *(Edward I)*, heroical romance (the lost *Turkish Mahomet and Hiren the Fair Greek)*, foreign history *(The Battle of Alcazar)*, and biblical history *(The Love of King David and Fair Bethsabe)*, His classical pastoral *The Arraignment of Paris* was presented by the Chapel children at court before Queen Elizabeth in the early 1580s. The play gives a familiar legend a novel topical twist. Paris, whose abduction of Helen prompted the Greeks to embark upon their siege of Troy, is arraigned before a court of the Olympian deities for having awarded the golden apple to Venus. The apple is reclaimed and the case submitted to Diana, goddess of chastity, for final adjudication. She chooses to award the prize to "the noble phoenix of our age, Our fair Eliza" and—as a final stage direction puts it—*"She delivereth the ball of gold to the Queen's own hands."*

Peele's *Old Wives Tale,* which survives in an abbreviated text probably acted by a company of adults while on provincial tour, blends folklore with romance, as three serving men find themselves lost in a dark wood and are brought to a smith's cottage, where their host's old wife, Madge, helps them wile away the long night with a winter's tale. "Once upon a time, there was a king, or a lord, or a duke, that had a fair daughter, the fairest that ever was, as white as snow and as red as blood; and once upon a time his daughter was stolen away, and he sent all his men to seek out his daughter, and he sent so long that he sent all his men out of his land." No sooner has the old woman begun her tale than the characters come alive on the stage—among them the wicked sorcerer Sacrapant, who had turned himself into a great dragon and carried away a king's daughter, Delia, and keeps her captive and under a spell deep in the forest; the Wandering Knight Eumenides, who loves Delia and seeks her rescue; the huffing braggart Huanebango; two sisters, one shrewish and pretty, the other hard-favored but agreeable; the Old Man of the Cross; even Booby the clown and the Ghost of Jack. There are a well for the Water of Life and a hidden flame, enclosed in glass, which must be extinguished if the enchanter's spell is to be broken. All of course ends happily—as in an old tale—and Madge (who has been dozing) is awakened to prepare breakfast before her guests depart. *The Old Wives Tale* casts a spell stronger and more durable than Sacrapant's.

Robert Greene

Of middle-class Norwich stock, Robert Greene prided himself on academic credentials from both universities: a B.A. degree from St. John's College, Cambridge, and incorporation as an Oxford Master of Arts. Abandoning his Norwich wife and children, he lived precariously by his pen in the capital. He wrote ceaselessly—minor fiction in the popular euphuistic and Arcadian modes; muckraking pamphlets (in an age without newspapers)

about the London underworld, which Greene knew from
firsthand experience; repentance tracts consisting of
thinly veiled autobiography; and, above all, plays, the
surest means for a writer to support himself in an age
in which copyright protected publishers rather than authors. He tried his hand at a variety of dramatic genres.
With *Alphonsus, King of Aragon* Greene paid *Tamburlaine* the tribute of imitation (''mighty Tamburlaine'' is
mentioned in the dialogue) as his conquering base-born
hero becomes a dispenser of crowns and kingdoms, and
in the end marries his principal enemy's daughter. *A
Looking-Glass for London and England,* written in collaboration with Thomas Lodge (also a University Wit),
accommodates the medieval Mystery play to the
sixteenth-century London stage, telling the story of Jo-
nah and holding up the wickedness of Nineveh as a
mirror for contemporary London. Greene's *Scottish
History of James the Fourth, slain at Flodden, inter-
mixed with a pleasant comedy presented by Oberon,
King of Fairies,* an extravagant pseudo-history, early an-
ticipates the later vogue of tragicomedy. Greene may
have also written *George a Greene, the Pinner of Wakefield,* which has some of the appeal of an old ballad.
The play nostalgically evokes yeoman virtues; at the
end, when King Edward asks George, after many wonderful exploits, to kneel and be dubbed a knight, the
pinner declines the honor:

Then let me live and die a yeoman still.
So was my father, so must live his son.
For 'tis more credit to men of base degree
To do great deeds than men of dignity.

Greene dramatized an episode from Ludovico Ariosto's
romantic epic, *Orlando Furioso*—for which the only reward his princely patron bestowed upon him was a
question, ''Where did you find so many stories, Master
Ludovico?'' The influence of *Tamburlaine* is once again
apparent, and perhaps also, for Orlando's madness, *The*

Spanish Tragedy. But the play for which Greene is today best remembered is *Friar Bacon and Friar Bungay*, which happily blends the malign wonders of necromancy with the virtuous wonder of romantic love. Through his magical incantations the fabled master of Oxford's Brasenose College can make women of devils and juggle cats into costermongers as Friar Bacon pursues his rivalry with the Suffolk conjurer Friar Bungay. Bacon has devised a prospective glass—is it a magic glass or forerunner of the modern telescope (the historical Roger Bacon [c. 1214–c. 1294] wrote a treatise on physiological optics)—and with his Brazen Head hopes to wall England around with impregnable brass. But the Friar's black magic is foredoomed to spectacular failure. "Time was," speaks the Brazen Head, lightning flashes forth, and a hand suddenly appears out of nowhere to smash the Head with a hammer. In the play's second action, Lacy, Earl of Lincoln, falls in love with Margaret, a humble keeper's daughter. He tests her constancy in much the same way as Patient Griselda's constancy is tested in Chaucer's *Canterbury Tales*. When Lacy seems to renounce her for a higher-born maiden, Margaret prepares to seek heaven's joy before earth's vanity, and to be shorn a nun. As she is about to enter the convent, the earl arrives booted and spurred, and his friend Ermsby tersely puts to the fair maid of Fressingfield the decision she must make:

> Choose you, fair damsel; yet the choice is yours,
> Either a solemn nunnery or the Court,
> God or Lord Lacy.

Margaret's answer must be short, and it is. "The flesh is frail," she confesses.

> That when he comes with his enchanting face,
> Whatsoe'er betide, I cannot say him nay.

Off goes the habit. Thus are secular values triumphantly reaffirmed. Romantic love, leading to wedlock, holds legitimate magical powers unmatched by Friar Bacon's dark arts, and furnishes *Friar Bacon and Friar Bungay* with its celebratory finale.

5

Shakespeare in London

The Upstart Crow

Greene is today best remembered not for *Friar Bacon and Friar Bungay* or exposés of London low-lifes, or even for his novella *Pandosto,* which in due course supplied Shakespeare with the principal source for a late romance, *The Winter's Tale,* but for a topically allusive—and abusive—broadside he included in his last pamphlet, written as he lay dying, reportedly of a surfeit of Rhenish wine and pickled herring but probably more likely of pestilence, London then being in the grip of a particularly virulent outbreak of the plague (eleven thousand deaths were recorded for 1593 alone). Now, in his *Groatsworth of Wit* (1592), Greene warns his friends, "fellow scholars about this city"—Marlowe and (probably) Nashe and Peele—against "those puppets . . . that spake from our mouth, those antics garnished in our colours," and particularly against one:

> an upstart crow, beautified with our feathers, that with his *Tiger's heart wrapped in a player's hide*, supposes he's as well able to bombast out a blank verse as the best of you; and being an absolute *Johannes fac totum*, is in his own conceit the only Shake-scene in a country.

The punning reference to a Shake-scene and the parody of a line from I.iv of *3 Henry VI* ("O tiger's heart wrapped in a woman's hide!'') identify the victim unmistakably. Less clear is the purport of the attack, couched as it is in obscurely allusive language; but the University Wit, with his Cambridge and Oxford degrees, seems to be sneering at a mere uneducated player who deigns to set himself up as a universal genius *(Johannes fac totum)* and to rival his betters by turning out plays in stilted blank verse. Conceivably Greene is also accusing Shakespeare of plagiarism, because crows (as a contemporary remarked) ''selected flowers from others' wit.'' However that may be, the notice pays hostile tribute to a successful competitor.

The *Groatsworth of Wit* evoked protest that, its author being dead, fell upon the head of the man who had prepared the manuscript for the press. Before the year was out, Henry Chettle, a printer who would in time himself become a prolific playwright, included in a prefatory epistle to his *Kind-Heart's Dream* a handsome apology to the actor-playwright:

> I am as sorry as if the original fault had been my fault, because myself have seen his demeanor no less civil than he excellent in the quality [i.e., acting] he professes. Besides, divers of worship have reported his uprightness of dealing, which argues his honesty, and his facetious grace in writing, that approves his art.

Narrative Poems

Who the ''divers of worship''—that is, sundry gentlemen—were who vouched for Shakespeare's good character, history does not record. We do know, however, that in the next year, 1593, he published a long narrative poem, *Venus and Adonis,* with a signed dedication to Henry Wriothesley, the third Earl of Southampton. Elaborately courteous but not servile, self-deprecatory but with an undertow of confidence, the tone with which the patron, then nineteen, is addressed does not argue close personal acquaintance:

> Right Honorable, I know not how I shall offend in dedicating my unpolished lines to your Lordship, nor how the world will censure me for choosing so strong a prop to suppost so weak a burden. Only if your Honor seem but pleased, I account myself highly praised, and vow to take advantage of all idle hours, till I have honored you with some graver labor. But if the first heir of my invention prove deformed, I shall be sorry it had so noble a godfather, and never after ear so barren a land, for fear it yield me still so bad a harvest. I leave it to your honorable survey, and your Honor to your heart's content, which I wish may always answer your own wish, and the world's hopeful expectation.
>
> Your Honor's in all duty,
> William Shakespeare.

The phrase "first heir of my invention" has given scholars pause; after all, Shakespeare had already had plays produced. Perhaps he thus described *Venus and Adonis* simply because it marked his debut as a published author. Or maybe he was distinguishing between a serious literary venture, properly launched in a printed book equipped with a dedication, and those ephemeral entertainments that the masses admired on Shoreditch or on Bankside. As an aspiring man of letters he may simply have accepted, as a fact of life, his age's condescending valuation of plays and playwrights. A warmer note enters into the dedication, the next year, of *The Rape of Lucrece* to the same nobleman. "What I have done is yours," Shakespeare concludes, "what I have to do is yours; being part in all I have, devoted yours."

Both poems issued from the press of a former Stratford neighbor, Richard Field, whose father's goods John

Shakespeare had appraised in 1592. Three years Shake-speare's senior, Richard had migrated to London in 1579 and set up shop in the Blackfriars. The author may well have corrected the proofs of the poems, which are freer from error than any of Shakespeare's plays issued during the author's lifetime. What subsequent dealings, if any, Shakespeare had with the earl can only be con-jectured. No further document links the two men, and Southampton is not one of the patrons to whom Shake-speare's old friends and colleagues, Heminges and Condell, dedicate the First Folio of his plays in 1623. Many believe Southampton is the Fair Youth celebrated in the Sonnets, and although this may be so, it cannot be proven.

Excellent in the Quality He Professes

In any event, nondramatic activities cannot for very long have absorbed Shakespeare's principal creative ener-gies. The plague eased, the playhouses reopened. On March 15, 1595, the Accounts of the Treasurer of the Queen's Chamber list William Shakespeare, William Kempe, and Richard Burbage—all three ''servants to the Lord Chamberlain''—as joint payees for plays per-formed the previous Christmas season before her maj-esty at her royal palace at Greenwich. This notice is the first to connect Shakespeare with an acting company, and it shows him already in an official capacity. Evi-dently he had become, at thirty, a leading member of the most esteemed troupe in the realm.

Scattered reports enrich our sense of Shakespeare's career as an actor. Traditions of uncertain reliability re-port that Shakespeare played ''kingly parts,'' that he stalked as the Ghost in *Hamlet,* and that he was the faithful old servant Adam in *As You Like It*—according to this intelligence, appearing ''so weak and drooping and unable to walk, that he was forced to be supported and carried by another person to a table, at which he was seated among some company, who were eating, and

one of them sung a song.'' Unlike Burbage or Edward
Alleyn, Shakespeare was not one of the celebrated actors of the period, although the gossip Aubrey, in his
Brief Lives, avouches that Shakespeare ''did act exceedingly well.'' Shakespeare performed in other men's
plays as well as in his own: in Ben Jonson's *Every Man
in His Humour* in 1598, and, five years later, in the
same dramatist's *Sejanus*. We know because Jonson included the cast names when in 1616 he brought together
his plays for the age's first dramatic folio. When, seven
years after Shakespeare's death, his old associates (following Jonson's precedent) gathered together his comedies, histories, and tragedies for the great First Folio,
they put Shakespeare's name at the head of their
prefatory list of the ''Principal Actors in all these
Plays.''

All in all, Shakespeare's contemporaries—so far as
their responses left an imprint—overwhelmingly, the
wretched Greene excepted, spoke well of the man and
his art. In his *Palladis Tamia,* or *Wit's Treasury,* Francis
Meres, a Master of Arts of both universities and a clergyman dwelling in London, includes a ''Comparative
discourse of our English poets, with the Greek, Latin,
and Italian poets'' in which he compares the best of his
contemporaries (as he saw them) with the ancients and
the masters of Renaissance Italy. A celebrated passage
enthusiastically cites Shakespeare:

As Plautus and Seneca are accounted the best for
comedy and tragedy among the Latins, so Shakespeare among the English is the most excellent in
both kinds for the stage. For comedy, witness his
Gentlemen of Verona, his *Errors,* his *Love's Labour's Lost,* his *Love's Labour's Won,* his *Midsummer's Night Dream,* and his *Merchant of
Venice;* for tragedy, his *Richard the 2.,* *Richard
the 3.,* *Henry the 4.,* *King John,* *Titus Andronicus*
and his *Romeo and Juliet.*

These, then, are plays—selectively limited to six comedies and an equal number of tragedies (the list here including histories)—known to have existed by 1599, when *Palladis Tamia* was printed. *Loves's Labour's Won*, which—no text having come down—may be an alternative title for an extant comedy, remains a much discussed puzzle.

Other voices include that of the obscure Anthony Scoloker. In his prefatory epistle to *Diaphantus, or the Passions of Love* (1604), Scoloker avers that a superior literary work should be (for example) "like friendly Shakespeare's tragedies, where the comedian rides, when the tragedian stands on tiptoe: faith, it should please all, like Prince Hamlet." Did the two men know one another, as the phrase "friendly Shakespeare" might suggest? In his popular *Remains of a greater Work concerning Britain* (1605), which rapidly passed through seven editions and issues, the distinguished antiquary William Camden cites Shakespeare—along with Sidney, Spenser, Jonson, and half a dozen others—as among the "most pregnant wits of these our times, whom succeeding ages may justly admire." An anecdote jotted down on March 13, 1602, by John Manningham in his commonplace book speaks of Shakespeare in a lighter and more personal vein. Manningham was then a young law student at the Middle Temple, where the previous month he had seen Shakespeare's *Twelfth Night* performed. The anecdote (which Manningham had from his roommate) brings together the leading dramatist and the leading actor of the Chamberlain's Men in an amorous context, with the dramatist wittily having the upper hand. "Upon a time, when Burbage played Richard III," Manningham writes,

there was a citizen grew so far in liking with him that before she went from the play she appointed him to come that night unto her by the name of Richard III. Shakespeare, overhearing their conclusion, went before, was entertained and at his game ere Burbage came. Then message being brought that Richard III was at the door, Shakespeare caused return to be made that William the Conqueror was before Richard III.

"Shakespeare's name William," Manningham helpfully adds.

In 1597 the company's ground-lease on their regular house, the Theater in the northern suburb of Shoreditch, expired, and when their efforts at renewal fell through, they dismantled the building and ferried the timber across the Thames to Bankside. That was the next winter. In 1598, during the Christmas holidays, there was "a great snow," with the Thames "nigh frozen at London Bridge" (as we learn in 1601 from John Stow's *An nales of England*): not the most practicable time to ferry timbers across the Thames. But that cruel winter the Chamberlain's Men did indeed eventually cart the timbers of the Theater across the Thames to Bankside. There they erected a new playhouse more splendid than any the capitol had yet seen. This house they called the Globe. (In October 1989 workmen uncovered, during bulldozing for an office building on the site of a former brewery in south London, near Southworth Bridge, vestiges—chalk blocks, wooden stumps, and old bricks—of a small section of the foundation of a stair turret on the east-north-east side, and sections of the adjacent foundations, of Shakespeare's Globe. The exploratory dig, as described by Andrew Gurr, a scholar actively committed to the pursuit, in *Shakespeare Quarterly* for Spring 1990, uncovered a small slice of the theater's perimeter wall and, more consequential, the brick foundation of a stair turret lobby—one of two such turrets at the Globe, giving access to the galleries opposite the stage—along with the foundation walls of a passageway running from the lobby into the yard. A good chance exists that altogether more than 40 per cent of the Globe's original circuit may be excavated. These are, of course, the remains of the second Globe, the playhouse depicted in 1647 by Wenceslas Hollar in his cel-

ebrated "Long View" of London from Bankside; but
the second Globe was built on the foundations of the
first. Also uncovered was a quantity of hazelnut shells,
the nuts having served more or less the same function
for Elizabethan audiences which popcorn, a much less
durable testimonial, serves for modern-day movie patrons.)

Most Elizabethan dramatists eked out their precarious
livelihoods as hirelings of the actors, but when the players set up the Globe, they also instituted a species of
proprietorship in which Shakespeare was entitled to 10
percent of the profits. The value of a share fluctuated
as the original holders decreased or augmented their
number. So too did the profits vary, depending upon
the house's takings; a plague season would be disastrous. How much did Shakespeare actually earn? Somewhat in excess of two hundred pounds, on average,
annually might be a reasonable guess: an excellent
income by Elizabethan standards—ten times what a
well-paid schoolmaster would make. As part owner,
Shakespeare would have had a voice in company policy.
Probably he helped stage his own plays and also those
of others. Above all, he was his troupe's regular dramatist, in the sense that he wrote exclusively for them:
their "ordinary poet," in Elizabethan theatrical parlance. He thus served his associates in a triple capacity:
as playwright, actor, and business manager. Historically, few writers (the ancients excepted) can have made
such a thoroughgoing commitment to the profession of
playwright.

6

The Lord Chamberlain's Man:
Early Plays

When Queen Elizabeth died in 1603, her Privy Council at once proclaimed the accession of James VI of Scotland as James I of England. On May 17, only ten days after his arrival in London, the Lord Chamberlain's Men became, by royal patent, the King's Men—a testimonial to their preeminence at their craft. Shakespeare's name appears near the head of the list in the warrant. The next year Shakespeare is the first mentioned of the nine players allowed scarlet cloth in order to participate, as Grooms of the Chamber, in the coronation procession, and the following summer the players waited for eighteen days upon the Spanish ambassador and his train at the queen's palace, Somerset House, which James had placed at the ambassador's disposal. Thus, a special relation was established early between the new monarch and his company. Although other troupes were beckoned to perform at Whitehall Palace or at Greenwich, the King's Men were there more frequently than all the others combined. According to one reckoning, they played at court 187 times between the issuance of the patent and the year of Shakespeare's death. Of the ten pieces shown during the year commencing November 1, 1604, seven were by Shakespeare, most of them past favorites—including *The Comedy of Errors, The Merchant of Venice,* and *The Merry Wives of Windsor*—but the king also watched the relatively new *Othello* and the new *Measure for Measure.*

No neglected genius discovered in after ages by a grateful world, Shakespeare prospered by the endeavors of his art. He invested shrewdly, nurturing the ties with his hometown. "He was wont to go to his native country [i.e., county] once a year," Aubrey noted in his *Brief Lives*. In 1597 Shakespeare purchased the Great House of New Place, the second largest in Stratford. The mansion, with its three stories and five gables, was warmed by ten fireplaces. It would remain Shakespeare's permanent residence until his death. He also required an address closer to work. From tax assessments we know that Shakespeare dwelt in London in the mid-nineties, first in St. Helen's, Bishopsgate, an upper-middle-class neighborhood not far from the Theater; later in the Liberty of the Clink on the Bankside, where, in nearby Southwark, stood the Globe.

In 1604, and for a time before and perhaps after, "one Mr. Shakespeare . . . lay in the house" of Christopher Mountjoy, a French Huguenot tire maker (i.e., manufacturer of ornamental headdresses) in Silver Street, center for the wig trade, in northwest London. A court action unravels the history of a courtship and its aftermath. The Mountjoys were keen to marry their daughter, Mary, an only child, to Stephen Belott, a former apprentice, then working for a fixed salary in the downstairs shop. But Belott held back until Madam Mountjoy persuaded Shakespeare to act as a matchmaker. So the depositions testify in *Belott* v. *Mountjoy*. The dramatist conveyed to Belott the father's promises with respect to the marriage portion and also word that, should she refuse the match, "she should never cost him, the defendant her father, a groat.* Whereupon, and in regard Master Shakespeare had told them that they should have a sum of money for a portion from the father, they were made sure by Master Shakespeare by giving their consent, and agreed to marry." The wedding duly took place. Later Belott and his father-in-law quarreled over the dowry and a promised legacy. Hence, eight years later, the suit. In his signed testimony Shakespeare, described as a gentleman of Stratford-upon-Avon, remem-

*A silver coin equal in value to four pennies.

bered that Mountjoy had promised Belott a dowry of
some sort, but what the amount was, and when it was
to be paid, he could not say, nor could he vouch that
the defendant had pledged the couple two hundred
pounds after his decease. Although Shakespeare's name
was set down for a second hearing, he did not again
testify. The court referred the case to the elders of the
French Church in London for arbitration. Of all the
Shakespeare records, only this case shows the playwright living amid the materials for domestic comedy.
The proceedings, for all their mercenary overtones, reveal the poet-dramatist of superhuman powers as a
somewhat baffled mortal, or (in the discoverer's words)
"as a man among men."

The brouhaha caused by performance of *3 Henry VI*
demonstrates that, less than twenty years after the first
public amphitheaters had opened their doors to the London public, the young Shakespeare had already become
a notable presence in the theater. (Incidentally, the last
two installments of *Henry VI* may well have preceded
the first segment in composition. Where is it written
that events being dramatized have to be dramatized
chronologically? A modern instance may suffice by way
of illustration. Lillian Hellman, who won enduring fame
with *The Little Foxes*, turned to the earlier history of
her vulturous predators in *Another Part of the Forest*.)
The London stage of the 1590s had never seen anything
quite as ambitious in scope as Shakespeare's early tetralogy *1-3 Henry VI* and *Richard III:* the first *Henriad,*
as students refer to these plays, dramatizing English history from 1422 to 1485.

Indeed, the world stage had seen little in scope to
compare with this undertaking since Greek tragedy—
e.g., Aeschylus's *Oresteia,* the only complete Greek
trilogy to have survived. These may be thought to have
provided a precedent, but the Elizabethans paid mainly
lip service to the Greek classics. In England the epic
transformation of Shakespeare's amorphous chronicle
sources found its only precedent in the Mystery plays
of the cathedral towns, of which Shakespeare had per-

haps himself witnessed a performance at Coventry as a boy. Only a few years ago the *Henry VI* trilogy (1590–92), after centuries of neglect, was, more or less intact, revived with spectacular success before enraptured audiences by the Royal Shakespeare Company performing at Stratford-upon-Avon and on tour.

A key scene in *1 Henry VI* (II.iv) shows Richard Plantagenet (son of the late Earl of Cambridge), the Duke of Somerset, and sundry other aristocrats gathered for convenience in London's Temple Garden. It is here that Richard plucks the white rose that would become symbolic of the Yorkist cause, and Somerset—adhering, as he claims, to "the party of the truth" (i.e., the Lancastrians)—plucks the red rose from the thorn. In time the Wars of the Roses—the burden of the *Henry VI* plays—would follow. Warwick puts on the white rose and prophesies—correctly, for in Elizabethan drama prophesies tend to become actualities—that

> this brawl today
> Grown to this faction in the Temple garden
> Shall send, between the red rose and the white,
> A thousand souls to death and dreadful night.
>   (II.iv.124–27)

For the rest, in the course of *1 Henry VI,* England's greatness abroad, namely in France, is lost because of division at home, as Joan la Pucelle, the peasant's daughter from Domrémy, rallies the French forces.

Born in 1412, and burnt at the stake in 1431, she would be known to posterity as Joan of Arc: declared venerable in 1904, blessed in 1908, and canonized as Saint Joan in 1924. To the English, however, Joan was a bane. In the play she conjures with fiends, to avoid burning denies her own parentage, and although unmarried whorishly claims she is pregnant: this is scarcely our Saint Joan. In its own day *1 Henry VI* made a great impression on spectators. In his famous tribute to the popularity of *1 Henry VI* the contemporary anti-Puritan satirist Thomas Nashe declares,

> How would it have joyed brave Talbot (the terror of the French) to think that after he had lain two hundred years in his tomb, he should triumph again on the stage, and have his bones new embalmed with the tears of ten thousand spectators at least (at several times), who, in the tragedian that represents his person, imagine they behold him fresh bleeding.

This passage, which occurs in *Pierce Penniless* (1592), recalls Act IV, scene vii, of Shakespeare's play in which, on a battlefield near Bordeaux, old Talbot, dying with his young son—his Icarus, his blossom—dead in his arms, frozen emblematically in the posture of a funerary sculpture, receives from Sir William Lucy his elaborate epitaph.

The first Henriad goes on to depict the marriage of King Henry and Margaret (daughter of the threadbare Reignier, Duke of Anjou), and the descent of a kingdom, under a monarch whose churchlike humors make him ill-suited to governance, into eventual anarchy and civil war: the matter of *2 Henry VI*. For a while York (as he confides to the audience) will be still, but in time he grapples with the house of Lancaster to make Henry perforce yield the crown. In the end York is captured by Queen Margaret's forces and made to stand upon a molehill; he is wiped with a napkin stained with his slain young son's blood and crowned with a paper crown before being stabbed to death by his triumphant enemies *(3 Henry VI*, I.iii).

The sequel play, *Richard III* (c. 1593)—at some 3,600 lines Shakespeare's longest drama except for *Hamlet*—has not suffered similar neglect on the boards and is the subject of a notable film directed and starred in by Laurence Olivier. Crookback Richard, the diabolical protagonist, cunningly rises to power. Thirty-two when he died, Richard had reigned for a mere twenty-six months, but Tudor apologists were not long in transforming the man into a monster. The Warwickshire antiquary John Rous, who died in 1491, reports that Richard—an Antichrist—poisoned his wife and incarcerated her mother for life, murdered his nephews, and killed (or had killed) that "holy man," Henry VI. Rous describes Richard—somewhat improbably—as having been "held for two years in his mother's womb, emerging with teeth and with hair down to this shoulder"; also as "small of stature, having a short figure, uneven shoulders, the right being higher than the left."

"Deformed persons are commonly even with nature; for, as nature hath done ill by them, so do they by nature, being for the most part (as the Scripture saith) 'void of natural affection'; and so they have their revenge of nature." Thus Francis Bacon—who was Shakespeare's exact contemporary and conceivably knew firsthand from performance the dramatist's *Richard III*—writes in his essay "Of Deformity" (1598). Shakespeare's Richard has his revenge on nature. Deformity has its own peculiar ethical symbolism, equating physical disfigurement with moral turpitude. Such an equation underlies the abuse heaped upon Richard; first in *3 Henry VI*, when he is Duke of Gloucester, and then in *Richard III*, even after he becomes ruler of all England: a whole menagerie is invoked for unflattering metaphors.

The preceding installment of Shakespeare's first tetralogy had ended with Edward IV back on the throne and looking forward to enjoying the pleasures of the court; pleasure was always his principal occupation. There is no interval in the continuing action that the long title of the early quartos sums up: *The Tragedy of King Richard the Third. Containing his treacherous plots against his brother Clarence, the pitiful murder of his innocent nephews, his tyrannical usurpation; with the whole course of his detested life, and most deserved death.* However evil himself, Richard is vastly amusing yet serves God's providential purpose: those who perish at his hands by and large deserve their fates as Richmond rises with aplomb to power. The end sums up all as on the eve of the battle of Bosworth Field Richard, assailed by a guilty conscience, endures nightmares. His antagonist, Richmond, on the other hand, enjoys sweet dreams: the scourge gives way to God's beneficent minister, and the Tudor age, which Richmond—now Henry VII—was to go to such pains to mythologize, has begun. With *Richard III* the myth found in Shakespeare its most complexly eloquent spokesman, although more than myth went into this compelling play.

Over the years sundry dramatic orphans—unascribed plays of the 1590s: history plays available in manuscript or in quarto playbooks—have been attributed in whole or in part on stylistic and/or thematic grounds to Shakespeare: *Edward III*, for example, or *Edmund Ironside*. The supporting evidence, while sometimes intriguing, remains speculative. In any event, *1-3 Henry VI* are not the earliest canonical plays. As a youthful dramatist Shakespeare tried his hand at comedy and tragedy as well as history.

Friendship, as exhibited in the relationship of Valentine and Proteus, furnished Shakespeare with his subject in *The Two Gentlemen of Verona* (c. 1593). Romantic love plays as important a role, but the claims of masculine friendship are the perspective from which love between the sexes is viewed. No great difference separates the vocabulary of the one theme from the other as "sweet Valentine" and his "loving Proteus" address each other in terms of mutual adoration approaching, at times, the religious. The play dramatizes an ideal betrayed. The very name Proteus—familiar enough in Elizabethan letters for a fickle, unstable friend, often a self-serving flatterer—forewarns as much. Separation serves as catalyst. In the first scene Valentine bids farewell to disconsolate Proteus, who will remain behind with his girlfriend, Julia, while his friend goes off "to see the wonders of the world abroad" (the play is, as much as anything else, about a young man's education). Once in Milan, Valentine promptly—and without violation of the accepted imperatives of idealized male friendship—falls in love with Sylvia, the Duke's daughter, and she with him. When Proteus arrives on the scene, dispatched by an authoritarian parent to further *his* education, he too finds Sylvia irresistible. If in the course of the *Two Gentlemen* Proteus does not run through quite all the sins, he manages to touch a number of bases. He is false to both friendship and love, Valentine and Julia, who, disguised as a boy, follows Proteus to Milan and eavesdrops as he woos Sylvia under her chamber window. In a forest near Mantua, Proteus's near rape of Sylvia is averted by Valentine's unforeseen intervention.

When the gentlemen reconcile, Valentine offers to give up Sylvia to his friend. However psychologically unreal to moderns, Valentine's gesture of renunciation would have been taken in stride by Elizabethans brought up on the conventions of friendship literature. Friendship is of course a universal of human experience and appears elsewhere in Shakespeare: in the *Sonnets*, for example, and in *The Merchant of Venice*, in which Antonio risks all—even his life—to further the matrimonial hopes of a friend wholly unlike him in temperament. In no other of Shakespeare's plays, however, is the theme so consistently center stage as in *The Two Gentlemen of Verona*, as friendship is by turns extolled, betrayed, and ultimately reaffirmed.

The first scene of *Titus Andronicus* (c. 1593) takes place before the Capitol in ancient Rome. To the accompaniment of drums and trumpets, the late emperor's two sons enter, by separate doors, with their patrician followers. Saturninus appeals on legalistic grounds—he is the firstborn—for the crown; Bassianus urges the moral claim of superior virtue. Each is in his own terms right. From the upper level of the stage—*Titus Andronicus* is a tragedy that fully exploits the resources of the Elizabethan playhouse—Marcus, the tribune of the people,

announces that their voices have been given to his
brother, the conquering general Titus Andronicus. In
an elaborate processional entry Titus returns in triumph
from his wars against the Goths, bringing back with him
Lucius and his three other surviving sons and a strikingly aloof figure, Aaron the Moor. Aaron says not a
word through this long scene, during which he twice
briefly departs, and need not to attract audience notice;
for he alone is "coal black"—a blackamoor—with a
fleece of woolly hair.

The characters to whom we are introduced have sufficiently Roman-sounding names, and the patricians and
tribunes of the people, returning legions, burial rites,
and great issue of imperial election—all these convey
the flavor of Roman history: late Roman history, one
gathers from the captive Goths who bedeck Titus's triumph. But it is mostly spurious history. In *Titus Andronicus* Shakespeare finds his own mode of savage
hilarity, perhaps best exemplified in the scene (III.i)
that has the Andronici—Titus, Marcus, and Lucius—
quarreling over who will have the privilege of sacrific-
ing his hand as ransom for Titus's sons. In the upshot,
Titus has his hand chopped off by the Moor (one of
many brutalities) while the others are temporarily offstage. Barely able to repress his glee, Aaron returns
with the sons' heads and the severed hand—which the
raped and mutilated Lavinia, like a faithful dog, carries off between her teeth. The Rome in which such
bestiality can occur is not the civilization of Cicero
and law and aqueducts, but the decadent empire of
Nero and the gladiatorial contests: "a wilderness of
tigers."

In the end the slain Tamora's corpse receives treat-
ment appropriate to her bestial nature (lustful and in-
satiable, she has consorted with the villainous Moor).
"No mournful bell shall ring her burial," Lucius, newly
declared emperor, decrees in the final speech of the
tragedy,

But throw her forth to beasts and birds of prey.
Her life was beastly and devoid of pity,
And being dead, let birds on her take pity.

The peculiar resonance of these lines owes more to
Shakespeare's vision than to literary or theatrical
sources. But if he here seems to look ahead to the modern theater of cruelty, he also expresses in the play a
characteristic interest in social order: Marcus, all passion spent, implores the sons of Rome "to knit again /
This scattered corn into one mutual sheaf."

Virtually ignored by professional theater folk for almost three centuries, *Titus Andronicus* returned triumphantly to the stage in 1955 in the celebrated Peter Brook
revival at Stratford-upon-Avon, and two years later in
London's West End, with Laurence Olivier as Titus, his
then-wife Vivien Leigh as Lavinia, and Anthony Quayle
as the Moor. The production demonstrated the enduring
stage vitality of this formerly contemned early Shakespearean tragedy, and revealed also how the dramatist
distances the barbarities by stylized dramaturgy and formal rhetoric.

In *The Taming of the Shrew* (c. 1594), on the day
appointed for his marriage to Katherine, the famous
shrew of Padua, Petruchio keeps the wedding party fret-
fully waiting. When he finally makes an appearance, he
is—as the page Biondello breathlessly announces—
mounted on a decrepit nag and grotesquely attired. The
groom's deportment in church befits his costume. At his
father-in-law's house, Petruchio boorishly passes up the
wedding feast, but before carrying his Kate off, he
pauses to deliver a manifesto to the assembled company: "I will be master of what is mine own. / She is
my goods, my chattels. . . . " Harsh doctrine, and ob-
noxious to modern sentiment, but for the period conventional enough and theologically sanctioned. Was
there not St. Paul's advice in his letter to the Ephesians:
"Let women be subject to their husbands, as to the
Lord; for the husband is the head of the woman, as
Christ is the head of the church"? Elizabethans of every

station knew Paul's words well; they heard them every time their preacher delivered from his pulpit "The Sermon of the State of Matrimony" from *The Book of Homilies*. The natural inferiority of women, ratified by scripture, was official Church of England doctrine. Yet paradoxically a woman, inferior to none, held greatest sway in the land. But in this freewheeling comedy the shrew is at length tamed.

The rather complex tripartite structure of the *Shrew* includes, besides the main plot and the assumed identities of the underplot, an overplot, or Induction, in which a Lord finds the tinker Sly in drunken sleep before a country alehouse and spirits him away to his own manor house, where he is transiently deluded into believing he is himself a lord. Despite the fantastic premise, these brief scenes have a persuasive verisimilitude. The Induction, itself illusion, introduces Sly and the playhouse audience to the more distanced illusion that the visiting players come to offer. The *Shrew* revels in the very idea of theater. Comedy, as the Messenger proclaims, has its own therapeutic function:

> Your Honor's players, hearing your amendment,
> Are come to play a pleasant comedy.
> For so your doctors hold it very meet,
> Seeing too much sadness hath congealed your
>   blood,
> And melancholy is the nurse of frenzy.
> Therefore they thought it good you hear a play
> And frame your mind to mirth and merriment,
> Which bars a thousand harms and lengthens life.
> (Induction, ii, 129–36)

In a supremely self-confident touch, Shakespeare has Sly quickly grow bored with the players' production. Few audiences have reacted similarly, nor have revivals been greeted by female activists marching in protest on opening night, although some have been predictably

discomfited by even bygone sexism. Much of course depends upon the presentation.

In the last scene of *Love's Labor's Lost* (c. 1594), the
locals undertake to entertain their courtly betters with
a Show of the Nine Worthies. Dusk gathers as the summer day wears on. When the frivolity is at its merriest
a black-suited messenger, Monsieur Marcade, enters
unheralded to notify the Princess that the king her father
is dead. Marcade has one of the most striking short
parts—a mere three lines—in all Shakespeare. After he
speaks all pastimes cease. The Princess and her retinue
immediately prepare for departure. And what of the
wooing games so optimistically undertaken? "Now, at
the latest minute of the hour," the king begs the ladies,
"grant us your loves." It is not to be; not so soon,
anyway. The lovers who had denied love with their academe must first perform a prescribed period of penance before their mourning mistresses will deign to
receive them as sweethearts. "At the twelvemonth's
end," Maria assures Longueville, "I'll exchange my
black gown for a faithful friend." The upshot is, in a
way, no surprise, for the title had forewarned that love's
labor would be lost. Still, while the play merrily proceeds, hope springs; and for Elizabethan comedy the
resolution is sufficiently audacious, straining against familiar limits of genre. Shakespeare savors his unortho-
doxy by having his most articulate character take note
of it. "Our wooing doth not end like an old play,"
Biron ruefully sums up:

Jack hath not Jill. These ladies' courtesy
Might well have made our sport a comedy.
                              (V.ii.875–77)

How different from *A Midsummer Night's Dream,* in
which Puck sings in very similar words of the more
usual comic disentangling: "Jack shall have Jill, /
Nought shall go ill" (III.ii.461–62).

Students have seen *Love's Labor's Lost* as teeming

with references to events, causes, and living persons, and sought to recover the meaning of private jokes made unintelligible by the passage of time. May not the witty boy Mote, twice called "tender juvenal" (i.e., juvenile), punningly represent the witty, university-trained Thomas Nashe, characterized as "gallant young Juvenal" by Meres in *Palladis Tamia?* Nashe took up arms against the Cambridge don Gabriel Harvey in pamphlet wars as vitriolic as they are obscure. Who, then, signifies Harvey in the play? Maybe Holofernes, whose affected language Harvey to a degree shared, and who was always to be seen in the company of his parson brother—the equivalent of Nathaniel? Others have urged other candidates; as far back as 1747 the editor Warburton opted, with characteristic dogmatism, for Florio: "By Holofernes is designed a particular character, a pedant and schoolmaster of our author's time, one John Florio, a teacher of the Italian tongue in London, who has given us a small dictionary of that language under the title of *A World of Words.*"

His scant plot gave Shakespeare ample leeway for reveling uninhibitedly in puns, conceits, parodies, and witty badinage. Some quibbles require patient historical explication for their multilayered meaning to be rendered accessible to the modern reader, but one wonders how much of the verbal high jinks escaped even Elizabethans in the rapid-fire give-and-take of the two hours' traffic of the stage. The larger contours of Shakespearean thematic topography remain clear enough, though. The lovers may send their mistresses' letters too long by half a mile, or cram as much rhyme on a sheet of paper as will fill both sides, margin and all, but in the end what speaks most eloquently, as the sage Boyet observes, is "the heart's still rhetoric." This truth the lovers, in the course of the play, learn. Biron resolves henceforth to woo "in russet yeas and honest kersey noes"; or, as he puts it—for all the gallants—after Marcade's announcement, "Honest plain words best pierce the ear of grief." So much they have come to know at least intellectually. Now they will have a year to ponder their lesson. The verbal revels are over.

But if at the end love's labor is lost, this is only temporary. Before dispersing, the audience is treated to a song of spring and winter, rather improbably written by—so we are told—the pedant and the curate, "the two learned men." The song transports us from Navarre's court to the homey seasonal realities of maidens bleaching their summer smocks in the sun, or milk coming frozen home in the pail, presaging the passage of the year and a day, which is after all, as Biron wryly observes, too long for a play.

Beginning at Windsor Castle in April 1398, when Henry Bolingbroke in the presence of Richard II leveled his accusations against the Duke of Norfolk, and ending with the aftermath of Richard III's defeat on Bosworth Field in August 1485, Shakespeare's two vast tetralogies present a consecutive narrative of almost a century of medieval English history. Only two of Shakespeare's history plays, *King John* and *Henry VIII*, stand apart from this grand sequence.

One of the more intriguing aspects of *King John* (c. 1595–96) is that it fails to mention—let alone dramatize—the most celebrated event of John's fairly long reign. By 1215, the year before his death, the king had squandered his resources in a futile war with France, quarreled with Rome by nominating a worthless favorite for the primacy, plundered the clergy who did not subscribe to his candidate, and (most infuriating) alienated subjects of all classes by his arbitrary despotism and exorbitant taxes. The stage was set for Runnymede. There, on June 15, in a meadow midway between Windsor and the barons' camp at Staines, King John and some forty hostile peers—acting on the advice of the lords spiritual and temporal, including the Archbishop of Canterbury, the papal legate, Pandulph, and the Earl of Pembroke—set their seals to the articles of Magna Carta, or the Great [large] Charter. The Charter denounced John's evil deeds and innovations, and reaffirmed neglected legal processes, although it did not

Mr. WILLIAM
SHAKESPEARES

COMEDIES,
HISTORIES, &
TRAGEDIES.

Published according to the True Originall Copies.

LONDON
Printed by Isaac Iaggard, and Ed. Blount. 1623.

William Shakespeare, *Comedies, Histories & Tragedies* (1623), title page (Courtesy Folger Shakespeare Library)

Exterior of the Birthplace, c. 1762 (watercolor by Richard Greene)
(Courtesy Folger Shakespeare Library)

Elizabethan schoolroom, from Alexander Nowell, *Catechismus breuis, Christianae disciplinac* (1573), title page (Courtesy Folger Shakespeare Library)

Richard Burbage (Courtesy Folger Shakespeare Library)

Edward Alleyn as Tamburlaine (Courtesy Folger Shakespeare Library)

Bankside amphitheaters (Wenceslaus Hollar, "Long View" of London, 1647) (Courtesy Folger Shakespeare Library)

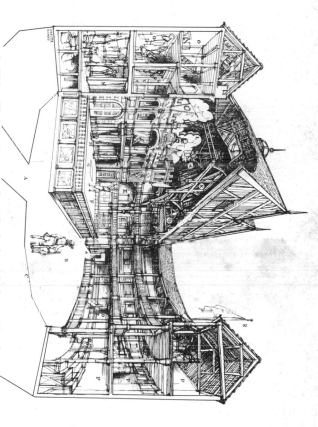

C. Walte-Hodges. *Interior of an Elizabethan Playhouse* (drawing)
(Courtesy Folger Shakespeare Library)

The Tragicall Historie of
the Life and Death of
Doctor Faustus.

With new Additions,

Written by C H. M A R.

Christopher Marlowe, *The Tragical History of the Life and Death of Doctor Faustus* (1631 ed.), title page (Courtesy Folger Shakespeare Library)

The Spanish Tragedi
OR,
Hieronimo is mad againe.

Containing the lamentable end of *Don Horatio*, and *Belimperia*; with the pittifull death of *Huronimo*.

Newly corrected, amended, and enlarged with new Additions of the *Painters* part, and others, as it hath of late been divers times acted.

LONDON,
Printed by W. White, for I. White and T. Langley, and are to be sold at their Shop over against the Sarazens head without New-gate. 1615.

Thomas Kyd, *The Spanish Tragedy* (1615 ed.), title page (Courtesy Folger Shakespeare Library)

THE
WORKES
OF
Benjamin Jonson

Benjamin Jonson, *Works* (1616), title page (Courtesy Folger Shakespeare Library)

Hamlet, 1604 title page
(Courtesy Folger Shakespeare
Library)

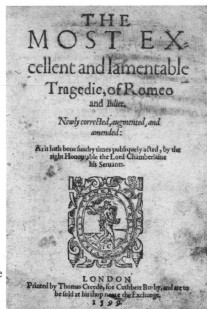

Romeo and Juliet, 1599 title
page (Courtesy Folger
Shakespeare Library)

Samuel Ireland, New Place, Chapel, Grammar School (1795)
(Courtesy Folger Shakespeare Library)

Shakespeare: the Chandos Portrait: Ozias Humphry's rendering,
1783 (Courtesy Folger Shakespeare Library)

go so far as to mandate habeas corpus writs or trial by jury.

"No free man," declares Article 39, "shall be seized or imprisoned, or stripped of his rights or possessions, or outlawed or exiled, or deprived of his standing in any other way, nor will we [the king] proceed with force against him, or send others to do so, except by the lawful judgement of his equals or by the law of the land." The king himself was subject to—rather than above— the law. Pope Innocent III might declare Magna Carta null and void, and excommunicate its signatories, articles would be added or deleted, there would be subsequent charters, but in time the document would come to be viewed as the cornerstone of the English constitution: the guarantor of individual liberty, foreshadower of the cease of absolutism. That heritage was not yet self-evident in Shakespeare's time, so it is understandable that an Elizabethan playwright might remain imaginatively unmoved by the Magna Carta. Only when the clouds of civil war gathered in the mid-seventeenth century and royalist was set against parliamentarian did Magna Carta begin to gather the hallowed associations for which it is now cherished.

Shakespeare's John is no Moses. The play's full title, *The Life and Death of King John,* implies that events spanning a seventeen-year reign, from 1199 to 1216, will be the dramatist's subject matter, and such is the case. Shakespeare, as was his wont, conflates and abridges events. As the play unfolds, the Bastard Faulconbridge serves as both chorus and participant, a young newcomer observing the dynamics of power. Before Angiers, he sees two rival kings, mighty opposites, appeal for recognition. Which side has the better claim to loyalty? Wait and see who proves the mightier, comes the answer from Hubert, the representative citizen on the battlements—"to him will we prove loyal" (II.i.271). Might makes right in a world of power. When the Citizen proposes a politic accommodation—a royal marriage in return for a dowry consisting of those provinces the English have shed their blood to protect—the gates of Angiers at last open, leaving the Bastard alone upon the stage to make his great speech on commodity (561-98), a catch-all word implying the workings of expedience, self-interest, and greed we have just seen displayed. The legate, Pandulph, who now makes his first appearance, uses commodity to achieve other ends, for he is totally committed to the rectitude of his cause: the supremacy of papal authority.

For John the turning point comes midway through the play, at III.iii, when he woos Hubert to do away with young Prince Arthur, the King's nephew, who (as a Plantagenet) has a claim to the throne. (Shakespeare's Richard III, another usurper, similarly—but less persuasively—woos Buckingham to murder the princes in the Tower.) Later we see the white-hot irons with which the suborned executioners plan to put out Arthur's eyes. It is a relative mercy that he leaps to his death from a wall. How the historical Arthur met his end is uncertain; one report holds that John ordered him blinded and castrated to incapacitate him from the obligations of sovereignty.

Thereafter it is downhill for John. He incurs the opposition of his nobles by extravagantly insisting upon a second coronation (the historical John was crowned four times), abuses Hubert for faithfully (so he thinks) carrying out his order respecting Arthur, and ignominiously yields up his crown to the papal emissary. Faced with death, John is unable to repent, and, like Marlowe's Mephistophiles in *Doctor Faustus,* finds hell is within him as, with burning bosom and parched lips, he gives up the ghost. In the play's last moments, his son, Prince Henry, the legitimate heir to the throne, stands by; the king has already given over command to the Bastard.

In the course of the play, "commodity" has taken its toll. The women have had cause to lament the price. Left in the lurch on her wedding day as her French husband decides to make war on her English uncle's kingdom, Blanche runs through her aria of grief (III.i); then Constance, separated from "pretty Ar-

thur," tears her hair in histrionic sorrow. But the
Bastard has the last word. In the presence of King
John's corpse he kneels to pledge "faithful service /
And true submission" to the new king, and in the
play's last—and most famous—lines, makes his ringing
patriotic affirmation: "This England never did, nor
never shall, / Lie at the proud foot of a conqueror . . ."
(V.iii.112–13).

Richard II (c. 1595) dramatizes an awesome historical occasion: the deposition of an anointed king. He
may have been by nature ill-suited to sovereignty and
his reign marred by extravagances and misdeeds, but,
the son of the heroic Black Prince and the grandson of
revered Edward III, Richard of Bordeaux held an indis-
putable hereditary title to the crown. His removal sig-
naled the interruption of a divinely sanctioned political
order. Before Parliament at Westminster Hall (IV.i),
Richard plays out his "woeful pageant." With ritualis-
tic solemnity and the conscious eloquence of which he
is master, he undecks himself: "I give this heavy weight
from off my head / And this unwieldy sceptre from my
hand, / The pride of kingly sway from out my heart"
(IV.i.203–205). The play chronicles Richard's fall and
Bolingbroke's rise. At Westminster Hall their destinies
intersect.

When *Richard II* begins, the King sits in state on a
great scaffold erected at Windsor Castle, with the lords
and prelates of the realm seated in their places, as Henry
Bolingbroke, Duke of Hereford, comes to level charges
against Thomas Mowbray, Duke of Norfolk. Bolingbroke's challenge, ostensibly directed against Mowbray,
levels equally at the King. Unsurprisingly, Richard, who
himself has blood on his hands—the blood of his uncle,
the overbearing Duke of Gloucester, slain at Calais by
Mowbray at Richard's behest—would like to forget about
the whole issue as soon as possible, and so he tries to
reconcile appellant and defendant. But matters have
passed beyond the point of no return, the king is not
inclined to have a commission investigate the charges
(the normal legal recourse), and so he sets up a trial by

combat. In Act I, scene iii, at Coventry, we go through
the full panoply of chivalric ceremony until Richard
throws down his warder, the staff or truncheon used by
a king when umpiring a trial by combat. The upshot is
ten years of exile for Bolingbroke and lifetime banish-
ment for Mowbray. Cunningly, Richard makes these
proud men, seemingly so hopelessly at odds with each
other, swear never to patch up their differences, or
"meet / To plot, contrive, or complot any ill, / 'Gainst
us, our state, our subjects, or our land" (I.iii.188–90).
Bolingbroke's sentence is then reduced by four years;
"such is the breath of kings." Richard's action in halt-
ing the joust at the last moment may appear to betoken
weakness and vacillation, and many have so concluded.
Yet at a single stroke he has managed to rid himself—
at least for the time—of two embarrassments: his ag-
gressive cousin Bolingbroke, who represents a direct
threat, and Mowbray, to whom he owes too much and
who has outlived his usefulness.

   Richard overplays his hand when, confronted with
the financial exigencies of his impending Irish wars, he
confiscates Gaunt's estate—the richest patrimony in the
realm—directly after the old duke dies. To fly in the face
of sanctioned laws of inheritance is to rend the very
fabric of society; as York puts it, to "take from Time /
His charters and his customary right." Ruling by divine
right, the king in his person represented the body politic
and was thus perfect and eternal, despite the accidents
to which his physical being was subject. God omnipotent alone was his master, Richard had earlier reminded
York, and would muster armies of pestilence against
any who dared lift vassal hands against his head. But
at his moment of supreme crisis no armies come to
Richard's defense. He is vulnerably mortal. And what
of Bolingbroke? A pragmatist unmesmerized by the
mystique of kingship, he has taken advantage of such
opportunities as have come his way. The new king does
not yet have the oppressive weight of past misdeeds to
reckon with. "God knows, my son," he will confess to
Prince Hal in *2 Henry IV,* "by what bypaths and indi-

rect crooked ways / I met this crown.'' About such
deeper currents *Richard II* is silent. Ahead lie Henry's
unquiet reign and his son's famous victories; then the
Wars of the Roses, the descent into anarchy, and the
rise of the tyrant—the tumultuous events that had absorbed Shakespeare when, early in his career, he em-
barked upon his first Henriad.

In the last scene of *Richard II,* with Bolingbroke now
crowned Henry IV, he laments that blood has sprinkled
him to make him grow, and vows to ''make a voyage to
the Holy Land / To wash this blood off from my guilty
hand'' (V.vi.48–50). In *1 Henry IV* (c. 1596) he is still
talking of going off to fight in the Crusades. But he will
never get there. Instead, shaken and wan with care, the
king eventually recognizes, in *2 Henry IV,* that the head
that wears a crown is destined to lie uneasy. To the
north gallant young Hotspur and the Percys threaten
with their Scottish forces; in Wales the wild Glendower
will not be contained. At home the king's son and heir,
Harry, Prince of Wales, carouses and makes merry
with his uncourtly chums. Three worlds converge in
the play: that of the royal court, that of the rebel nobility, and that of the tavern merrymakers in Eastcheap, of whom Falstaff is the principal: not only witty
in himself (as eventually he will sagely point out) but
also the cause of wit in others, bringing together physical corpulence with energizing lightness and dexterity
of mind.

But Prince Hal is the pivotal figure. That all will turn
out well we are apprised by his soliloquy at the end of
Act I: He will throw off his loose behavior, and his
reformation, glittering over his fault, will show more
goodly ''than that which hath no foil to set it off'':

> I'll so offend to make offense a skill,
> Redeeming time when men think least I will.

(Time will turn out to be an important consideration
in this play and its successor.) Hal's soliloquy has, as

one would expect, engendered much commentary, but none with greater acuity than Samuel Johnson's in his 1765 edition of Shakespeare. "This speech," Dr. Johnson wrote, "is very artfully introduced to keep the Prince from appearing vile in the opinion of the audience; it prepares them for his future reformation; and, what is yet more valuable, exhibits a natural picture of a great mind offering excuses to itself, and palliating those follies which it can neither justify nor forsake."

When war comes, Falstaff misuses his power of impressment to round up a pitiful company of scarecrows, and delivers his catechism on honor, that "mere scutcheon" (V.i.140–41). In the end, on the killing field of Shrewsbury, Hotspur receives his mortal wound from Prince Hal. "O Harry, thou hast robbed me of my youth!" he cries; for him time has reached its stop. Meanwhile, Falstaff plays dead, only to opportunely rise up. "The better part of valor is discretion," he sums up, "in the which better part I have saved my life." So he prudentially stabs Hotspur's still-warm corpse and slings it over his back. Prince Hal, who fathoms all, is yet willing, for his part, to gild Falstaff's lie with "the happiest terms I have." Thus is the most made of Hotspur's valor and Falstaff's ripeness.

Bad news travels with proverbial speed. So does false news. To the latter phenomenon Shakespeare testifies through the allegorical figure of Rumor, who comes on stage to deliver the Induction to the sequel play, *The Second Part of Henry the Fourth, continuing to his death, and coronation of Henry the Fifth* (so the title page of the 1600 quarto in part reads), a play in which conceptions—and misconceptions—guide the action of a complexly orchestrated history. In the Induction, Rumor, allegorically painted full of tongues, runs before King Henry's victory at Shrewsbury, to report—falsely— that Hal and the King have been slain. Rumors have repercussions: old Northumberland (Hotspur's father) lying "crafty-sick," throws in his lot with the traitorous Bishop of York. Meanwhile, rumors do Falstaff good service; but, as the stern Chief Justice bitterly remarks, the fat knight is "as a candle, the better part out."

Advancing age and its deprivations figure prominently in the dramatic mix: as Hastings puts it, "We are time's subjects, and time bids us be gone" (I.iii). The king is sick. In the Boar's Head, the Eastcheap tavern of Falstaff and his cronies, music plays, Doll Tearsheet—Sir John's mistress and a doxy who drinks too much—sits on Falstaff's knee, but it grows late and he laments, "I am old, I am old," and she bids "sweet John" a tearful farewell as he goes off to the wars. When we last see Tearsheet (V.iv), the constables have delivered her to the beadle, "for the man is dead that you and Pistol beat amongst you," and she has "whipping-cheer" to look forward to. In Yorkshire, Coleville of the Dells, a knight who unfortunately throws in his lot with the rebels and—misled by the fat knight's spurious celebrity—yields to him, is for his pains sent off to execution by Hal's brother, Prince John of Lancaster (IV,iii).

In Gaultree Forest in Yorkshire (IV.ii), Hal's younger brother, John, in contrast to his sibling a cold-blooded Machiavellian politician, parleys with the rebel leaders Mowbray, Hastings, the Archbishop of York, and others. Lancaster listens patiently to their recitation of grievances, promises redress, and bids them, as tokens of "restored love and amity," to disperse their power: after all, they have his princely word. The armies are forthwith discharged, upon which the rebels are arrested and hauled off to the executioner's block, Lancaster meanwhile assuring them that he will keep his word "with a most Christian care"—but as traitors they will taste their due. The drum strikes up: "God and not we hath safely fought today," Lancaster piously concludes. In the theater this scene still has power to disturb.

In Gloucestershire Falstaff and the Inns of Court cronies of his youth reminisce. "Jesu, Jesu, the mad days that I have spent," recalls Justice Shallow. "Death is certain." Looking to enlist half a dozen men for the king's forces, Falstaff for a consideration exempts the likeliest possibilities, ending up with his ragtag crew for his nation's defense. This is Falstaff's army. He has heard the chimes at midnight (the title of Orson Welles's celebrated film about Falstaff); they belong to his past. In the end Henry IV dies, and Henry V is crowned king. Falstaff—persuaded that the laws of England are at his commandment—has taken horse for the event.

In the last lines of the last scene of the play, the king and his erstwhile companion confront each other. "My king! My Jove! I speak to thee, my heart!" And the newly crowned king, resplendent in his coronation robes and diadem: "I know thee not, old man. Fall to thy prayers. . . ."

> I banish thee, on pain of death,
> As I have done the rest of my misleaders,
> Not to come near our person by ten mile.
> For competence of life I will allow you,
> That lack of means enforce you not to evils.
> And, as we hear you do reform yourselves,
> We will, according to your strengths and qualities,
> Give you advancement.   (V.v.48,64–71)

Thus does the sovereign, who will in due course become the hero king that triumphs at Agincourt, decree the rejection of Falstaff. From the first the event has shaken up audiences, as the Epilogue's promise to continue the story, "with Sir John in it," manifests. In fact Shakespeare did not continue the story, and 2 Henry IV and its denouement have been much discussed. They are likely to continue being so.

The reenactment of an incomparable moment of national greatness achieved with the active support of higher powers has recommended Henry V (c. 1599) for patriotic occasions. Laurence Olivier's 1944 film, dedicated to the "Men of the Royal Air Force," helped to stimulate English patriotism on the eve of the Allied

invasion of Europe in World War II. Yet the play has
also appealed to postwar audiences with no illusions
about imperial missions. War may be glory, but it is
also hell. Early on, Canterbury holds out the prospect
of blood and sword and fire. Exeter, in Act II, forewarns the French king of bereavements to come: "the
widows' tears, the orphans' cries, / The dead men's
blood, the pining maidens' groans." As his men prepare to scale the walls of Harfleur, Henry delivers his
ringing call, "Once more unto the breach, dear friends,
once more"; but no sooner has the cannon roared than
the sorry crew of Nym, Bardolph, Pistol, and Falstaff's
page—Prince Hal's old companions from the tavern-
haunting days—come on to furnish their thematic counterpoint, complaining that the knocks are too hot, ex-
pressing their longing for a pot of ale and safety. Such
dear friends as these must be whipped like dogs and
riffraff unto the breach. The king's appalling ultimatum
before Harfleur (III.iii), evoking the horrors of murder,
spoil, and villainy that attend the sack of cities, is no
less weighted with eloquence than the preceding exhor-
tation to conquest.

If the besieged suffer, so do their tormentors. Winter
comes on, sickness grows, lawlessness breaks out. Bardolph robs a church of a pax—a metal disk with an
engraved Crucifixion kissed by priest and communi-
cants at mass and, old associations with Prince Hal
notwithstanding, he is sentenced to be hanged. Later
we learn that Nym too has been executed. Before Agincourt, Williams's thoughts dwell on ultimate matters as
he describes a Judgment Day such as a latter-day Spanish master, Francisco Goya, might have painted—"when
all those legs and arms and heads, chopped off in a
battle, shall join together at the latter day, and cry all,
'We died at such a place,' some swearing, some crying
for a surgeon, some upon their wives left poor behind
them, some upon the debts they owe, some upon their
children, rawly left." As the battle progresses, it in-
tensifies in ferocity. Rampaging French deserters
slaughter the boys guarding the English luggage; en-

raged, Henry orders all his prisoners' throats to be cut. Historically, a platoon of armed peasants—not deserters—did pillage the baggage train, but Henry more likely ordered the massacre by his execution squad of archers to forestall inadequately guarded prisoners from attacking his rear with salvaged weapons when the third French division charged. The charge never came. Holinshed, divining the king's true motive, shakes his head over the fact that a virtuous and charitable prince should give an order so "contrary to his accustomed gentleness."

If war serves as catalyst for bravery and cowardice, it also sets off the human comedy. Henry's heroic figure bestrides the play, but a richly varied assemblage of minor characters disport themselves in the long shadow he casts. His captains provide happy opportunities for dialect humor: Scots, Irish, and Welsh. (The French princess's accent, and her English lesson in III.iv, vary the linguistic bill of fare.) Of Henry's captains, Fluellen stands out. Sir Roger Williams (1540?–1595), a valorous, eccentric, and bluntly outspoken Welsh officer from Monmouthshire, may have served as his prototype. Sir Roger, who saw duty on some of Henry V's battlefields, in 1590 published *A Brief Discourse of War . . . With his opinion concerning some parts of the Martial Discipline*. Pistol's antics, carried over from *Henry IV*, bring another native dialect into the mix: the swaggering humors of "a counterfeit cowardly knave." Trifling properties provide the pretext for parallel exercises in comic manipulation: Fluellen's leek, with its Welsh associations, worn to get back at Pistol for anti-leek, anti-Welsh effrontery; the gages exchanged by Williams and his incognito sovereign before Agincourt.

Paradoxically the character who moves us most poignantly in *Henry V* never appears, although Shakespeare had originally planned otherwise. The dancer who speaks the Epilogue to *2 Henry IV* had promised, "If you be not too cloyed with fat meat, our humble author will continue the story, with Sir John in it, and make you merry with fair Katherine of France. Where, for anything I know, Falstaff shall die of a sweat, unless already 'a be killed with your hard opinions.'' Why did Shakespeare change course? Any answer must be guesswork; the premeditations of art perforce give way before the pressures of the creative moment, and Shakespeare had now and then to risk disappointing audience expectation. Dr. Johnson, commenting on the Hostess's report of Falstaff's death (II.iii), draws an instructive moral: "Let meaner authors learn from this example, that it is dangerous to sell the bear which is not yet hunted, to promise to the public what they have not written." Yet Falstaff, dying offstage, comes as vividly to life as any character in literature.

Tested in the crucible of awesome responsibility, Henry emerges as the virtuous warrior king, humane and magnanimous when circumstances permit. "For conclusion," his chronicler sums up, "a majesty was he that both lived and died a pattern in princehood, a lodestar in honour and mirror of magnificence." Shakespeare paused over this passage; Holinshed's "lodestar in honour" became in the Epilogue, "this star of England." Thus do Shakespeare's chronicle source and chorus assess Henry's character, and countless theater spectators have ratified the verdict with their applause. But not everyone is this king's enthusiast. Writing in the Romantic Age, William Hazlitt observed in his *Characters of Shakespeare's Plays* (1817):

> Because he [Henry] did not know how to exercise the enormous power, which had just dropped into his hands, to any one good purpose, he immediately undertook (a cheap and obvious resource of sovereignty) to do all the mischief he could.

Others have voiced similar misgivings.

Still, Henry has not wanted distinguished advocates. Writing in 1947, in the afterglow of the Allied triumph over Nazism, a great Shakespeare scholar, John Dover

Wilson, saw Henry's spirit as breathing in Winston Churchill; the king's petition before battle—"And how thou pleasest, God, dispose the day" (IV.ii.i.133)— becomes "a statement of the ultimate heroic faith, a faith which, like that of the martyrs, puts him who holds it beyond reach of mortal man." In such contraries does criticism rejoice, and by admitting subversive counter-currents, Shakespeare invites liberty of interpretation. Each reader and viewer must decide for himself whether the hero is an exemplary Christian prince or self-righteous imperialist, or some combination of both, and his play a sublime testimonial to national purpose or an exercise in wonderfully eloquent but essentially mere-tricious jingoism—or any of the innumerable gradations between these polarities.

In an introductory volume such as this, only passing reference to Shakespeare's deployment of source mate-rials is possible, but it should come as no surprise to readers to hear that his reading—and acquaintance with contemporary drama—was ample. Thus he knew plays by rival companies on the hero king who had been a madcap youth, but who had triumphed in the battle-to-end-all battles at Agincourt. In the 1580s (for example) the Queen's Men had performed the anonymous *Famous Victories of Henry V* at the Bull Inn. The same com-pany, however, owned an earlier play on Henry that the playhouse entrepreneur Philip Henslowe noted in his *Diary* account book. From *The Famous Victories* (printed in 1598) Shakespeare profited, e.g., the scene in which the French king's prudence is contrasted with the Dauphin's uncouth rudeness in underestimating his English adversary (II.iv). But when it came to English (and Scottish) history, Shakespeare mainly trusted to the 1587 edition of Raphael Holinshed's *Chronicles of England, Scotland, and Ireland,* although he also profited from the posthumously published *Union of the Two Noble and Illustre* [i.e., illustrious] *Families of Lancaster and York* of Edward Hall (c. 1598–1647) and *The Chronicles of England* of John Stow (c. 1525–

1605). For his last English history, *The Famous History of the Life of King Henry the Eighth*, or *All Is True*, Shakespeare still depended mainly on Holinshed, although characteristically supplemented from other sources.

7

The Lord Chamberlain's Man: Mid-Career Plays

An artist's manipulation of his sources can sometimes
bring striking revelations. Take *Romeo and Juliet*
(c. 1595), for instance. Shakespeare took the plot of his
tragedy mainly, perhaps exclusively, from the long poem
by Arthur Brooke, who died young, *The Tragical History of Romeus and Juliet* (1562), itself a version of a
recent Italian *novella* of Matteo Bandello. But the dramatist manages without Brooke's Puritan moralizing, a
moralizing that surfaces as early as Brooke's prefatory
epistle "To the Reader":

> . . . to this end (good reader) is this tragical matter
> written, to describe unto thee a couple of unfortunate
> lovers, thralling themselves to unhonest desire, neglecting the authority and advice of parents and
> friends, conferring their principal counsels with
> drunken gossips and superstitious friars (the naturally
> fit instruments of unchastity), attempting all adventures of peril, for the attaining of their wished lust,
> using auricular confession (the key of whoredom) for
> furtherance of their purpose, abusing the honorable
> name of lawful marriage, the [i.e., to] cloak the
> shame of stolen contracts, finally by all means of unhonest life, hasting to most unhappy death.

Shakespeare takes a different view of his lovers and their
destiny.

The play from the beginning has been one of Shakespeare's most popular. The first quarto of 1597 contained the title-page boast that the tragedy "hath been often (with great applause) played publicly," and—before the playhouses were shut down in 1642—there had been (besides the First Folio of 1623) four more quarto editions on the bookstalls. Besides constant revivals at universities and Shakespeare festivals, the play has inspired a multitude of versions in other media. On film (for example) Theda Bara performed the heroine in a silent version in 1916, while an early sound film directed by George Cukor (1936) featured Leslie Howard and Norma Shearer as the relatively superannuated lovers, with John Barrymore as Mercutio. More recently, Franco Zeffirelli, in 1968, starred two attractively youthful actors, Leonard Whiting and Olivia Hussey, as the lovers, who looked more suitable for the parts than they sounded. But the film was a great box-office success with young cinemagoers who had never seen Shakespeare professionally performed. The BBC did not cover itself with glory with its version for the Time-Life Shakespeare Plays, 1979–85. *Romeo and Juliet* has also inspired ballets; a dramatic symphony by the Romantic composer Hector Berlioz (1803–69), *Roméo et Juliette;* and music-hall takeoffs; its inspiration lies behind Leonard Bernstein's much-applauded *West Side Story.*

The essential action is economically set forth in the opening Chorus (in form a sonnet): the "ancient grudge" in Old Verona, the "pair of star-crossed lovers," the overthrow that "doth with their deaths bury their parents' strife." What the Prologue makes no effort to convey is the incandescence of the doomed youthful love to which untold generations of viewers have responded. Nowhere is that love more expressively conveyed than when Romeo first lays eyes upon Juliet at the festivity at the Capulet house. They meet, and in another sonnet, this one in the form of a duet, profess romantic love in the imagery of religious adoration: "If I profane with my unworthiest hand / This holy shrine . . ."(I.v.95–96). *Romeo and Juliet* was probably written in 1594 or 1595, when the playwright had lately turned thirty; later, when he was himself middle-aged, he would dramatize, more profoundly, the passion of a pair of middle-aged lovers in *Antony and Cleopatra*.

If *Romeo and Juliet* is a youngish man's love tragedy, *A Midsummer Night's Dream,* written at around the same time, is a fantastic love-comedy, and has been almost as popular. The three pairs of lovers play their hands, as do Oberon, the King of the Fairies, and his inamorata Titania, Queen of the Fairies. Through the artifice of Puck, a "sprite" in the service of Oberon, the base mechanical Bottom's head is magically transformed into an ass's head, upon which Titania, having had magic love juice applied to her eyes by Oberon, becomes smitten with him. Thus Bottom too has his midsummer night's dream. He awakens to hilariously ponder "Bottom's Dream" (IV.i). The rustics' play, intended to grace the nuptials of Duke Theseus and the Queen of the Amazons, is a comical counterpart to what takes place tragically in *Romeo and Juliet:* Pyramus, thinking his Thisbe dead (her mantle had been torn by the Lion), stabs himself, and Thisbe, thinking her lover dead, commits suicide with Pyramus's "trusty sword," but not before bidding her friends farewell: "The tragedy ends, / Adieu, adieu, adieu." *A Midsummer Night's Dream*, then, testifies to a truth that comes as no surprise: that Shakespeare did not take an overly solemn view of his own incomparable genius.

The *Dream* has several times been filmed for cinema or for television. A 1935 film version, directed by Max Reinhardt and William Dieterle, is notable mainly for the performances of the young James Cagney as a vacuously self-possessed Bottom, Mickey Rooney as a street-smart Puck, and Joe E. Brown as Quince flourishing a huge fake flower in the part of Thisbe. In Peter Brook's gymnastic *Dream* (1970)—much applauded by some critics and taken by others as a nightmare—the fairies' costumes brought to mind circus clowns or oriental acrobats; a huge white box of a set had trapezes, swings, and ropes: for all the world, a gymnasium or circus, making extraordinary athletic demands of a cast not of professional athletes but actors. The American Repertory Theatre's film of the comedy included interpolated music and songs from Purcell's *The Fairy Queen,* but was no more than a film of the stage revival. Peter Hall's film, designed mainly for the small screen, emphasized close-ups and featured Judi Dench, captivating as a nude queen of Fairies.

In *The Merchant of Venice* (c. 1596–97) the mutual antagonism of Antonio and Shylock—gentile and Jew, native and exotic alien, merchant and usurer—is of long standing. A kinder gentleman than Antonio may not tread the earth, yet when he and Shylock meet, as they often do in the Rialto, Antonio's customary civil demeanor deserts him; he spits on Shylock's beard and gabardine, excoriates him as misbeliever and cutthroat dog, and kicks him like some mongrel cur (happily, not in view of the audience). That Shylock should feel "a lodged hate and certain loathing" (IV.i.60) for the man who treats him thus is not surprising, but their enmity also has a strong economic motive. For Shylock, Antonio represents unfair competition: he lends money gratis, lowering the rate of usury in Venice, and imperiling Shylock's sole source of livelihood. Why, Antonio asks, should a barren metal breed offspring, i.e., interest? This objection to moneylending is philosophically at least as old as Aristotle, and in the Middle Ages became proverbial wisdom. Wearing their identifying badges of shame, Jews—the "race accursed"—were variously expelled or forcibly converted to Christianity, massacred or (the lucky ones) confined to urban ghettoes. In England, Jews, who had begun settling not long after the Norman conquest, undertook the moneylending that canon law prohibited Christians from practicing. With leases on the shire for security, Jewish moneylenders made advances to the crown, so that the king could pursue his wars and crusades. Housewives pawned their pots and pans to the moneylenders for ready cash; priests and religious houses, their Gospels and holy relics. Almost anything might serve as security—jewelry, loads of hay, knightly armor, and, best of all, houses and land.

Not all Jews turned to moneylending, however. Some became physicians of note to whom even popes turned for medical care. Others, less fortunate, eked out a living as peddlers. Of whatever means, they lived apart in special streets known as the Jewry. In London, on the west side of Westminster Hall, the Jews had their own exchequer, which supervised financial transactions and served as a channel of communication between Jewry and the crown. In time, however, a statute was issued by which Jews were forbidden, just as Christians immemorially were, from lending money at interest. Existing contracts became no longer enforceable. That was in 1275. Anyway, by then Italian bankers, the Lombards, had supplanted the Jews. Their economic utility exhausted, the Jews were fifteen years later expelled from England by Edward I. They lingered in consciousness as the bogeymen of anti-Semitic folklore.

"It follows from all of this," a distinguished authority on Jewish history, Solomon Grayzel, has written, "that neither Marlowe nor Shakespeare could have been acquainted with a Jew and that Shylock was therefore a purely imaginary character." The actual facts are somewhat more complicated: A colony of Jewish, or crypto-Jewish, merchants in fact went about their business in London in Shakespeare's day. Roderigo Lopez, of Jewish origin, was a baptized New Christian and regular communicant. In 1594, with his enemy the Earl of Essex sitting in judgment, Lopez confessed to high treason to avoid torture, after which he was hanged, and, while still alive, castrated, disemboweled, and quartered. "At the gallows," an Elizabethan chronicler records, "Lopez declared that he loved the Queen as well as he loved Jesus Christ, which coming from a man of the Jewish profession moved no small laughter in the standers-by." Once a Jew, it seemed, always a Jew. Like all Londoners, Shakespeare would have known about the Lopez sensation. Whether he was aware of the handful of crypto-Jews in his midst we cannot say.

Moneylending for profit went on in Shakespeare's England, but the usurers were Christians. Such transactions, although deemed illegal, were widespread, and in the early 1570s—as has recently come to light—Shakespeare's father, John, more than once faced prosecution in the Exchequer for usury. The Chamberlain's Men would build the Globe playhouse with money borrowed on interest. Be that as it may, Shakespeare's Jewish usurer has long held, for innumerable readers and spectators, an immediacy and reality that transcend the purely imaginary. Yet Shylock figures in but five of the play's nineteen scenes, has only some 360 of the 2,700 lines, and does not appear at all in the last act. He is also old, a social outcast, and scapegoat. Jessica—his own flesh and blood—absconds with her father's ducats to marry a Christian; later we hear that, honeymooning in Genoa, she has exchanged Shylock's turquoise—the ring that as a bachelor he gave his Leah—for a monkey. In his own behalf Shylock is an intelligent and eloquent advocate, noting correctly that, while the Venetians beseech him to show mercy to a delinquent debtor, they at the same time keep slaves that they treat no better than their asses or mules.

What moderns have found most disquieting is Antonio's insistence that Shylock turn Christian. In Shakespeare's day, however, the democratic ideal of religious freedom was not yet part of the ideological landscape, and by embracing Christianity, willingly or no, Shylock is being offered his only chance of escaping eternal damnation. Antonio's friend, Bassanio, like Portia's wealthy suitors, has been faced with the choice of caskets—gold, silver, or lead—fantastically dictated by her deceased father's will. In his moment of truth, Bassanio correctly chooses lead; he can distinguish between appearance and reality—he knows that "all that glistens is not gold"; is not so enamored of himself as to pick the silver chest, whose legend reads, "Who chooseth me shall get as much as he deserves"; and is willing to give and hazard all by staking his fortune on a base metal. Mercenary motives may not be absent from Bassanio's initiative, but Portia constitutes a fairer prize than the dross that entices the other suitors.

The Merry Wives of Windsor (c. 1597) is unusual among Shakespeare's comedies; in some ways, unique. It is his only comedy to have a native English setting: Windsor and environs, at the time a village on the south bank of the Thames, some twenty miles from the capital, and the seat of one of the royal palaces. Containing a larger—much larger—proportion of prose than any other play in the canon, *The Merry Wives* is notable also for its topicality and colloquial specificity. The comedy is steeped in contemporary English life: we hear of Herne's oak in Windsor Little Park, of Datchet Mead, and of the Thames flowing close to hand. Above all, we are sensible of Windsor Castle and its choir. For good reason. Near the end of the play (V.v.) a passage alludes specifically to "the several chairs of order" and the motto of the Order of the Garter, the highest chivalric order in England: *"Honi soit qui mal y pense"* ("Ill be to him who evil thinks").

Now, in 1597 at Windsor Castle, the seat of the order, George Carey, the second Lord Hunsdon—Queen Elizabeth's cousin, the Lord Chamberlain, and the patron of Shakespeare's troupe—was installed in May as Windsor Knight of the Garter. That year the queen was not herself present at the ceremonies, but she attended the Garter Feast at the Palace of Westminster on April 23, Saint George's Day. *The Merry Wives* was possibly written for this ceremonial occasion.

In 1702—a little over a century after Shakespeare wrote *The Merry Wives*—the critic and neoclassical playwright John Dennis wrote that this comedy "hath pleased one of the greatest Queens that ever was in the world: This comedy was written at her command, and by her direction, and she was so eager to see it acted, that she commanded it to be finished in fourteen days, and was afterward, as tradition tells us, very well pleased at the representation." To which Nicholas Rowe, Shakespeare's first editor, added seven years later, that "Elizabeth was so taken with Falstaff that she commanded Shakespeare to continue with him for one more play and show him in love.''

Love it isn't in *The Merry Wives,* but rather the corpulent old rogue's lust. He addresses identical amatory missives to Mistress Ford and Mistress Page—the merry wives of the title—and must perforce endure their comical revenge: Falstaff is obliged to seek cover from an irate husband in a basket of soiled linen, which is dumped forthwith in a muddy ditch; to disguise himself as Mother Prat, the notorious witch of Brentford, and to be driven off by Ford in a shower of blows; finally, to wear a pair of horns and in his disguise be pinched black and blue by supposed elves and hobgoblins in the forest at midnight. This Falstaff is not the witty rogue we have previously encountered but a more conventional comic butt, just as Ford is, with his tantrums: the conventional jealous husband, to be suitably purged. A number of the characters—Pistol, Nym, Mistress Quickly, etc—are already familiar from *1* and *2 Henry IV.* But we hardly recognize the hostess of Falstaff's Eastcheap tavern in the hostess of Dr. Caius, the irascible Frenchman who makes fritters of the English language.

The Merry Wives has not inspired nearly the same degree of critical interest as the other comedies, although it has scarcely been neglected by Shakespeareans. Popular on stage, it was cannibalized by Boito's libretto for Verdi's great opera *Falstaff.* At the end of the play the young lovers of the underplot, Fenton and that ''pretty virginity,'' Anne Page, are matrimonially united, so all can now ''go home, / And laugh this sport o'er by a country fire; / Sir John and all'' (V.v.24–42).

Shakespeare was always drawn to the big themes. *As You Like It* (c. 1599) is Shakespeare's version of pastoral. The dramatist draws upon a tradition going back to the Bucolics of the Greek poet Theocritus in the third century B.C. Theocritus's forest, unlike the one in *As You Like It,* holds no threatening beast of prey. Miraculously, sheep tending requires no menial hired hands.

The pastoral thus enshrines the urban sophisticate's nostalgic vision of a golden world that never was. Nostalgia has always exercised powerful attractions. The Happy Shepherd in a late nineteenth-century poem by William Butler Yeats might sing, "The woods of Arcady are dead / And over is their antique joy"; but in the Renaissance the antique joy was far from over. With "Come live with me and be my love," Christopher Marlowe gave Elizabethans the quintessential pastoral lyric. In *As You Like It* Shakespeare remembers Marlowe (who died young in 1593) by having his shepherdess Phebe refer to the "dead Shepherd" and recite a line for which he was famous: "Who ever loved that loved not at first sight?" (III.v.82).

Running through the play is the great antithesis between the natural and the artificial. The clash between two ways of life is seen on several levels: the opposing values attached to civilized society (the court or great country estate) and simpler living (the open pastures and forest encampment); in the strife that sets brother against brother and parent against child; and in the contrast between courtships that are based upon genuine emotion (Orlando and Roslind) and those which are formalized affairs (Silvius and Phebe). The various levels are not kept distinct in the play; disorder in the one is likely to parallel disorder in another. Encapsulating a rich literary heritage in popular dramatic terms, *As You Like It* is the exemplar of pastoral in English best loved by readers and theater audiences alike.

Much Ado About Nothing (c. 1598–99) offers two narrative lines of approximately equal dramatic weight: the one—involving Claudio and Hero—melodramatic and conducted with the formal eloquence of blank verse; the other—the Beatrice-Benedick story—a happy experiment in high comedy, deploying vivacious conversational prose. The two stories take up contrasting pairs of lovers. The first story is conventional, with clearly traceable sources and analogues; the second allows the dramatist to give free rein to original (indeed anti-conventional) characters who obviously engaged him—

as they do us. Both plots hinge upon deceptions either maliciously intended to separate lovers or benignly calculated to unite them.

Structurally *Much Ado About Nothing* is highly integrated. Opposing stratagems come to the fore in immediately succeeding scenes (II.i, II.ii). In the church all the characters arrive at a turning point. Beatrice and Benedick affirm their mutual love. Impetuously he declares, "Come, bid me do anything for thee." Her simple rejoinder, "Kill Claudio," and his reply, "Ha! Not for the wide world"—for Claudio is his best friend—make for an arresting moment. Usually audiences react with a curious mixture of shock and amusement, for the play here teeters dangerously on the thin line dividing comedy from potential tragedy. Only a self-assured master can carry off successfully such a theatrical gamble. Succeed Shakespeare does. He did not invent the species of romantic comedy in which lovers conduct their courtship in what might be termed (in legal parlance) an adversary relationship. Before him, John Lyly had delighted in witty duels between the sexes in his stylish, if bloodless, comedies. Shakespeare treated the battle of the sexes with farcical gusto in *The Taming of the Shrew:* Petruchio tames his Kate, but the conquest implies mutual attraction despite his avowed aim to wive it wealthily in Padua and her evident aversion to being bought and sold as a marriage commodity. The high comedy of *Much Ado About Nothing* represents the Shakespearean apotheosis of the idea of (in a phrase of the period) the mad couple well matched.

As such, it pointed a way to playwrights who followed. In William Congreve's *The Way of the World* (1700), with its celebrated "proviso" scene, with urbane wit and elegance Mirabell and Millamant set forth their matrimonial preconditions. "These articles subscribed," Millamant concludes her inventory, "if I continue to endure you a little longer, I may by degrees dwindle into a wife." To which Mirabell rejoins, "Well, have I liberty to offer conditions—that when you are dwindled into my wife, I may not be beyond measure enlarged into a husband?'' Their provisos agreed upon, they seal their bargain with a kiss.

Sophisticated love games were hardly a distinguishing feature of the Victorian stage, but in Oscar Wilde's trivial comedy for serious people, the repartee bubbles frothily for three acts, until Jack Worthing realizes for the first time in his life the vital importance of being Earnest, and thus wins his Gwendolen, who has known it all along. In our own century, sex duels have sparkled in the comedies of—among others—George Bernard Shaw. "The life force enchants me," Tanner protests helplessly to Ann in *Man and Superman* (1903): "I have the whole world in my arms when I clasp you. But I am fighting for my freedom, for my honour, for my self, for one and indivisible." It is a struggle Tanner is happily destined to lose, just as before him it had been lost by Beatrice and Benedick and the rest who have taken their place in a great tradition of English comedy.

The first record of what is, in all probability, Shakespeare's *Julius Caesar,* occurs in 1599 in the travel book of a Swiss physician visiting London. "On the 21st of September, after dinner, at about two o'clock," wrote Thomas Platter of Basel, "I went with my party across the water; in the straw-thatched house we saw the tragedy of the first Emperor Julius Caesar, very pleasingly performed, with approximately fifteen characters; at the end of the play they danced together admirably and exceedingly gracefully, according to their custom, two in each group dressed in men's and two in women's apparel." The dance which so engaged Platter was the jig that usually followed the main attraction. The playhouse "across the water" on the south bank would have been the newly erected Globe, its bright straw contrasting with the weathered thatch of the surrounding roofs. *Julius Caesar* may well have inaugurated the new theater. The play stands poised midway between earlier Shakespearean tragedy and the astonishing sequence of tragedies beginning with *Hamlet.*

In a modern history—for example, W. H. McNeill's well-regarded *Rise of the West*—Julius Caesar may rate no more than brief mention as an extralegal upstart, but for Shakespeare's age, and for some time before and after, Caesar's was the most imposing name in secular history. Almost everywhere his legions marched—in Gaul, Spain, Britain, Asia Minor—he came, saw, and conquered *("Veni, vidi, vici,"* as he tersely put it himself.) Yet no more spectacular instance existed of the vanity of human wishes and the fickleness of Fortune— a goddess best known for that trait—than the cutting down of the great Caesar at the very height of his worldly fame and power.

Such a figure is destined to lead a life of myth as well as of verifiable fact. Caesar contributed to the process himself by claiming descent from the goddess Venus and the Dardanian Anchises, parents of Aeneas, the legendary founder of Rome. He aspired to divinity; specially consecrated priests served this godhead, and at the temple of Quirinus he set up his statue, with the inscription "To the unconquerable god." Caesar lusted after absolute power and would have transformed Republican Rome into an authoritarian monarchy without constitutional safeguards. On the ides (15th) of March in 44 B.C., the blood of the unconquerable god flowed, as he lay dying in the Capitol at the base of the statue of the same Pompey he had humbled in the Civil Wars.

In *Julius Caesar*, Cassius' rallying cry over the fallen leader, "Liberty, freedom, and enfranchisement!," affirms the conspirators' Republican program. But although they slew Caesar, Caesarism lived. It was the Republic that was dead, for Rome ahead lay the transient glories of the Augustan age and the *Pax Romana*—the peace imposed by the Empire upon its dominions—and the evil days of Caligula and Nero.

Imperious Caesar is dead before the drama bearing his name has reached the halfway point. He has only one-hundred fifty lines all told. But Caesar, looming larger than life, stands at the center of the play. "Why, man," complains Cassius enviously, yet with due awe,

> he doth bestride the narrow world
> Like a Colossus, and we petty men
> Walk under his huge legs and peep about
> To find ourselves dishonorable graves.
>   (I,ii,135–38)

The conspiracy—its inception, implementation, and aftermath—has no other end than elimination of Caesar and what he represents. The play, with its three phases, dramatizes the enterprise's failure. As Brutus, beholding the dead bodies of Cassius and Titinius, is moved to exclaim,

> O Julius Caesar, thou art mighty yet!
> Thy spirit walks abroad, and turns our swords
> In our own proper entrails.   (V,iii,94–96)

Arrogant and grown superstitious, the aging Caesar has his share of infirmities—he is deaf in one ear and subject to epileptic seizures. But Caesar is a shrewd assessor of character, intuitively sensing the danger posed by Cassius and correctly placing most trust in that sensual reveler Antony. He is also susceptible to flattery; as Decius Brutus, one of the conspirators, wryly observes, ". . . when I tell him he hates flatterers, / He says he does, being thus most flattered." Living, this most masterful of men is vulnerably human; dead, Caesar is invincible.

Brutus is not. High-minded in his devotion to established Republican principles, Brutus has the consolations of his Stoic philosophy, and so, outwardly at least, can take calmly word of his beloved wife Portia's death. Others defer to his moral superiority. But along with this superiority goes a streak of self-righteousness, and the noble Brutus makes one practical mistake after the other. He rules against having Antony fall with Caesar, mistakenly confident that "Antony is but a limb of Caesar." (Antony himself displays no such fastidiousness; in the Proscription scene (IV,i) he goes along with the projected murder of his own nephew, and of Cicero, greatest of Roman orators, who played no part in Caesar's assassination.) Against advice, Brutus allows Antony to make the funeral oration, which turns the tables on the conspirators. And despite the counsel of a more experienced soldier, he chooses to stake all at Philippi—a decision that delights his antagonists. Never does Brutus, a moral man, visibly confront the great moral question of whether ends justify means; whether political assassination—especially when the victim is not a monster—can ever be honorable. In a crucial meditation (II,i, 110–40), although he has already decided, Brutus wrestles with the bloody deed's justification, focusing on Caesar's itch for a crown and ignoring the simple fact that this leader already wields absolute power; the rationalist argues, unreasonably, that murder is warranted because of what Caesar might do, not what he has indeed done. It is not in this play's mode that Brutus, like other Shakespearean tragic heroes, should arrive at the self-knowledge that the Greeks termed *anagnorisis*.

Cassius, at least in the earlier part of the play, suffers in comparison with his co-conspirator. Clearly he detests Caesar and is his envious detractor. With Brutus, Cassius plays an unengaging tempter's role; ". . . it is meet," he allows in soliloquy, "that noble minds keep ever with their likes; / For who so firm that cannot be seduced"—a tacit admission of his own lack of nobility. Yet we do not question Cassius' devotion to the old Republican order, nor does he make any bid for personal power or preeminence. A realist, he knows from the outset that what the conspirators intend is "most bloody, fiery, and most terrible." But Cassius, too, is humanly vulnerable, and never more sympathetic than in the Quarrel scene (IV,iii), in which his desperate eagerness to be loved is painfully evident. In the end, after he has fallen upon the sword that he used to kill Caesar, "the last of all the Romans" is, not once but three times, eulogized by Titinius and Brutus and movingly garlanded with a wreath of victory.

From his first speech—"When Caesar says 'Do thus,' it is performed"—Antony's total devotion to his leader is manifest. In the funeral pulpit, he displays unexcelled gifts for demagogic manipulation in a cause in which he believes passionately. At the end, he pays splendid tribute to Brutus, the foe he has so relentlessly pursued. But young Octavius is now Caesar; he gives the orders, and Antony obeys. It is Octavius who invites those that served Caesar now to serve him. Appropriately he has the last word in *Julius Caesar*.

With *Hamlet,* a century was ending or a new one beginning: 1600 is as likely the year of composition as any. The play may well have engendered more commentary and controversy than any other ever written. The late F. P. Wilson, the much-revered Merton Professor of English literature at Oxford University, once noted that someone trying to read everything ever written on *Hamlet* would have no time to read anything else—including *Hamlet.* The play is the vehicle for the biannual *Hamlet Studies,* published for over a decade now at the University of New Delhi in India (there is no more international literary subject than Shakespeare), and billed—no doubt accurately—as "the first journal devoted exclusively to a single literary work."

Another *Hamlet,* since lost, preceded our *Hamlet.* In 1596 Thomas Lodge—the erstwhile law student at Lincoln's Inn and swashbuckling privateer who sailed to the Canary Islands and South America, and the man of letters whose prose novella *Rosalynde* furnished Shakespeare with his principal source for *As You Like It*—described in *Wit's Misery* (1596) a countenance "pale as the visard of the ghost which cried so piteously at the Theatre like an oyster wife, *Hamlet, revenge.*" The phrase "Hamlet revenge" would become a byword. In another famous passage, this one from Robert Greene's *Menaphon,* we hear of "many good sentences, as *Blood is a beggar,* and so forth; and if you entreat him [i.e., one of the "shifting companions"] fair on a frosty morning, he will afford whole hamlets, I would say handfuls, of tragical speeches." This unpublished and also since lost play, presumably (although not certainly) not by Shakespeare, has come to be known as the *Ur* [i.e., original] *Hamlet*. It testifies—and other evidence is not far to seek—to the great and continuing popularity of tragedies on revenge themes, a popularity not too unlike the twentieth-century vogue of the western on screen and television.

Few plays have raised more questions than Shakespeare's *Hamlet*. One distinguished modern critic, Harry Levin, has said that *"Hamlet* is the most problematic play ever written by Shakespeare or any other playwright."* One is not inclined to disagree. Levin has written a well-received book entitled *The Question of "Hamlet."* Indeed, the play begins with a question. On a bitter cold night, when the clock has just struck twelve, a sentinel asks—in the first line—"Who's there?" The question poses questions, for it is asked by Bernardo, come to relieve Francisco, who is standing guard at Elsinore Castle. Normally one would expect the man on duty to put the question to the new arrival, not the other way around. Other questions follow as the play unfolds, including that most celebrated of all questions in all theatrical literature, "To be or not to be, that is the question."

This one poses great philosophical issues, for in the Prince of Denmark the tragedy has a philosophical protagonist. Structural issues too, as the rising action carries us through the play-within-the-play, with the theater audience watching Hamlet and Horatio and the court watching King Claudius watching the players perform their knavish piece of work, the murder of Gonzago. Shakespeare was from early on in his playwriting career drawn to the possibilities offered by theatrical metaphors and by interior actions—through the prayer scene, when king and prince are alone together on the stage for the first and only time, to the dramatic climax in the Closet Scene, when Hamlet's weapon passes through the arras and pierces the eavesdropping Polonius, shedding blood for the first time and providing Claudius with his instrument, the aggrieved son who will dare to avenge his father's unwitting murder. For the student the very fame of the play, in which so many lines have become familiar quotations, may be a deterrent to coming to grips with it. But in the playhouse—wherever—after myriad performances in myriad languages, even in Danish at Elsinore Castle, *Hamlet* remains pristine. So too in the classroom. We are always, in effect, seeing it or reading it or discussing it for the first time.

Twelfth Night (c. 1601) begins with music, establishing a melting mood, which we take at face value at our peril. The opening speech shows Duke Orsino luxuriating in the exquisite sensations of amorous deprivation. An invitation to take up the manly sport of hunting is politely deflected with a *hart/heart* quibble and an allusion to the mythical hunter Actaeon who, having glimpsed the chaste goddess Diana naked, was turned into a stag and hunted down and slain by his own hounds: an emblem—dear to Elizabethan sonneteers—of Eros denied for the man; marriage and motherhood for the woman. The duke is the prisoner not, as he fancies, of the unreciprocating Countess Olivia but of the romantic idea of the self he has fashioned. Another prisoner of the self, Olivia, is, as the duke's follower Valentine enters to report, in thrall to grief. She mourns her deceased brother; also, we later learn, her father dead in the same year. Immured within her own house, her face covered by a veil, Olivia purposes to remain cloistered for seven years, keeping memory green by watering "once a day her chamber round / With eye-offending brine." The picture conjured up of a young woman, apt by nature for wedlock, consecrating herself to an artificial program of ritualized weeping, is, like Orsino's devotion to his indifferent love object, more than faintly absurd, although by no means ignoble.

Thus, in a poetically charged brief scene of only forty-two lines does the dramatist set up his amused examination of Renaissance self-fashioning. As the action proceeds, the countess will be liberated from her bondage and Orsino from his, but they will not be freed for each other.

The countess's steward, Malvolio, is utterly without a sense of humor, a deficiency that ranks high in the Shakespearean hierarchy of disabilities. Olivia's waiting-gentlewoman, Maria, calls Malvolio "a kind of Puritan," but quickly retracts the intended slight as too flattering: "The devil a puritan he is, or anything constantly but a time-pleaser." Master below stairs, the steward dreams of becoming, by his mean-spirited exercise of limited authority, the master above: a consummation to be had only in the unlikely eventuality that he achieves matrimony with his mistress. "O, you are sick of self-love Malvolio," Olivia chides with unwonted harshness, "and taste with a distempered appetite." For his malady the prognosis is negative. Unloved and unloving, Malvolio aspires to fashion a self bearing scant relation to the reality, social and personal, of his situation. When he bursts in upon the late night revelers—Sir Toby, Sir Andrew, Maria, and Feste—as they uproariously tipple and sing, and denounces them for making an alehouse of his lady's house, Malvolio oversteps a steward's proper bounds (Sir Toby is, after all, the countess's uncle), and sets in motion the mechanism of retribution that gives the underplot its principal thrust.

With *As You Like It* and *Much Ado About Nothing,* *Twelfth Night* concludes a triad of comedies that criticism has termed happy. Shakespeare, however, presumably did not compose these plays seriatim; that's show business. Celebrating as it does festive release, the spirit of *What You Will* (as the alternative title puts it), *Twelfth Night* may indeed be reckoned joyous. Yet the fool Feste has his melancholy strain—some critics think him the most melancholy of Shakespeare's clowns—and the degree of discomfiture suffered by Malvolio has disturbed readers and audiences, and, indeed, disturbs other characters in the play. Even Sir Toby, prime instigator of revenge, is uneasy: "I would we were well rid of this knavery," he muses as his victim cowers miserably in his dark room. "I say there was never man so abused," Malvolio cries, and Olivia later echoes his words: "He hath been most notoriously abused.'' Hers are almost the play's last words. The duke fittingly gives the final speech, remembering those who have suffered and hailing his new ''fancy's queen.'' After all the rest have gone, Feste remains to sing the last tune of this delightfully tuneful comedy. His song traces the ''Ages of Man'' as summed up by Jaques in *As You Like It*, and signals the end of this revel—''our play is done''— preparing the audience to venture forth once again into the non-festive world of wind and rain.

When *Twelfth Night* first appeared on the stage of the Globe playhouse, the Virgin Queen had reached, for the time, a great age, perhaps sixty-seven. Her hair was ''of an auburn color but false,'' her teeth black from sucking sugar (an English self-indulgence), but she still might appear in bare-breasted attire when the fancy took her. In February 1603 she fell irrecoverably ill. She had procrastinated in naming a successor, but as her ministers crowded around, she finally whispered to Cecil, her principal secretary, ''I will that a king succeed me, and who but my kinsman the King of Scots.'' On March 24 she died, her Privy Council at once proclaimed the accession of James VI of Scotland as James I of England, and Sir Robert Carey had his horse saddled to bear the tidings to Edinburgh. In London bonfires blazed in the streets. Thus ended the Tudor dynasty, and thus began the reign of the house of Stuart, amid popular rejoicing over the peaceful change of crowns. The Jacobean Shakespeare was in the wings.

8

His Highness's Servant:
From *Measure for Measure*
to *Timon of Athens*

When a creative act took place can have interest in its
own right. Such is the case with our next play. The
Revels Accounts, which recorded expenses for royal entertainments, testify that *Measure for Measure* by
"Shaxberd" was played before the king and court at
Whitehall Palace on St. Stephen's Night, 1604. Shakespeare probably wrote the play earlier in the season for
presentation at the Globe playhouse, intermittently
opened to the public as the plague loosened its grip on
the capital. This was a time when a momentous public
drama was being enacted on a larger stage. Queen Elizabeth I had died the preceding year, and her Privy
Council had immediately proclaimed the accession of a
new monarch. Elizabeth had reigned for almost half a
century; most of her subjects had never known another
monarch. What would the uncouth Scot—so he impressed many Englishmen—who replaced her be like?
Would he be severe or accommodating? And what about
those innumerable statutes, for long uninvoked, that
cluttered up the lawbooks? Questions to be asked when
an administration changes.

The new king soon gave a hint of future policy.
Shortly after he had started out in April 1603, gallantly
accompanied by multitudes of nobility and gentlemen,
on his royal progress from Edinburgh to London, at
Newark-upon-Trent a "base pilfering fellow" was
caught cutting a purse amid the enthusiastic throng and
was hanged forthwith at the king's command. Before
departing, however, he ordered all the prisoners held in
Newark Castle to be set free. Justice and mercy, Jaco-

bean style: such issues, always of absorbing public interest, must have had a special piquance when *Measure for Measure* was composed. They retain their hold as in the theater we watch the play unfold almost four centuries later.

In the great central scenes of *Measure for Measure* Claudio's sister, Isabella, who is a novice in a convent and about to take her final vows, is called upon to plead for the life of her errant brother, guilty of a sin that her religious commitment has led her to detest. As the action progresses, Angelo—one who "never feels / The wanton stings and motions of the flesh"—is irresistibly, and sexually, attracted to the chaste Isabella; an attraction which a strumpet could never have stirred in him, for it is her very purity that arouses the beast in Angelo. "We are all frail," he comes to realize. A simple yet profound truth.

Isabella must decide whether to save her dear brother's life by the "abhorred pollution" of her own body to satisfy the deputy's lust. Does the end justify the means? For her it does not. Her decision is as unambiguous as it is inevitable: "Then, Isabel, live chaste, and brother, die: / More than our brother is our chastity" (II.iv.184–85). For Isabella chastity would appear to be a matter of the body only, not also of the spirit residing in that body, whatever may befall the body itself. Other views were possible. For the Renaissance the great exemplar was the Roman matron Lucrece, who chose death after being violated by Sextus Tarquinius, a king's son inflamed by her beauty. Shakespeare had recounted her story in his long narrative poem, *The Rape of Lucrece*. An obscure preacher, Thomas Carew, in a godly sermon printed in the same year that King James made his royal progress to London, took up the case of this celebrated figure from antiquity: "Lucretia and certain heathen women killed themselves that they might not be defiled with soldiers, not knowing that the body is not defiled, if the mind be chaste." A similar view had been expressed in the previous century by the biblical translator and religious controversialist William

Tyndale in *The Obedience of a Christian Man.* "She sought her own glory in her chastity and not God's," Tyndale writes.

> When she had lost her chastity, then counted she herself most abominable in the sight of all men, and for very pain and thought which she had, not that she hath displeased God but that she had lost her honour, slew herself. Look how great her glory and rejoicing therein, and much despised she them that were otherwise, and pitied them not, which pride God more abhorreth than the whoredom of any whore.

Yet Isabella approves the bed-trick by which Mariana snares the fiancé—the same Angelo—who had once discarded her.

Fierce and unyielding as Isabella may well appear to be, her refusal to yield her virginity to Angelo in order to save her brother is, judged by the logic of dramatic events, correct. For self-sacrifice would not have achieved its end: Having slept with Mariana but believing that he has indeed enjoyed Isabella's body, Angelo not unreasonably suspects that the outraged brother who has purchased his life at the expense of a sister's shame might well in time come to meditate revenge. And so—contrary to his undertaking to Isabella—the deputy orders Claudio to be executed forthwith and the severed head brought to him as proof that the command has been carried out. (This turn of events comes as a surprise to the duke, who with Isabella had anticipated a happy outcome; and when he suggests that Barnardine—a condemned murderer—be executed instead and his head sent in place of Claudio's, Barnardine stubbornly refuses to cooperate on grounds that he has been drinking all night and is not fit to die, a conclusion with which the duke must reluctantly agree. His power in Vienna may be absolute, but the duke shares in the fallibility to which all mortals are subject.) In the end, however, Isabella is not too proud to go down on her knees at the behest of Mariana, who now has a husband to preserve, to beg clemency for the very man she has every reason to believe had her brother killed.

There are different kinds of law. The old Mosaic law, validating an eye for an eye and tooth for a tooth, provides *Measure for Measure* with its title. It is invoked for the first and only time in the duke's pronouncement as the play draws to a close: "An Angelo for Claudio, death for death!" (V.i.411–12). But the title also recalls another dispensation in the Sermon on the Mount as set forth in Matthew's gospel: "Judge not that ye be not judged; and with what measure ye mete, it shall be measured to you again." The severity of the old law is mitigated by the new.

A manuscript play in the British Library in London, "The Book [i.e., the playhouse manuscript] of Sir Thomas More," provides the much gone-over and altered text of a play originally written by Anthony Munday and Henry Chettle, perhaps with assistance from another dramatist. Subsequently several playwrights—Chettle again, Thomas Dekker, perhaps Thomas Heywood, and the author of the so-called Addition IIc, comprising three pages plus a single speech prefix ("all"), amounting to 147 lines ascribed to "Hand D"—sought to rescue a play that was in trouble. Today many scholars believe that Hand D belongs to William Shakespeare on the basis of handwriting (mainly the six authenticated signatures), the spelling links with printed texts deriving (so far as we can tell) from Shakespeare's own papers, and diction and imagery. In all, contributions to the "Book of Sir Thomas More" were eventually made by six different hands, apart from annotations by the Master of the Revels, Sir Edmund Tilney (d. 1610), who remained in office for thirty years, having been appointed in 1579.

Based mainly on Holinshed's *Chronicles* and the manuscript *Life of More* by More's son-in-law, William Roper, "Sir Thomas More" deals with episodes in the life of More (1478–1535), ending with his execution on the scaffold. Tilney's censorship focused mainly on the so-called "Ill-May Day" scene of the London rioters—William and his wife, Doll, and the others—resolved that "on May Day next in the morning they go forth a-maying but make it the worst May Day for the strangers" (i.e., alien residents). Hence the "ill-May day," requiring the anxious city authorities to dispatch More as peacemaker. Shakespeare—if, indeed these pages are his—may not have known the play as a whole; probably he was once again the seasoned professional called upon to revise a scene, now lost, by another hand. Another passage in the play—a soliloquy by More after being appointed Lord Chancellor—has also been ascribed to Shakespeare, although this is in the hand of a professional scribe.

Firsthand study of "Sir Thomas More" has been handicapped as a result of a misguided early attempt to protect the manuscript. Around the middle of the nineteenth century, some unknown person pasted thick, semi-opaque paper on both sides of six of the crumbling leaves, and also patched holes with gummed paper; a case of the cure being worse than the disease. With the passage of time the tracing paper as might have been expected but was not—darkened, and the paste thickened, leaving much of the writing illegible. The mutilation affected two of the three pages of Addition IIc.

When did Shakespeare take part in the revision of "Sir Thomas More," if indeed he took part? Like so much in Shakespearean scholarship, any suggestion can be no more than speculative. Some think the revision took place in 1593, when the Lord Strange's Men, with Shakespeare possibly transiently one of them, were amalgamated temporarily with the Admiral's company. But in the view of others, stylistic considerations point to a later date for the "Ill May-Day" scene.

In the summer of 1600 the Admiral's Men, biding their time until their new playhouse, the Fortune, opened, went on tour, and their impresario, Henslowe, for a while made a few diary entries of payments to his chronically indigent playwrights. Did they, for the nonce, offer their wares to the rival Chamberlain's Men? If "Sir Thomas More" was written then—and this is only speculation—its theme of rebellion and execution would assume an ominous topical significance. For on February 8, 1601, the charismatic but unstable Earl of Essex—the queen's disgraced former darling—made his unsuccessful bid for supreme power. The prime movers of the failed insurrection were executed in February and March of 1601. "God for pity help these troublous times," beseeches a sheriff of London in "Sir Thomas More" after the collapse of the May Day insurrection, "the streets stopped up by gazing multitudes." The streets were indeed stopped up by gazing multitudes in 1601.

Or was "Sir Thomas More" set aside altogether in the light of Tilney's objections, to be taken up at a more propitious time? After all, it was More's refusal, as Lord Chancellor, to subscribe to the Act of Supremacy that led to his imprisonment and execution at the behest of Henry VIII. A martyr of the Roman Catholic Church, More would in time be canonized, but while a Tudor reigned, the man who defied the queen's father—and the basis for his defiance—would remain anathema to a censored drama. Thomas More may have been a man for all seasons, but he was a man more for some seasons than for others. Only when the death of the Virgin Queen resulted in the extinction of the Tudor line did a play on the rise and fall of Sir Thomas More cease to be a source of political discomfiture. Still, this play was destined to remain an intent that perished by the way.

Only a short interval apparently intervened between *All's Well That Ends Well* (c. 1604) and the joyous comedies that preceded. Like them, it dwells on the perturbations of courtship and marital choice, the stuff of romantic comedy. Within the broad perimeters of convention, however, Shakespeare follows the imperatives of his own imaginative vision, his characters moving beyond the stereotypes of romantic idealization. Helena, a huntress chaste and fair, sets her sights on her matrimonial quarry and captures her dubious prize. Led unwillingly to the altar, Bertram declines to consummate the union and sends his wife packing. Ultimately she prevails by means of the bed-trick—that is, by substituting herself for the young woman her estranged husband is angling (with promises of matrimony) to seduce. Thus does all end well.

Not surprisingly, many critics over the years have found the work unsettling. Some have viewed it as a "dark comedy" or, more usually, a "problem play." The dramatic historian F. S. Boas first spoke of Shakespeare's problem plays in 1896 when he grouped *All's Well* with *Measure for Measure, Troilus and Cressida,* and *Hamlet.* "Throughout these plays," Boas wrote, "we move along dim untrodden paths, and at the close our feeling is neither of simple joy nor pain; we are excited, fascinated, perplexed, for the issues raised preclude a completely satisfactory outcome, even when, as in *All's Well* and *Measure for Measure,* the complications are outwardly adjusted in the fifth act."

The familiar figures of fairy tale loom at once larger and simpler than real life. In *All's Well,* however, Shakespeare's art, subsuming folk motifs, acknowledges human singularity and the particulars of place and time. Whether the setting be the palace of the counts of Roussillon, the French king's glittering court at Paris, or the camp outside Florence, his play depicts a worldly Renaissance milieu with recognizable specificity.

The generations have their spokesmen: the elders, in the bereaved countess, ailing sovereign, and Lord Lafeu, ancient but hale (his name allusively signifies "fire" and possibly also "the late," i.e., "deceased," alluding to his age); the young, in Bertram and Helena and the parcel of noble bachelors who grace the court and go off to seek glory on a foreign field. Bertram's worthless follower, Parolles, foppishly bedecked with scarves, enriches the thematic counterpoint with an underplot built around his unmasking. The social classes too are represented. Lavache ("cow," and perhaps relates to *lavage*—"slop"—too), the household jester at Roussillon, views the human comedy from his own drily amused and world-weary vantage point. In Florence the widow Capilet, of genteelly straitened circumstances, dwells with her dowryless daughter, Diana, and makes ends meet by lodging pilgrims on the way to Saint Jaques le Grand at her inn beside the city gate. There are pages and attendants, a steward, messengers, soldiers, neighbors, and friends. As readers—or viewers—we attend the flow of commentary by which Shakespeare's characters size up one another and events. "The web of our life is of a mingled yarn, good and ill together," remarks the First Lord Dumaine; "our virtues would be proud if our faults whipped them not, and our crimes would despair if they were not cherished by our virtues" (IV.iii.74–78). The fabric of *All's Well* testifies to the rich texture of life in the process of being lived.

Bertram is from his first stage entry, specifying *"young Bertram,"* notable especially for his youth. Along with everyone else gathered at Roussillon for a family occasion, he wears mourning. The play thus begins, like *Hamlet,* written slightly earlier, in the aftermath of the death of a father. Just how old Bertram is, the text fails to indicate, but he is yet a minor and under the guardianship of the King. Now, at his sovereign's command, he is about to set out for Paris, a departure that, like Laertes's in *Hamlet,* evokes parental concern. " 'Tis an unseasoned courtier," Bertram's mother—perhaps the most empathetic matron in Shakespeare—worries aloud.

With good cause. Bertram's crisis comes quickly when the King decrees that Bertram take Helena as his wife. Helena is unacceptable in his eyes not so much for any personal deficiencies as by reason of her inferior social caste as a poor physician's daughter. Bertram goes on to behave badly in a variety of ways. Exercising the absolute authority of a Renaissance husband, he dismisses Helena without even the good-bye kiss she pathetically craves, and spares himself embarrassment by instructing her—cruelly through an intermediary—to assume responsibility herself for her precipitous departure from court. Helena's dowry, generously provided by the King, Bertram spends to outfit himself for a foreign military adventure undertaken expressly to put distance between himself and a detested wife. When confronted with his misdoings, he libels Diana, the virtuous maiden he has attempted to corrupt, as "a common gamester of the chase," and lies about the love tokens he believes they have exchanged. His brutish behavior, so unlike the winning ways of Shakespeare's earlier lovers, Orlando and Benedick, is in large measure responsible for the critical unease *All's Well* has stirred.

It is a curious comedy, written at a time when the playwright's most urgent creative energies were being absorbed by the great sequence of tragedies beginning with *Hamlet*. As chief architect of her own love plot, his Helena looks back to previous heroines, such as Rosalind in *As You Like It*. Bertram is, like Claudio in *Much Ado About Nothing*, let off more generously than he strictly deserves. The play also contains premonitions of Shakespeare's late romances, in which renewed hope follows spiritual regeneration, and painful separations end in reunion. In *All's Well* the imaginative range of Shakespeare's material—realistic, romantic, and fairy tale—elicits a correspondingly diverse mix of styles. The verse, although in Shakespeare's mature manner, assumes a distinctive spare eloquence in this play. At times it is gnomic or incantatory; a letter takes sonnet form. The prose—of which there is almost as much as verse—has an idiomatic vitality, and in the drum scenes Shakespeare allows himself a riotous excursion into pure gibberish. In such a context paradoxes flourish. The yarn of *All's Well* is richly varied, challenging and rewarding interpretation.

Critics have often classed *Troilus and Cressida* as one of Shakespeare's "problem plays," and of problems—

both textual and interpretative—it has more than a sufficiency. The play was entered not once but twice (in 1603 and 1609) in the Stationers' Register, where printers, before the advent of modern copyright legislation, would stake a claim for the manuscripts in their possession. *Troilus* first saw print in a quarto edition in 1609. In the 1623 First Folio the play was originally intended to appear after *Romeo and Juliet*, but (as things worked out) *Timon of Athens* came next, and *Troilus* appears, for the most part unpaginated, between *Henry VIII* and *Coriolanus;* in other words, in a no-man's land between the Histories and the Tragedies.

In the Folio—but not the quarto—a Prologue, armed for battle, puts in an appearance from which we learn that Paris has ravished Helen, Menelaus's queen, and that the instruments of cruel war have set forth to ransack her from Troy, within whose strong walls she is now immured; but Troilus and Cressida—the dual protagonists of the play—are not so much as mentioned. In the Folio, but not in the quarto, the full title is *The History of Troilus and Cressida.* An unsigned dedicatory epistle to the quarto, addressed by "A Never Writer to an Ever Reader," praises the play as an uproarious comedy: "none more witty than this" one, "never clapped-clawed [i.e., applauded] with the palms of the vulgar, and yet passing full of the palm comical," as good as the best comedies of Plautus and Terence. The author, whoever he was, has never written anything wittier.

The 1603 Register entry refers to *Troilus* "as it is acted by my Lord Chamberlain's Men," and the original quarto title page—afterward canceled—presents the play "as it was acted by the King's Majesty's Servants at the Globe." So *Troilus was* clapper-clawed by the vulgar after all, or (as the never-writer puts it) "sullied with the smoky breath of the multitude." He refers also to the "grand possessors' wills." Who were they? Maybe Shakespeare originally wrote the play for private performance. If so, it is not the only Elizabethan play that had more than one venue.

When was *Troilus and Cressida* written? An ingenious parallel has been made between the sulking Achilles of the play and Essex's absenting himself from the court in 1598; moreover, George Chapman dedicated his first Homer translation to the earl, that "most true Achilles." Then was Shakespeare mocking at Essex in 1598 or 1600, not long after the earl's return from Ireland? If so, then how square this with the playwright's unmistakable laudation of Essex in the Prologue to *Henry V*? More likely *Troilus* was written in 1602–3. With such perplexities does scholarship disport itself.

The play's high-sounding polysyllabic Latinate diction is consonant with private performance. Witness Troilus's response upon realizing that "All's done," as Ulysses, another bystander, remarks; that Cressida has indeed abandoned him for another lover. He stays, as he tells Ulysses,

> To make a recordation to my soul
> Of every syllable that here was spoke.
> But if I tell how these two did co-act
> Shall I not lie in publishing a truth?
> Sith yet there is a credence in my heart,
> An esperance so obstinately strong,
> That doth invert th' attest of eyes and ears,
> As if those organs had deceptious functions,
> Created only to calumniate.   (V ii 113–21)

Did ever disappointed lover thus unload himself? Not any other of Shakespeare's.

The matter of Troy—as students refer to the complex of myth and literature—has engaged Western civilization for almost three thousand years, ever since the Greek bard Homer enthralled an aristocratic audience in Asia Minor with his *Iliad*, which recounted with matchless tragic grandeur the wrath of Achilles and the deaths of Patroclus and the Trojan hero, Hector; Troilus, Priam's youngest son, is no more than mentioned as a gallant warrior. The Trojan war figures also in Virgil's *Aeneid,* with which Shakespeare was familiar, and in the *Metamorphoses* of Ovid, Shakespeare's favorite classic, which he knew both in the original Latin and in Golding's English translation. The matter of Troy was medievalized by Chaucer in his long poem *Troilus and Criseyde,* based on Boccaccio, in which love and chivalry vie with heroic warfare as the focus. In *The Testament of Cresseid* Robert Henryson (c. 1425–c.1506) furnishes a grimly moral epilogue to Chaucer's poem, as Cresseid, now a leper, beseeches alms with her cup and clapper, until one day the knight Troilus, riding by in triumph from Troy, spies her and—not recognizing her but being somehow reminded of Cresseid—casts to her a purse full of gold and jewels before riding on. In 1598 Chapman published the first installment of his English translation of the *Iliad,* consisting of seven books (1, 2 and 7–11), just a few years before Shakespeare turned to the matter of Troy for a Renaissance English tragedy. The tragic interfacing of love and war is present from the first speech of his play. ''Call here my varlet, I'll unarm again,'' Troilus bids Pandarus, Cressida's uncle; ''Why should I war without the walls of Troy / That find such cruel battle here within?''

Troilus and Cressida begins in medias res. The siege of Troy has gone on for seven long years. From the outset Cressida has known that her love affair with Troilus will be consummated: she plays a waiting game for whorish reasons, for ''men prize a thing ungain'd more than it is.'' Even without the services of Pandarus as go-between—his name would give an unbecoming word, *pander,* to the language—she would have bedded Troilus. In time Cressida will be returned to the Greek side and will take a new love. When she makes her first appearance in the Greek camp, the men size her up quickly. In turn they line up to taste her lips. No sooner has she gone than Ulysses gives his side's verdict: ''There's language in her eye, her cheek, her lip; / Nay, her foot speaks.'' Set such women down, he concludes, "For sluttish spoils of opportunity / And daughters of the game" (IV.v.55–63). A trumpet flourish follows, betokening the entrance of Trojans, and in Shakespeare's extraordinary auditory pun all shout, "The Troyans' trumpet," i.e., the Trojans' strumpet.

In a time of truce Achilles, the chief Greek warrior, indolently keeps to his tent, engaging in badinage with Patroclus, who is, as the scabrous Thersites puts it, "Achilles' brach," or bitch: that is, his homosexual lover. Such a motif is rare in Shakespeare. When the Trojan warrior Aeneas comes to the Greek camp bearing a challenge from Hector, his high-sounding chivalric rhetoric mystifies the unchivalric Greeks. "This Trojan scorns us," their general, Agamemnon, remarks, "or the men of Troy are ceremonious courtiers." Aeneas's challenge is directed to any Greek "that holds his honor higher than his ease," and is in fact aimed at the sulking Achilles. Ulysses, the shrewdest of the Greeks, who delivers his great, long speech on degree, sees an opportunity to arouse Achilles to action by choosing the "dull brainless Ajax" to meet Hector in the exhibition tourney. Characteristically for this play, nothing comes of the stratagem.

In the Trojan camp Cassandra, gifted with prophetic powers that are doomed to be ignored, cries unheeded, "Troy burns, or else let Helen go." Reason requires that they do just that, but the Trojans are committed to a "mad idolatry" that makes the service greater than the god. "Nay, if we talk of reason," Troilus declares, "let's shut our gates and sleep" (II.ii.46–47). He carries the day. Troy is destined to burn.

In another great, long speech Ulysses pays tribute to Time, which has "a wallet at his back, / Wherein he puts alms for oblivion" (III,iii.145–46). The ruins of time are a familiar Shakespearean theme in this in some respects uncharacteristic play, a theme that

Shakespeare had employed to advantage in *2 Henry IV*. Many a Greek and Trojan lies dead since Ulysses and Diomedes made the embassage that resulted in the abduction of Helen. The walls and proud towers of Troy will in time kiss their own feet: "The end crowns all, / And that old common arbitrator, Time, / Will one day end it" (IV,v.222–24). Before that day comes, Cressida will betray Troilus's love, and Achilles and his fierce Myrmidons will cold-heartedly slay Hector, who has doffed his helmet and hung his shield behind him. "I am unarmed;" he beseeches Achilles; "forgo this vantage, Greek" (V.viii). The Greek does not forgo it. Of such stuff are heroes made. The sun begins to set; ugly night comes on. Pandarus has the last word, coming on to ask the "good traders in the flesh" in the audience to give some groans for their bones aching from venereal disease. Meanwhile, Pandarus will sweat (also a result of venereal disease) and in time bequeath his diseases. Thus, unedifyingly, does *Troilus and Cressida* conclude.

The Tragedy of Othello the Moor of Venice, the second of Shakespeare's mature tragedies and from the first enthusiastically received on the boards, was performed before the first Stuart monarch in the Banqueting House at Whitehall on November 1, 1604. Presumably it had already been acted at the Globe. The author's main source was Giraldi Cinthio's *Hecatommithi (The Hundred Tales),* a collection of linked tales, like the *Decameron,* these reputedly told aboard a ship sailing from Rome to Marseilles. Here Shakespeare found the story of Disdemona (as the name is spelled in Cinthio) and the Moor of Venice—either in the original Italian or in the 1584 French translation—as well as his scheming ensign (or standard-bearer), the ensign's wife, and his corporal, "who was very dear to the Moor." Disdemona excepted, all the characters are unnamed. Shakespeare seems to have taken his information about the Turkish invasion of Cyprus from Richard Knolles's *History of the Turks,* first published in 1603; so *Othello* may well have been completed not earlier than 1604. The dramatist was more than once drawn to revise plays that his company had already acted. *Othello* was such an instance. Thus, Desdemona's willow song (IV.iii) was not from the first present, and Emilia's role in the closing scenes was originally slighter.

In plays of the period Moors, especially blackamoors, or Negroes, as distinguished from the Middle Eastern tawny Moors (and Othello *is* black), are characteristically lecherous and villainous, as, for example, Shakespeare's own Aaron in *Titus Andronicus*, who yet demonstrates a humanizing paternal devotion. Shakespeare envisages his Othello as an exotic hero-soldier, the general brought on board by the potentates of Venice—at this time still a great, albeit decaying, maritime power—to rescue the state in a potentially devastating war with Turkey. Yet Othello remains the foreigner. He is set apart from Desdemona as regards country and culture, race, and age, for (as he himself says) he "has declined into the vale of years." Desdemona, on the other hand, is the Venetian magnifico's daughter, her father's joy. Yet this is self-evidently a love match. As the bride forcefully declares before the assembled Duke and grandees, "I saw Othello's visage in his mind" (I.iii). Desdemona's primary loyalty lies not with her father but with her husband (when Cinthio's tale begins, the Moor and his wife have already happily settled into married life).

No Shakespearean tragic hero undergoes as much debasement as Othello, who falls into his obscene trance—babbling about handkerchiefs, confessions, noses, ears, and lips: the sex act. With Iago he kneels as they take their "sacred vow" to pursue to execution their "tyrannous hate" (III.iii). In the presence of the Venetian ducal emissary (her father's kinsman) Othello strikes Desdemona. To Iago, once her blood is made dull with sex, she will no longer look delightedly upon the devil. But Iago, not Othello, is the devil. Near the very end of the tragedy, before Othello takes his own life, he surveys the manacled Iago: "I look down towards his feet"—that is, to see whether they are, as the devil's supposedly were, cloven hooves— "but that's a fable." Iago, Vice-like, is indeed a species of devil in this allegory of evil, as Bernard Spivack entitles his well-known monograph on the Vice-like origins of the Iago character.

"Perdition catch my soul," Othello has declared, "but I do love thee! And when I love thee not, / Chaos is come again (III.iii.90–92)." Chaos indeed comes. The antagonist, like Richard III a superficially engaging presence, takes the audience into his confidence. He has a much larger part than the hero in this, Shakespeare's most concentrated tragic drama. To the other figures he is honest Iago, ready (if need be) to raise his glass and sing his song. "I am not what I am," he tells the "gull'd gentleman" Roderigo in the first scene: not "what I *seem,*" but "what I *am.*" In Exodus 3:14 "God said to Moses, I am who I am." In Iago the sacred becomes malignantly profane. Yet although voluble regarding others and himself, he remains a blank. "Demand me nothing," Iago growls in his last speech. "What you know, you know." As in a very different context, the rest is silence. On the motives for his evil, Iago comments explicitly enough, yet he tells us nothing; this, in Coleridge's celebrated aperçu, is "the motive hunting of motiveless malignity."

Othello begins in the midst of conversation, with Roderigo, the sponged-upon, declaring to the sponger, "Tush, never tell me!" Iago tells him anyway. From the first moment this play never lets up. Time is compressed, not (taken literally) permitting Desdemona to have bedded Othello's lieutenant even had she been so inclined. In due course, a single fragile property will arrest audience attention, the handkerchief that the Egyptian who could almost read the thoughts of people gave to Othello's mother, the handkerchief with "magic in the web of it." There is magic too—magic aplenty— in the web of the tragedy.

We encounter it as we listen to the Othello music when the Moor speaks. As men with lights and weapons draw on both sides, the battle-scarred general, however alien and outnumbered, is not to be ignored. "Keep up [i.e., sheath] your bright swords," Othello commands, "for the dew will rust them" (I.ii.58). In the Venetian senate chamber Desdemona declares her love for the black foreigner, and the signiors reaffirm their confidence in Othello by assigning the command at Cyprus to this soldier of fortune who has known slavery and cannibals and men whose heads grow beneath their shoulders, and is as yet unvanquished by all "the battles, sieges, fortunes" of life he has experienced. For Desdemona, whom he holds spellbound, he embodies the romantic ideal. But Othello is also self-idealizingly vulnerable and no match for a super-subtle Italianate villain. Once we touch down in the Cyprian castle garrison we are in an unabashedly masculine environment with an occupying army and few women: only the occasional officer's wife, such as the commanding general's and his ensign's, or the camp prostitute, such as Bianca. It is an environment, however familiar to the military, beset with temptations and dangers.

An elegy by a contemporary refers to "the grieved Moor" as a famous role of Richard Burbage, the stellar actor of Shakespeare's troupe. We first hear of a notable black actor in the part when Ira Frederick Aldridge (c. 1805–62), an American, debuted as Othello at the Royalty Theatre in London, and subsequently was applauded by the crowned heads of Europe when he performed on tour. Eventually Aldridge became a naturalized British subject; in those days a black actor could not perform in legitimate theater in the United States. In this century, black as well as Caucasian actors have been celebrated for their Othellos, among them Paul Robeson, who memorably took the part in 1942 opposite the young José Ferrer's Iago in the Margaret Webster revival on Broadway (Webster herself played

Emilia). James Earl Jones has also acted Othello, with Christopher Plummer as Iago.

In *Northrop Frye on Shakespeare*, the critic's most recent book (1986), Frye, whose varied learning—mythological, anthropological, archetypical—always commands respect, speaks (justly, I feel) of *Hamlet* as "the central Shakespeare play for the nineteenth and early twentieth centuries, when so many cultural factors revolved around the difficulties of uniting action and the consciousness of action," whereas "[i]n the existentialist period of this century this theme was still in the foreground, but, with a growing sense of the absurdity of trying to rationalize a world set up for the benefit of predatory rulers, *King Lear* began to move into the centre in its place." Surely, for moderns *King Lear* has indeed been the central Shakespearean tragedy.

Yet the play opens like nothing so much as an elemental fairy tale: There was once a very old king who wanted to rest, so one day he summoned his three daughters before the whole court and asked, "Which of you shall we say doth love us most for she will inherit the most opulent third of the kingdom?" Two of the daughters professed boundless love, but the third and youngest, who most loved her father and was most loved by him, would say nothing. If the love test sounds folkloristic, such is indeed the case, as is abundantly recognized: There are many ancient European and Oriental antecedents about good and bad children, and about filial ingratitude. There is the Goosegirl-Princess, who told her father she "loved him like salt," and Cinderella (the most famous such story, at least in the West), who was mistreated by her ugly sisters.

Sometimes an actual event may impinge upon the creative act. In October 1603—about a year before Shakespeare began *King Lear*—one Brian Annesley was reported to be unfit to govern either himself or his estate. Two of his daughters tried to have him certified as lunatic, but the youngest daughter—Cordell—appealed against such a verdict. In time, Cordell would wed Sir William Harvey, the stepfather of the Earl of Southampton, and regarded by many as the Mr. W. H. who was the "only begetter" of Shakespeare's *Sonnets*. In *King Lear,* as is characteristic of supreme drama, the topically particular conjoins with the universal.

The Lear of the play is more than fourscore. He has long since reached the age—as Freud puts it—when he would do well to "renounce love, choose death, and make friends with the necessity of dying." Yet only now does he learn what poor naked wretches feel. "I have ta'en / Too little care of this." Only now does pomp take physic, and thus undergo cure. The play dramatizes, with awesome power, the education of an eighty-year-old.

In introducing the Fourth Act, Edgar—having been declared an outlaw and disguised himself as a mad beggar—gives thanks for the consolations of philosophy. "To be worst," he comforts himself,

> The lowest and most dejected thing of fortune,
> Stands still in esperance, lives not in fear.
> The lamentable change is from the best;
> The worst returns to laughter.

But Edgar has not yet experienced the worst: no sooner has he thought this than he sees his father enter poorly led by an anonymous Old Man, a sometime servant; a realization that prompts him to reflect,

> World, world, O world!
> But that thy strange mutations make us hate thee,
> Life would not yield to age.

But Edgar does not yet know that his father has been blinded, a realization that understandably prompts him to reflect, "Who is't can say 'I am at the worst'? / I am worse than e'er I was." And his father now is led to conclude that man is a worm, and to express the most nihilistic sentiment in all Shakespeare: "As flies to wanton boys are we to th' gods; / They kill us for their sport.'' Yet the scene, expressive of a pre-Christian world in which the gods figure so prominently, witnesses the reconciliation process; the play is not over until it is over.

Terrible events will follow. In the last moment, Lear, himself soon to die, enters carrying his slain good daughter. *King Lear* offers no easy answers, only profound mysteries, not all of them comforting. In *Nosce Teipsum* (''Know Thyself''), a philosophical poem on the nature of man and the soul—or the mind, to use a modern secular approximation—Sir John Davies, almost Shakespeare's exact contemporary, sums up thus: ''And to conclude, I know myself a man / Which is a proud, and yet a wretched thing.'' So we may conclude about the human condition as we experience a play we justly recognize as a monument of Western civilization.

King Lear indeed presents man in this dual condition, proud yet wretched. In the first scene a great king, still full of glorious state, can swear ''by the sacred radiance of the sun''; the setting is King Lear's palace, but in this visionary kingdom Stonehenge cannot be far away. Yet, in the oft-quoted words of a distinguished Shakespearean, *''King Lear* is a Christian play about a pagan world; and the fact that Shakespeare can assume in his audience a different religious standpoint from that of any of his characters gives him a peculiar freedom, and makes possible an unusual complexity and richness.'' Shakespeare fully avails himself of this freedom. He wrote the play more than half a century before Thomas Hobbes in *Leviathan* offered a bleak materialist and pessimistic philosophy depicting the life of man as ''solitary, poor, nasty, brutish and short,'' and as the ''general inclination of all mankind, a perpetual and restless desire after power that ceaseth only in death.'' It is a point of view that Shakespeare's bastard Edmund, that ruthless materialist striver after power and possessions, would understand well even if he would not express it in similar words. *Nature* is his word when we first encounter Edmund: "Thou, Nature, art my goddess; to thy law / My services are bound" (I.ii). The word *nature*, in its various forms and combinations, will occur more than forty times in *King Lear*. It is the Nature that signifies the law of the jungle to which the Bastard vows allegiance. This too is what this inexhaustible masterwork forces readers and audiences to contemplate.

Considerations of space have prevented me here from elaborating on Lear's faithful follower, Kent, or on the Fool with his bitter repartee on Lear's folly in disowning Cordelia a projection of his master's submerged self—and his dropping out of the play when Cordelia returns to England. Nor has there been space to comment on the storm with its metaphysical dimension, or on the Morality tradition that feeds into the conception of Lear, who may be reckoned another, more sublime, counterpart to the King of Life (see page 67). I have often thought that in Elizabethan tragedy all roads lead to *Lear*.

The tragedy has formidable problems that challenge the textual scholar as well as the literary critic. For *King Lear* has come down to us in two radically different versions, and it is now felt that the Quarto version (first printed in 1608) offers an authoritative text that Shakespeare revised two or three years after the play was first written and produced. For the version first published in the 1623 Folio, a more obviously theatrical text, the playwright cut some three hundred lines and modified his script by altering (for example) the characterization of Albany and Edgar. In other words, a substantive recasting of certain aspects of Shakespeare's original script took place, and to conflate the two versions, as editors until very lately have tended to do, is, in effect, to create a play that never was. Among Shakespeare's mysteries not the least profound are the textual mysteries.

At under 2,300 lines, *The Life of Timon of Athens* is—excepting only *Macbeth*—Shakespeare's shortest tragedy. It also offers an abundance of confusion and, despite scholarly diligence, seemingly intractable problems. First printed in the 1623 Folio, *Timon* occupied the place originally set aside for *Troilus and Cressida*, a space that had somehow to be filled, although the brevity of *Timon* created problems of its own. Maybe, had special circumstances not obtained, the play would not have been included at all. When was *Timon* written? That there is no record of any early performance does not help in fixing a date. The tragedy can be assigned— to be sure, only speculatively—to around the same time that Shakespeare wrote *King Lear:* 1605 may do as a guess, but no more than that.

The play's irregularities are apparent to any attentive reader. Here it will suffice to cite only a few of many. Some of the blank verse is accomplished in the mature Shakespearian mode; other lines scarcely scan. Certain passages—such as the emblematic opening scene involving the Poet, Painter, Merchant, and Jeweler (also a Mercer who remains mysteriously silent)—are polished. Other scenes have only limited issue, like those involving the heroic and mistreated captain Alcibiades in the underplot: unfairly banished by the Athenian senate, he is driven "worse than mad." Taken in conjunction with the Timon story, the Alcibiades story opens up the possibility of a fully orchestrated double plot, such as Shakespeare had triumphantly deployed in *King Lear.* But Alcibiades has only one more appearance before the play's end, as the gates of a chastised Athens are opened before him, and he reads the epitaph of the "noble Timon" and vows to use the olive with the sword before bidding the drums strike. Prose will suddenly give way to iambic pentameter passages. "Yonder comes a poet and a painter," Apemantus notifies Timon in his cave in the woods; but the Poet and Painter do not make their entrance for almost two hundred lines, after the entrance and exit first of the banditti and then of Flavius, Timon's faithful steward. In the last speech Alcibiades reads, in succession, two varying epitaphs on Timon's gravestone on the sea's edge. The author never took the pains to regularize the forms of some of his characters' names. Thus, Ventidius—one of the false friends, whose debts Timon had, when rich, once paid, but now refused him a like sum when Timon is in need—is also designated as Ventidgius or Ventigiud; Apemantus also appears as Apermantus.

To look after such fine tuning, Elizabethan playwrights usually did not bestir themselves, but *Timon* has so many roughnesses and loose ends that one is forced to suspect that the tragedy was never acted in the form in which it has come down. In an important essay, written half a century ago, the late Una Ellis-Fermor makes the point well: She views *Timon of Athens* as "a play such as a great artist might leave behind him, roughed out, worked over in part and then abandoned, full of inconsistencies in form and presentation, with fragments (some of them considerable) bearing the unmistakable stamp of his workmanship scattered throughout." To see evidences of the supreme Western dramatist in the act of creation has its own special fascination—as well as its possible pitfalls.

Take the issue of the talents. A talent was an ancient weight and money of account of varying value among Assyrians, Greeks, Romans, and other peoples; it is mentioned often in the Bible and in Plutarch's writings, and is generally taken to have the value of a hundredweight of silver: a considerable sum. In *Timon* Shakespeare (and his collaborator—if he had one) had fluctuating notions of a talent's worth. Sometimes it represents a considerable sum, just five or six talents being cited as an appropriate number (I.i): elsewhere Timon asks the Athenian senators for one-thousand talents. Or we may hear, in III.ii, of "fifty" or "fifty-five hundred talents"—does this signify fifty *or* five hundred? In the same scene the playwright throws in the sponge and speaks vaguely of "so many" talents. In a brilliant essay, "Shakespeare Learns the Value of Money," in *Shakespeare Survey 6* (1953), the late T. J. B. Spencer accounts for these discrepancies in the tragedy by the hypothesis that "in the course of writing the play Shakespeare (i) became aware that he did not know the value of the talent, (ii) found out this piece of information from some person or book, and (iii) then in several places got his figures right.''

Because of inconsistencies of style—in addition to numerous confusions and loose ends—not a few students have seen *Timon* as a collaboration. Several contemporary dramatists have been proposed for an adjunct role—Heywood, Chapman, Field, etc.—but most notably the young Thomas Middleton, junior to Shakespeare by sixteen years. For Middleton arguments have been made, denied, and lately made again in the *Complete Oxford Shakespeare* (1986) and in the *Textual Companion* (1987) to that edition.

The historical Timon made a powerful impression on his own and after-times. He actually lived in fifth-century Athens, not far from the Acropolis. After his death, Timon became the stuff of legend. Poets made him the subject of epigrams and epitaphs. In his comedies Aristophanes more than once referred to him, as did other Greek playwrights in lost comedies of which records have come down. In the first century A.D. Plutarch introduced the Timon story into a digression in his *Life of Antony*, Shakespeare's principal source for *Antony and Cleopatra*. When Antony forsakes the company of his friends to dwell in a house actually placed in the sea, he let it be known (Plutarch holds) ''that he would lead Timon's life, because he had the like wrong offered him, that was before offered unto Timon: and that for the unthankfulness of those he had done good unto, and whom he took to be his friends, he was angry with all men, and would trust no man.'' Plutarch's account has no suggestion that Timon has fallen from great wealth or that, far from inflexibly demanding solitude, he has encountered a procession of visitors. In the second century A.D.—the silver age of Greek literature—Lucian of Samosata, a Syrian living in Athens who made the satiric dialogue into an important literary form, introduced, in his *Timon, or the Misanthrope*, Timon the prodigal reduced to poverty by flatterers who now neglect him but who flood back when he happens to dig up a treasure of gold. On the Lucianic version Shakespeare based the plot of his Timon. Although in the early seventeenth century no English translation of Lucian's dialogue is known to have existed, Latin, French, and Italian versions were available, so Shakespeare may have readily become generally familiar with the Timon legend.

With him the dramatist creates a tragic hero who can only lurch from one extreme to its opposite. In his glory days this noble Athenian bestows costly gifts, pays the debts of others, provides one of his servants with the means to marry a rich old Athenian's daughter, and patronizes munificently all the poets, painters, and tradesmen who come flocking to him. He never stints. In his evil days Timon becomes, as he himself avers, Misanthropos, who hates mankind. He keeps to his woodland cave. To Alcibiades, who stops to visit him as he goes marching with fife and drum to take Athens, Timon gives newfound gold to pay his soldiers. "Make large confusion," he bids Alcibiades, "and, thy fury spent, / Confounded be thyself!" To Alcibiades's mistresses, a brace of sluts, he gives gold and bids them spread venereal disease. "Down with the nose—/ Down with it flat; take the bridge quite away." (Syphilis frequently cost the infected profligate his nose.) The whores should be whores still:

> Plague all,
> That your activity may defeat and quell
> The source of all erection. (IV.iii.163–65)

Strong stuff. The churlish philosopher sums up Timon's nature thus: "The middle of humanity thou never knewest, but the extremity of both ends" (IV.iii). Timon's steward remains a humanizing presence. Dismayed by his master's extravagance, Flavius tries his best to restrain him and, after Timon's ruin, divides his last remaining money among the servants; at the end he feels impelled to visit Timon in his cave, where "this one honest man'' is the only caller Timon fails to abuse. *The Life of Timon of Athens,* however imperfect its state, has greater fascination than a multitude of more perfectly wrought works. About this play, as about so much else in Shakespeare, we can be certain only that we have not yet heard the last word.

9

His Highness's Servant:
From *Antony and Cleopatra*
to *Pericles*

The better part of a decade separates *Antony and Cleopatra* (c. 1606) from Shakespeare's earlier Roman play dramatizing the convulsion of state attendant upon a dictator's assassination. With *Julius Caesar* completed, ahead lay the crowning tragic sequence beginning with *Hamlet* and continuing with *Othello, King Lear,* and *Macbeth*. Now, with the last behind, the sequence was almost completed. Only the briefest historical interval, however, separates the two Roman plays. Antony grieved over Brutus, his fallen adversary, on Philippi field—the last scene of *Julius Caesar*—in 42 B.C. Now master of the eastern part of the Roman world, Antony a few months later watched entranced as Cleopatra sailed up the river Cydnus in her golden barge, the episode recalled by Enobarbus: "The barge she sat in, like a burnished throne, / Burned on the water: the poop was beaten gold. . . ." Generations of undergraduates who have neither read nor seen Shakespeare's *Antony and Cleopatra* have encountered T. S. Eliot's allusive deployment of Enobarbus's speech in *The Waste Land* (ll. 77ff)—part of what Eliot referred to as his "bricolage"—in which Cleopatra betokens the pinnacle of romance and glamour from which modern society, with its dissociation of sexuality from its cultural and religious moorings, has become alienated.

In terms of event, *Antony and Cleopatra* is less tumultuous than its predecessor. The audience sees soldiers on the march, and hears drums and trumpets—the alarums of war—but the battles take place offstage. A retreat is sounded *"afar off"*; another stage direction specifies *"alarum far off, as at a sea fight."* For the last scenes the action settles into the monument and its environs, in which Cleopatra, pursued by Octavius Caesar to grace his Roman triumph, has immured herself. To her is hoisted up the dying Antony. Here she voices her incomparably moving epitaph over the dead hero. Here too she puts on her robe and crown, and places the poisonous serpent to her breast. The most constricted stage space suffices for an image—both verbal and visual—that is transcendent: at once regal, erotic, and maternal, and transfigured by death's imminence. Even the chill Caesar, gazing upon Cleopatra's corpse, is not immune to her spell. "She looks like sleep," he marvels,

> As she would catch another Antony
> In her strong toil of grace. (V.ii,345–47)

Although *Antony and Cleopatra* has had more than its share of spectacular stagings, the human drama remains intimate, not unsuited to the spare physical resources of a studio theater, as modern production has demonstrated. Shakespeare's art—and Shakespeare's "wooden O"—was ample enough to accommodate the epic confrontations leading up to Agincourt in *Henry V* as well as the muffled encounters of *Antony and Cleopatra*.

Yet of all Shakespeare's tragedies, this one embraces the most spacious terrain geographically; in effect, much of the civilized world, as the ancients understood it. The forty-three scenes shuttle among Alexandria and Rome and Caesar's camp near Actium. The word "world," appearing over forty times (more often than in any other play in the canon), resonates through the text. Other words, such as "earth," "heaven," "sun," and "moon," enhance the aura of cosmic immensity. In Act IV, scene iv, heaven and earth tangibly meet when a company of four soldiers (as a stage direction specifies) *"place themselves in every corner of the stage,"* thus transforming the playing area into the earth's four corners, while the *"music of hautboys"* (i.e., oboes) issues from beneath the stage, signifying that the god Hercules, from whom Antony claimed descent, has abandoned his erstwhile favorite. Hyperbole, in such a context, becomes a favored rhetorical device. Antony is "the greatest soldier of the world," and the queen his lover "a wonderful piece of work," whose person beggars all description.

Writing not long before the events Shakespeare chronicles, the Roman poet Lucretius in his philosophical poem on the nature of the universe, *De Rerum Natura*, had speculated on the ceaseless motion of the atoms, infinite in number, making up the cosmos. No single thing abides, Lucretius concludes, but all things flow. So too does *Antony and Cleopatra* embody the ariable flux of human existence. Antony, before the play opens, has left behind his wife in Rome to fulfill a grand amour in Alexandria. While he makes love, Fulvia makes war. She dies, and Antony leaves Cleopatra to remarry, prudentially, a Roman matron noted for her "holy, cold, and still conversation." No sooner wed, he is—unsurprisingly—back in Cleopatra's arms. The only hope for permanence lies in some pagan Elysium:

> Where souls do couch on flowers, we'll hand in hand,
> And with our sprightly port make the ghosts gaze.
> (IV.xiv.51–52)

"I come my queen" Antony, resolved on death, promises, and Cleopatra, also about to die, utters almost the same words: "Husband, I come." Antony has had to choose between the greatest empire the world had known and history's most alluring woman. He is loser and gainer, perhaps a not inappropriate outcome for one whose "taints and honours / Waged equal with him," as Maecenas, one of Caesar's men, sums up Antony's character. In such contradictions does *Antony and Cleopatra* rejoice.

As the title indicates, the play, like Shakespeare's earlier love tragedy *Romeo and Juliet,* has dual protagonists. If Cleopatra overcame no kingdoms through the force of arms, she has subdued not less effectively than her imperial contemporary, Julius Caesar, the imaginations of those who followed. Cleopatra VI—hers was the customary name for queens in the Ptolemaic succession—was born in 69 B.C., and at seventeen became joint sovereign over Egypt with her younger brother. As custom decreed, she would marry the sibling boy king, and he would in due course conveniently disappear. The Romans called Cleopatra an Egyptian as a term of abuse, but she was in fact half Greek and half Macedonian, and in her veins flowed—albeit many generations removed—the blood of Alexander the Great. If Cleopatra's ruthlessness and lust for power astonished contemporaries, no less did her intelligence and wit. The numerous languages she had mastered included Hebrew, Persian, and Arabic. A seventh-century Coptic bishop, John of Nikiu, praised her as "the most illustrious and wise among women." In another age Cleopatra might have strolled with philosophers in the groves of academe, but as things stood, she would be best remembered for her effect on her lovers.

When Caesar, as overlord of Egypt, arrived in Alexandria, his client-queen had herself rolled into a carpet and smuggled into his presence—an episode recalled in the play. At twenty-one Cleopatra proceeded to conquer the potentate who had come and seen and conquered. Returned to Rome as dictator, Caesar furnished his mistress with a residence in the gardens on the other side of the Tiber, and at his new temple of Venus genetrix— the divinity from whom he claimed descent—he dedicated to her a golden statue. She always preferred gold, so it is fitting that the language lavished on her by Shakespeare should be golden. Cleopatra might now dream of joining East and West, and becoming empress of the world. That dream was dashed on the ides of March, 44 B.C., when assassins' blades cut down Caesar in the Capitol. (Shakespeare failed to mention Cleopatra when he dramatized these events in *Julius Caesar.* He had enough to occupy him without her.) Cleopatra fled to Egypt and shrewdly took no sides in the power struggle that ensued.

At Ephesus, a few months after his victory at Philippi, Marc Antony was hailed as a manifestation of the divine Bacchus. It was fitting that the god of wine, associated with fertility, should meet Venus, and Cleopatra was so adorned when she appeared on the river Cydnus. Thus, once again did she conquer, and her lover, whose current wife came of plebeian origins, had a queen for a paramour. Their relationship would endure, on and off, for over a decade. She bore Antony twins, Alexander Helios and Cleopatra Selene, their names avouching kinship with the twin deities of Sun and Moon. When, in 34 B.C., Antony defeated the Armenian host, he held his triumph not, as immemorial custom dictated, along the Sacred Way to Rome, but on Alexandria's long, broad avenue, up to where Cleopatra, seated aloft on her golden throne, received homage as "Queen of Kings" and true incarnation of Isis, daughter of the Sun god Re and champion of women. For state occasions she would henceforth go robed as the new Isis, an antique goddess miraculously reincarnated as a flesh-and-blood modern female.

She was thirty-nine when she expired on her couch of gold. Caesar could now rejoice in the possession of the treasure of the Ptolemys to reward his hungry legions, and take comfort from the elimination of Ptolemy Caesar, whose name and parentage might eventually have proved inconvenient. In recognition of his services to the state, the Roman senate would confer on him the title Augustus, and he would be the first of Rome's emperors, a greedy, cruel, and superstitious man, but wise and politic as a ruler. Whether deified or no by the sacred serpent, Cleopatra lived on in legend. In the eastern part of the empire, as early as the first century A.D., she was being praised as an alchemist, able to make gold, a recipe for which she conveniently left behind. Cleopatra was also credited with a treatise on cosmetics and coiffure, and another on weights, measures, and coinage in Egypt. And is she not to be credited with the canal bringing water to Alexandria, as well as the lighthouse and palace and other great monuments of the past? Not unexpectedly, Romans took a different view of Cleopatra. In his *Pharsalia* Lucan describes how Caesar, inveigled by Cleopatra's beauty, squandered on her the wealth of the world he had plundered; for Horace she was the "mad queen" with Antony for her servile plaything. In the Middle Ages, Dante placed Cleopatra in the second circle of Hell with Helen and Dido and other carnal sinners.

To the Romans in Shakespeare's play, Cleopatra is no better than a courtesan: a "strumpet" or "trull." Octavius Caesar bluntly assesses his brother-in-law's conduct ("He hath given his Empire / Up to a whore"); and Antony, in his misery and rage after the Actium fiasco, denounces "this foul Egyptian" as a "triple-turned whore"—a whore who has made the rounds of lovers, turning from Pompey, from Julius Caesar, and finally from himself. Cleopatra seems to endorse the Roman view of her life-style when she speaks of herself as one who trades in love (II.v.2). Full of games and sport, she will hop forty paces through a street, or play transvestite games with her lover, dressing him like a woman and wearing his man's sword. Yet she is always "Royal Egypt, Empress!" Empress she may be, but before that Cleopatra is a woman—

No more but e'en a woman, and commanded
By such poor passion as the maid that milks
And does the meanest chares.   (IV.xv.72–74)

In a man's world that places a premium on female youth and beauty, she finds herself "wrinkled deep in time." Like the Cleopatra of history, the Cleopatra of the play resorts to feminine wiles and uses them superlatively well. And however mutable and inconstant she is, she remains, in the end, true to her Antony.

The world of power and policy, which so engaged his creator when he composed his English history plays, had lost none of its fascination for Shakespeare. The great centerpiece of *Antony and Cleopatra*, the scene in which the three world-sharers meet aboard Pompey's galley (II.vii), contains no mention of Cleopatra, nor does the brief scene, often omitted from production, that follows, in which Ventidius, marching in triumph through Syria, calls it a day rather than risk becoming his captain's captain. These episodes contain their own powerful evocation of the public world that Rome represents. Public and private, Rome and Egypt, receive the full measure of Shakespeare's artistry in *Antony and Cleopatra*.

First performed in 1606, *Macbeth* is the shortest and most concentrated of Shakespeare's tragedies—at not much more than 2,100 lines just over half the length of *Hamlet*—but its brevity and familiarity do not mean that it is one of Shakespeare's less difficult plays. On the contrary, *Macbeth* derives its dramatic power from its complex imagery and compression of language. Despite its brevity, the play has a relatively large number of scenes: twenty-eight, all told. These, for the most part, are not elaborately constructed, as those depicting the play-within-the-play in *Hamlet* or the blinding of Gloucester in *King Lear*. The tragedy illustrates Shakespeare's fascination with the criminal mind; or, rather, the mind that becomes criminal. In the first act, a bleeding Captain, fresh from the battlefield, can speak of "brave Macbeth," "valor's minion," and Ross, a Scottish nobleman, describes his general admiringly as Bellona's bridegroom, Bellona being the goddess of war.

Yet Macbeth's crimes—and they are many—are those of a brutal despot. His first victim is Duncan, who is not only his king, but also his kinsman and guest. In the first part of *The Divine Comedy* Dante pays special attention to the hierarchy of sin. In the *Inferno* there are nine circles of hell. In the upper circles the punishments are not terribly severe, but—lower and lower—below the burning fires that our imagination usually associates with Hell, comes ice. These are the calculated crimes of cold blood. Among the sinners in the frigid ninth circle are Judas, Brutus, and Cassius: Judas, who betrayed the church, and Brutus and Cassius, who lifted daggers against the empire. The basest crimes are those committed against benefactors or hosts, kinsmen, and country. In murdering Duncan, Macbeth is simultaneously guilty of all three of these outrages. If he were to have a place in Dante's Hell, it would be there at the bottom.

With the knocking on the palace gate, the nameless Porter suddenly and briefly surfaces between the regicide and its aftermath to discourse drunkenly on—among other things—lust, impotence, and urine—and then goes off (II.iii), never to be heard from again. Dramatic necessity beckoned him to put in his solo appearance, as a great Shakespearean, Edward Capell, first noted in the eighteenth century; for Macbeth must be offstage at this juncture in the rising action in order to clean himself up and change costume after the bloody episode that has preceded. Of course it was Shakespeare's way to make theatrical necessity serve the purpose of dramatic art. With the Porter, the everyday, none too soon, makes its entry into *Macbeth*. From time immemorial, Hell has had its entrance gate. At the outset of the Third Canto of Dante's *Inferno*, the narrator—simultaneously Everyman and Dante Alighieri the Florentine—pauses before the words written in dark characters but nonetheless visible in the starless night: THROUGH ME THE WAY INTO THE WOEFUL CITY. . . . The episode clearly associates the Macbeths' palace with Hell: the scene is indebted to medieval plays on the theme known as "The Harrowing of Hell," in which the gates of Hell are battered. The Porter alludes to the "porter of hell gate," and he asks, "Who's there in the name of Beelzebub?"

There are other analogous allusions, some submerged, in the tragedy. At Inverness Castle, in Act I, after hautboys play and servants with dishes and the service cross the stage, Macbeth enters to deliver his

first soliloquy. "If it were done when 'tis done, then
'twere well," he avers, "it were done quickly." At the
Last Supper, in the Gospel according to St. John (XIII:
27), we read, "And after the sop Satan entered into
him. Then said Jesus unto him, 'That thou doest, do
quickly.' " Like Macbeth, Judas Iscariot absents himself before the meal is over. The scene in *Macbeth* thus
depicts the last supper of King Duncan, about to be
betrayed by his subject Macbeth. (Abraham Lincoln, all
his life an ardent admirer of Shakespeare's works, ru-
minated on the assassination of King Duncan just a week
before he was himself assassinated in Ford's Theatre in
Washington.)

Yet as loathsome as Macbeth's deeds are, he somehow remains within the bounds of human sympathy. We
retain this noble view of Macbeth—or at least a sem-
blance of it—even when he makes his descent from nobleman to tyrant. Macbeth retains our sympathies also
because he recognizes the consequences of his crimes.
Shortly after the murder of Duncan, after the act has
come to light, we hear Macbeth voice sentiments that
cloak him in moral virtue:

> Had I but died an hour before this chance,
> I had lived a blessed time; for from this instant
> There's nothing serious in mortality:
> All is but toys. Renown and grace is dead,
> The wine of life is drawn, and the mere lees
> Is left this vault to brag of.   (II.iii.93–98)

Spoken in the company of his lady, Banquo, and other
noblemen of Scotland, these lines are deceitfully intended to impress the onlookers in the aftermath of the
king's murder, but they ironically reveal a profound truth
about Macbeth's situation. Had he indeed died before
he killed Duncan, his life would have been (so far as
we can tell) happy and virtuous; but by killing his king
he has in effect destroyed what remains of his own life.
Throughout the latter part of the play, Macbeth is aware

of the enormity of his deed: He cannot freely give up the crown, nor can he deceive himself.

James I, a Scot who held the English crown from 1603 to 1625, took a special interest in demonology, on which he fancied himself an authority (he wrote a treatise on the subject). In the prophetic Show of Eight Kings (IV.i), the last to appear is King James with a prospective glass in his hand, prophesying the union of England and Scotland, then very much a topic under discussion. To insist—as some authorities do—that *Macbeth* was especially written for the king's entertainment is perhaps to press a claim too far, but the Scottish setting and the use of witchcraft to enhance the theme do reflect a professional dramatist catering to topical concerns when those concerns coincide with his own artistic purposes. And the three witches are, to be sure, a powerful emblematic device.

When Macbeth dies, he dies friendless, without love; as king, he is dressed in borrowed robes, as one of the play's most striking (and by now most familiar) metaphors holds. He has become a ruthless despot whose bond is not with the people who serve him but with a dark and icy underworld: He has made his tragic descent from a ''worthy gentleman'' to an ''abhorred tyrant'' and, finally, to a ''dead butcher.'' Near the end, ruminating on the death of his wife, he says:

> She should have died hereafter;
> There would have been a time for such a word.
>   (V.v.17–18)

''She should have died hereafter''—the line resonates. Does it mean that Lady Macbeth should have died later, after the din of battle had subsided? Or that, like all mortals, she had to die someday? Or that she should have died at a time when death had some significance? The line may have any one or more of these meanings. What is certain is that for Macbeth life has become

                                              a tale
Told by an idiot, full of sound and fury
Signifying nothing.   (V.v.26–28)

Here the life-enhancing resonance of the language gives
the lie to the nihilism to which that language attests.

   In 1609 *The Late and much admired play called Pericles, Prince of Tyre. With the true relation of the whole
history, adventures, and fortunes of the said Prince: As
also, the no less strange and worthy accidents in the
birth and life of his daughter Marina* was first printed,
*"As it hath been divers and sundry times acted by his
Majesty's Servants at the Globe on the Bankside,"* after
being entered the preceding year in the Stationers' Register. Evidently one of the most popular plays of the
period, *Pericles* ushered in the dramatic romances of
Shakespeare's last phase. In the next age Dryden would
confidently assert that "Shakespeare's own muse her
Pericles first bore; / The Prince of Tyre was elder than
the Moor"; and indeed there are narrative and thematic
anticipations of the play as early as the youthful *Comedy
of Errors,* with the disastrous sea voyage that separates
Aegeon from his wife, Aemilia, and her taking refuge
in a convent, much as Pericles' mourning wife, Thaisa,
becomes a votaress in the temple of Diana, likewise in
Ephesus.

   Yet *Pericles* (c. 1606–8) is the one canonical play to
be excluded from the First Folio. From the Second as
well; nor was the play originally included in the 1662
Third Folio, but admitted with six apocryphal plays in
the 1664 reissue of this edition. A reason for the early
editors' decision is not far to seek. The 1609 and subsequent quartos show manifest signs of corruption, and
may well have been put together from memory. The
play is, moreover, a collaboration, probably with
George Wilkins—the playwright, pamphleteer, and
novelist—who published in 1608 *The Painful Adventures of Pericles, Prince of Tyre,* "Being the true history of the Play of *Pericles,* as it was lately presented
by the worthy and ancient poet John Gower."

With Gower the play has its Presenter and recurring
Chorus, "To sing a song that old was sung," to glad
the ear and please the eyes. That song, we learn, has

> been sung at festivals,
> On ember-eves and holy-ales;
> And lords and ladies in their lives
> Have read it for restoratives.
>   (Cho., I.5-7)

Why Gower? A friend of Chaucer and joint dedicatee
of that poet's *Troilus and Criseyde,* Gower was himself
a prolific versifier: the author of long poems in rime-
royal or octosyllabic couplets, best known for his *Con-
fessio Amantis*, consisting of 141 stories (octosyllabic
couplets again): the confessions, as the frame has it, of
the lover Amans to Genius, a priest of Venus. One of
these, the "Appolonius of Tyre" story, became the
principal vehicle of *Pericles*. Unsurprisingly, an engraving of Gower—staff and posy in hand—adorns the title
page of Wilkins's *Painful Adventures*. But this romance
is older than Gower: indeed, some hundred medieval
Latin versions have come down. Chaucer alludes to the
story—unfavorably—in the Introduction to the *Man of
Law's Tale,* and in the Renaissance adaptations in verse,
prose, and drama proliferated in sundry tongues. But
the earliest extant version, probably of Hellenistic origin, goes back to the ninth century. However, the main
source of *Pericles*, duly acknowledged by its creator,
was Gower.

It is a tale of abundant wanderings and miraculous
escapes. To Antioch Prince Pericles comes to solve King
Antiochus's riddle: a riddle that the venturer must either
solve or sacrifice his own life, as the grim looks of the
severed human heads that bedeck the palace testify—
not an unfamiliar sight to Londoners crossing London
Bridge in Shakespeare's time, for the heads of executed
felons were displayed on poles to warn wayfarers. But
the king has incestuously mated with his own daughter,

and to that circumstance the riddle's hidden significance testifies: not so hidden that Pericles fails to fathom it. Many strange adventures follow, conveyed by choruses, dumb shows, and narrative. In Tarsus, Pericles's ships, groaning with corn, rescue a famine-starved populace. At Pentapolis he dons his rusty armor to contest a tournament that the great King Simonides holds to celebrate his daughter Thaisa's birthday, and Pericles wins both the tourney and Thaisa's love.

There are more journeys; a storm at sea; the shipboard delivery of a daughter, appropriately named Marina; and the mother's apparent—but not actual—death. Thinking herself a widow, Thaisa becomes a votary at the temple of Diana at Ephesus, where she eventually ends up. Abducted by pirates and sold to a bawd in Mytilene, Marina—a bona fide virgin—finds her maidenhood up for auction. But her virtue is triumphant. "If fires be hot, knives sharp, or waters deep," she protests,

> Untied I still my virgin knot will keep.
> Diana aid my purpose! (IV.ii.154–56)

Diana indeed comes to the rescue. In the brothel Marina converts the lecherous, cynical clients to a life of virtue. Even the governor, Lysimachus, come to enjoy a young virgin, is thunderstruck by Marina's virtue:

> Had I brought hither a corrupted mind,
> Thy speech had altered it. Gold, here's gold for
>   thee.
> Persevere in that clear way thou goest,
> And the gods strengthen thee! (IV.vi.110–13)

Marina is no doubt bad for the whorehouse business: a peevish baggage capable of freezing the god Priapus and undoing a whole generation, as the pander's servant, Boult, complains.

Finally, on board Pericles's ship off Mytilene, the king—for he has become that—who for three months has not spoken to a soul and has taken sustenance sufficient only to prolong his grief, is reunited with his long-missing daughter. Pericles now hears (as he believes) the music of the spheres. He sleeps, and Diana, the goddess of chastity, appears to him in a vision. Prince Lysimachus will wed Marina, now his betrothed, at Pentapolis, and Pericles will clip his hair, which for fourteen years no razor has touched. Thus are age and youth—father and daughter—juxtaposed and reunited. The supernatural finds its way into the mundane. If the conclusion of *Pericles* haunts us with its beauty, it does so in the manner of Shakespeare's late romances, as *The Winter's Tale* and the others do. Elsewhere in this play we see the hand of Shakespeare's journeyman collaborator, Wilkins, a fellow playwright with the King's Men who had lately written a superior domestic drama, *A Warning for Fair Women*. In other scenes we discern the hand of the supreme master. Such, on occasion, is the nature of the collaborative enterprise.

10

His Highness's Servant:
Last Hurrahs

The year 1609 saw the publication of the first quarto edition of *Shakespeare's Sonnets,* as *Never before Imprinted,* bringing together a collection of 154 sonnets. Evidently this publication, entered in the Stationers' Register on May 10, was unauthorized, for the volume shows clear evidence of not having been proofread by the author. The limits of composition have been much discussed, as has the identity of the mysterious Mr. W. H., "the only begetter of these ensuing sonnets," cited in the dedication furnished not by the poet but the printer, Thomas Thorpe. (In 1598 in *Palladis Tamia* Francis Meres refers to Shakespeare's "sugared sonnets among his private friends," and two of those sonnets— 138 ["When my love swears that she is made of truth"] and 144 ["Two loves I have, of comfort and despair"]— first appeared in the 1599 *Passionate Pilgrim,* an unauthorized anthology ascribed to Shakespeare on the title page, but mainly consisting of poems by other authors.)

With *Coriolanus* (c. 1608) Shakespeare bade a permanent farewell to tragedy and to Thomas North's justly renowned translation of Plutarch's *Lives of the Noble Grecians and Romans,* which served him well for four plays on classical themes. Ahead lay the dramatic romances. For *Coriolanus,* Plutarch's life of Caius Martius Coriolanus was apparently Shakespeare's sole source, except for the fable of the Belly and the Body's members, which the worldly-wise Menenius Agrippa, Coriolanus's patrician friend—one "that hath always loved the people," and a man "that converses more with the buttock of the night than with the forehead of the morning"—uses to keep enthralled (and pacify) the mutinously hungry Roman plebeians (I.i.27–164), just as he has since enthralled countless viewers and readers of *Coriolanus*. The fable *is* to be found in Plutarch, who only passingly alludes to Menenius as "one of the pleasantest old men" in the senate. For the passage Shakespeare also made use of William Averell's *A Marvelous Combat of Contrarieties*, printed in 1588—the year of the Armada—and intended as a warning against sedition. But Menenius's long speech is a characteristically Shakespearean labyrinth of recollections. Besides North and Averell, the dramatist recalled William Camden's more recent *Remains of a greater work concerning Britain* (1605), for Camden's paraphrase (ultimately deriving from the Latin of John of Salisbury) of words describing the body's "instruments." From Philemon Holland's translation of Livy (1600) he derived the suggestion that the belly distributes the "rivers of your blood," flowing through all "the cranks and offices of man"; indeed, through the entire organism. A bravura performance, Menenius's speech yet never lacks immediacy.

The historical Caius Martius was later called Coriolanus, an addition with which he was entitled to augment his name so that he might always be nobly known for his stunning—and bloody—victory in battle against the Volscian capital of Corioli in 493 B.C., more than four centuries before Julius Caesar was assassinated in Rome on the ides of March of the year 44 B.C. By the time of the Caesars, Coriolanus had become a semilegendary symbol of patrician resistance to the intensifying demands of the rabble, who had lately found spokesmen in the two tribunes they were given to represent their interests.

Thus, in *Coriolanus* Shakespeare goes back to classical beginnings; before Rome had become an imperial power; with *Julius Caesar* and *Antony and Cleopatra* he showed Rome before the end of the Republic. In all, Shakespeare touches down upon a vast expanse of Western history—in *King Lear* upon the legendary pseudo-history of Britain; in *Cymbeline* upon a mix of classical and early British history, along with romance; in *Macbeth* upon medieval Scottish history; in his plays on the Wars of the Roses and their aftermath upon actual English history. With *Henry VIII,* or *All Is True,* he would also—at the end—turn to the reign of a Tudor monarch.

The martial hero of Corioli comes to be excoriated as an enemy of the people—to cite the title of Henrik Ibsen's 1887 play—just as (in a much lesser compass) Dr. Stockmann is hounded out of their midst by "the compact majority" of his little town when he discovers that the drainage system on which the town depends financially is defective. Hence it is that Dr. Stockmann comes to his realization that "a minority may be right—a majority is always wrong." In *Coriolanus* the destructive tensions from which violence arises have their origins not in drainage but in class—in the mutual antagonism of plebeians and patricians—and in the tragic protagonist's choleric nature.

"Now in those days," according to Plutarch (in the North translation), "valiantness was honored in Rome above all other virtues, which they called *virtus,* by the name of virtue self, as including in that general name all other special virtues besides." Of valiantness Caius Martius has more than a sufficiency, indeed he commits his whole being to the martial prerogatives idealized by his society. His valor is beyond reasonable human expectation. Of the other virtues—of *virtus*—specialization has resulted in shortcomings. Back in the Roman Capitol after victory at Corioli, Cominius—one of the generals against the Volscians—tells the assembled dignitaries that Coriolanus's

> sword, death's stamp,
> Where it did mark, it took; from face to foot
> He was a thing of blood, whose every motion
> Was tim'd with dying cries: alone he enter'd
> The mortal gates of th' city, which he painted

With shunless destiny, aidless came off,
And with a sudden reinforcement struck
    Corioles like a planet.   (II.ii.108–15)

But Coriolanus pays for superhuman valor with personal limitations, which are as grand in scale as his warrior's heroism. He holds in contempt his own soldiers and the Roman citizenry, who (not unnaturally) want the state's amply stored wheat at their own rates. Of self-discovery, or *anagnorisis*, Coriolanus can even at the end claim little. "What is the city but the people?" rhetorically asks Sincinius Velutus, tribune of the people, as he is surrounded by a rabble of plebeians: a question that Coriolanus would never think to ask in this intensely political play.

For Coriolanus, martial heroism takes its toll on everyday humanity, on the bread and cheese of life. This is most expressively conveyed in a fleeting moment at Corioli, when—after the trumpets have sounded and Caius Martius has, for what he did before Corioli, been honored with the added surname Coriolanus—he pauses to ask his general, Cominius, to give freedom to the poor man who once had used him kindly and given him a bed in Corioli, and now, taken prisoner, had cried to Martius. "Well begg'd!" is Cominius's response, and another general, Titus Lartius, asks, "Martius, his name?" But Martius has forgotten the name of the prisoner he had hoped to free. "I am weary, yea, my memory is tired; / Have we no wine here?" (I.ix. 89–90). Time to repair to the tent to be looked after. The forgetfulness is Shakespeare's invention.

In another tent outside Rome (IV.vii) the Volscian general, Tullus Aufidius, the unsuccessful veteran of many losing battles against Caius Martius and from the first his implacable foe (I.x.17–27), pauses to reflect at length on the nature of the tragic hero, as exhibited in the character of Coriolanus. Normally one would expect such a speech in an Elizabethan play, conducted without an interlocutor, to take the form of a soliloquy, but the commander is speaking in the presence of his unnamed

Lieutenant, who is given eleven fairly nondescript lines, whereas Aufidius's dissection of Coriolanus's nature occupies twenty-nine. Aufidius's speech is, in effect, a quasi-soliloquy, a species of self-communing on his part. As the preeminent practicing dramatist of the age (indeed, of all time), Shakespeare presumably took an interest in dramatic theory, but usually his comments are made only in passing; he had enough fish to fry without getting waylaid.

So much interest attaches to the passage—expressed in the idiomatic yet convoluted and image-laden style of Shakespeare's most mature verse; a style which, while constituting a challenge to the reader in the study is in performance immediately accessible to the auditor—that extended quotation is justified:

> Whether 'twas pride,
> Which out of daily fortune ever taints
> The happy man; whether defect of judgment,
> To fail in the disposing of those chances
> Which he was lord of; or whether nature
> Not to be other than one thing, not moving
> From th' casque [i.e., general's helmet] to th'
>   cushion, but commanding peace
> Even with same austerity and garb
> As he controlled the war; but one of these,
> As he hath spices of them all,—not all.
> For I dare so far free him—made him feared,
> So hated, and so banished. But he has a merit,
> To choke it in the utt'rance. So our virtues
> Lie in th' interpretation of the time;
> And power, unto itself most commendable,
> Hath not a tomb so evident as a chair
> T'extol what it hath done.
> One fire drives out one fire; one nail, one nail;
> Rights by rights founder, strengths by strengths do
>   fail.   (IV.vii.37–55)

Of course the character of the speaker to an extent inevitably conditions our response. Aufidius *is* Coriolanus's enemy. The interplay of character and personality between these two formidable adversaries—in some ways alike, in others utterly unlike; both worthy but one distinctly worthier than the other—offers striking opportunities for stage directors, opportunities of which they have not been reluctant to take advantage. In Terry Hands's Royal Shakespeare Company production of *Coriolanus*, which debuted in 1977 and toured across much of Europe with extraordinary success, Hands choreographed the storming of Corioli as Caius Martius (Alan Howard)—in black leather and covered with blood—encountered Aufidius (Julian Glover) in the identical costume: Martius's mirror image. Mirror image but not mirror image.

Threatened with being cast to destruction from the Tarpeian rock, Coriolanus leaves Rome, an exile, to join forces with Aufidius and march upon the capital; only to relent before his formidable mother Volumnia's entreaties and offer Rome an advantageous peace. Aufidius reacts as one might expect. "Out of that," he says in an aside, "I'll work / Myself former fortune." In the end Aufidius infuriates Coriolanus by addressing him as "thou boy of tears"—just as earlier, in the Roman Forum, the plebeians had infuriated him by accusing him of harboring tyrannical ambitions. To the conspirators of Aufidius's faction Coriolanus says, "Cut me to pieces, Volsces. Men and lads, / Stain all your edges on me. Boy? False hound!" The conspirators draw, and indeed cut Coriolanus to pieces. Aufidius, standing on him, finds that his rage is at last spent.

> Though in this city he
> Hath widowed and unchilded many a one,
> Which at this hour bewail the injury,
> Yet he shall have a noble memory.
>   (V.vi.150–53)

Although funeral music was seldom heard on the Elizabethan stage, a death march is sounded to conclude

Coriolanus, which brings to a conclusion Shakespeare's career as a tragedian no less innovatively, in its own way, than *Titus Andronicus* had initiated it.

"The Tragedy of *Coriolanus*," wrote Dr. Johnson—always to be taken respectfully as a critic—"is one of the most amusing of our author's performances." Amusing? Surely not, except for isolated moments, mirth provoking. Indeed, Johnson goes on to cite "the old man's merriment in *Menenius;* the lofty lady's dignity in *Volumnia;* the bridal modesty in *Virgilia;* the patrician and military haughtiness in *Coriolanus;* the plebeian malignity and tribunition insolence in *Brutus* and *Sicinius*"; these "make a very pleasing and interesting variety: and the various revolutions of the hero's fortune fill the mind with anxious curiosity." Of anxious curiosity there is plenty in *Coriolanus*. It *is* an unsettling play that, on a world basis, has appealed powerfully to audiences in the aftermath of war. The German poet-playwright Bertolt Brecht—a Marxist—at his death left behind an unfinished adaptation. And the play has also stirred great actors to give of their best. In 1959 Albert Finney understudied the late Laurence Olivier as Coriolanus in Peter Hall's revival at Stratford-upon-Avon. "He makes the climaxes higher and he makes the depths of it lower," said Finney, "than you feel is possible in the text."

No specific notice has come down of any performance of *Cymbeline* (c. 1610–11), either at the court or in the playhouse from Shakespeare's own age, but in his manuscript *Book of Plays*, now in the Bodleian Library at Oxford, Simon Forman—magus, lecher, and unlicensed medical practitioner who may well have killed fewer patients than many of his fellow physicians—included notes of performances he had witnessed, probably all at the Globe, of some of Shakespeare's plays. These include a paragraph "of Cimbalin king of England." Stylistically and thematically, *Cymbeline* belongs with the other dramatic romances of Shakespeare's last period. Characters do die—Cymbeline's enterprisingly wicked queen (not his first wife) and her unenterprisingly wicked son, Cloten, who, "too bad to report," lusts after his stepsister Imogen.

In Elizabethan comedies characters don't die, but in tragicomedies—of which *Cymbeline* is an instance—they may. Yet not every dramatist took the same view of the genre as Shakespeare. "A tragicomedy is not so called in respect of mirth and killing," writes John Fletcher—who would in time collaborate with Shakespeare—in his preface "To the Reader" of *The Faithful Shepherdess* (c. 1608), "but in respect it wants deaths, which is enough to make it no tragedy, yet brings some near it, which is enough to make it no comedy, which must be a representation of familiar people, with such kind of trouble as no life be questioned, so that a god is as lawful in this as in a tragedy, and mean people as in a comedy." Fair enough for many tragicomedies, but not an entirely accurate description of Shakespeare's.

What happens in *Cymbeline* is too diversely complicated to lend itself to brief summary, but the play, characteristically for Shakespearean romance, has more than one sensational *coup de théâtre*. Thus, in Act IV Imogen, the king's daughter, hungry and tired and sick at heart after wandering through the mountainous Welsh countryside, unwittingly takes the drug intended by the queen to poison her, but which is in fact a sleeping draft—and falls instantly into a trance. Meanwhile, Cloten—disguised in the attire of Imogen's husband, Posthumus, "a poor but worthy gentlemen"—is slain and decapitated. Believed dead, Imogen is buried in a rustic grave bedecked with flowers, with the headless corpse of her presumed husband alongside. She awakens, and in a long soliloquy (forty-one lines) shares with the audience her discovery: ". . . his Jovial [i.e., like that of Jove, king of the gods] face—/ Murder in heaven? How? 'Tis gone." Imogen falls upon the body. Standing in the audience, Dr. Forman was duly impressed. He notes how the young woman "chanced to fall on the cave where her two brothers were, and how by eating a sleeping dram they thought she had been dead, and laid her in the woods, and the body of Cloten by her, in her love's apparel that he left behind him. . . .'' Forman must have seen *Cymbeline* before September 12, 1611, as he died that day, possibly by suicide.

Imogen's supposed death inspires a haunting dirge:

> Fear no more the heat o' th' sun
> Nor the furious winter's rages,
> Thou thy worldly task hast done,
> Home art gone and ta'en thy wages.
> Golden lads and girls all must,
> As chimney-sweepers, come to dust.
> (IV.ii.258–65)

The stanzas give utterance to a profound commonplace, that Death—the Great Leveler—comes to all, regardless of appearance, station, or even (in some instances) age. Of course, since the supposed decedent is not in fact dead, the obsequies are artificial, in much the same way that Shakespeare has Juliet's family react to her supposed demise.

Even more striking is the upshot of the wager between Posthumus and Iachimo—an Italianate villain if ever there was one—that the latter can persuade Imogen to sacrifice her chastity; such (Iachimo maintains) is female frailty. In Act II, scene ii, of *Cymbeline* Iachimo emerges from the chest in Imogen's bedchamber, lit by a single flickering taper; he makes notes of the surroundings—the window, the adornment of the bed, the painted arras—and, more especially, of the sleeping girl with the mole on her left breast; then he removes her bracelet and tiptoes back into the chest, closing the lid over his head. True, Shakespeare's plays lent themselves to performance in diverse venues, but for such a scene the ambiance of the enclosed, candlelit Blackfriars theater offered advantages over the comparative vastness of the Globe. Still, it was probably at the Globe that Forman was stirred when the Italian, ''in the deepest of the night, she being asleep, he opened the chest and came

forth of it, and viewed her in her bed, and the marks of
her body, and took away her bracelet, and after accused
her of adultery to her love, etc."

In *Cymbeline* one sometimes has a sense of a time
machine gone haywire; pseudo-history has its innings.
In Holinshed's *Chronicles of England, Scotland, and
Ireland,* to which Shakespeare turned as a matter of
course when English history concerned him, he learned
of the reign of "Kembeline or Cimbeline the son of
Theomantius," a reign supposedly dating from 33 B.C.
to soon after the birth of Christ. Real history plays its
part in the play too. "Now say, what would Augustus
Caesar with us?" asks Cymbeline at the start of Act
III, scene i. To which Caius Lucius, a Roman general
come to England with a peremptory demand, replies:

> When Julius Caesar, whose remembrance yet
> Lives in men's eyes and will to ears and tongues
> Be theme and hearing ever, was in this Britain
> And conquered it, Cassibeland thine uncle,
> Famous in Caesar's praises no whit less
> Than in his feats deserving it, for him
> And his succession granted Rome a tribute,
> Yearly three thousand pounds, which by thee lately
> Is left untendered.   (III.i.2–9)

When the scene moves to Rome itself, we somehow find
ourselves in an urbane Renaissance context—this plot
strand drawing, directly or indirectly, from the *Decameron* of Giovanni Boccaccio (1313–75), a caper with
which Machiavelli might have felt at home. Still elsewhere, when we encounter Guiderius and Arviragus,
the king's sons kidnapped in infancy and rustically
reared in a Welsh fastness, the green world enters into
Cymbeline, as it had entered *As You Like It* (much more
prominently) a decade earlier.

With Imogen's wicked stepmother and Cloten we enter a fairy-tale-like world with folklorish elements rem-
iniscent of Grimm's Snow White. Centuries before

Bruno Bettelheim explored, in a classic study, the importance of fairy tales, Shakespeare understood well the uses of enchantment. At the end, we are conveyed to a supra-terrestrial world not unlike that of the Stuart masque, to which the commercial theater could not but respond. We hear solemn music. Sicilius Leonatus, Posthumus's father, enters "as in an apparition": an old man attired as a warrior, leading in by his hand an ancient matron, Posthumus's mother. Others follow, with more music. They circle round Posthumus as he lies sleeping. Ultimately, Jupiter descends from the heavens *"in thunder and lightning, sitting upon an eagle; he throws a thunderbolt. The ghosts fall on their knees."* The Thunderer speaks, after which the holy eagle returns to his crystalline palace. The marble pavement now closes; Jupiter has entered his radiant roof. In a long concluding scene about five hundred lines — revelations are made, truths disentangled, and we hear "the tune of Imogen." The sheer number of final twists and turns is breathtaking; only a master would have attempted so much.

Over the centuries, readers and viewers have responded diversely to this diverse play. Before the advent of Victorian sentimental romanticism, Dr. Johnson in 1765 said in his end note: "to remark the folly of the fiction, the absurdity of the conduct, the confusion of the names and manners of different times, and the impossibility of the events in any system of life, were to waste criticism upon unresisting imbecility, upon faults too evident for detection, and too gross for aggravation." Imogen's tune did not harmonize with the neoclassical sensibility. Tennyson, however, relished *Cymbeline,* to the extent that (so his son informs us) he had a copy of the play buried with him. And Tennyson's contemporary, the poet Algernon Charles Swinburne, concluded his *Study of Shakespeare,* in 1880, "upon the name of the woman best beloved in all the world of song and all the tide of time; upon the name of Shakespeare's Imogen." For Swinburne—as for Tennyson and countless other Victorians—the tune of Imogen was a celestial harmony.

Let Henry James, less effusive than Swinburne, have the penultimate word. In 1896 he reviewed Sir Henry Irving's production of *Cymbeline* for *Harper's Weekly*. "The thing is a florid fairy-tale," James wrote, "of a construction so loose and unpropped that it can scarce be said to stand upright at all, and of a psychological sketchiness that never touches firm ground, but plays, at its better times, with an indifferent shake of golden locks, in the high sunny air of delightful poetry."

Johnson, Swinburne, James. In the next age the modern (and postmodern) sensibility would be stirred in new ways by the last plays and by the evolution of Shakespearean tragicomedy. You pay your money and you take your choice. Meanwhile, in the theater, the headless corpse and the sleeping girl with the spotted mole on her left breast have continued to stir spectators ignorant of—and indifferent to—the high road of academic Shakespeare criticism. At the Royal Shakespeare Theatre in Stratford-upon-Avon—the RSC's major house—the Bill Alexander staging of *Cymbeline* in 1989 had John Carlisle riveting as a suitably unillusioned, world-weary Iachimo transiently frisking with a black trollop; among other incongruities, Jupiter failed to make his spectacular climactic descent in this production of what is, these days, a relatively infrequently revived play.

Unlike many dramatists, Shakespeare seems on the whole to have concerned himself little with the titles of his plays. The protagonists' names for the tragedies, reigning monarchs for the English histories; these suffice. As regards the comedies, Shakespeare can be—at least seemingly—offhand: *Much Ado About Nothing*, *As You Like It*. The title of *The Winter's Tale* (c. 1610) has, however, a suggestiveness reinforced by textual reference. Asked by his mother in the nursery to sit by her and her ladies, and amuse them with a tale, young Mamillius volunteers,

A sad tale's best for winter. I have one
Of sprites and goblins.   (II.i.25–26)

Late in the play, after the king's long-lost daughter has
been recovered, an anonymous Gentleman marvels,
"This news, which is called true, is so like an old tale
that the verity of it is in strong suspicion" (V.ii.29–
31). Twice again—at V.ii.65 and V.iii.117—we hear of
"an old tale." A winter's tale was a catch phrase for an
incredible story—the very word *tale*, then as now, could
signify something untrue—suitable for nothing better
than to wile away a long winter's evening by the chim-
ney corner. For his play Shakespeare invented a fairy-
tale world—albeit without sprites or goblins—in which
the constraints of narrative realism need not apply.

A seizure of sexual jealousy, as resistless as it is un-
countable, grips Leontes, king of Sicily, suddenly; or
so it seems—has he managed up to this point to conceal
his true feelings? He watches, himself unnoticed, while
wife Hermione and guest smile, while her white hand
innocently clasps his; he hears her address Polixenes as
"friend"—in Elizabethan parlance an equivocal word
that could mean "lover." "Too hot, too hot," Leontes
exclaims aside: the first intimation that the fit is on him.
He goes on to ask his trusted lord, Camillo, to poison
Polixenes, and when the two sensibly decamp, Leontes
is certain that he is indeed a cuckold.

The ruler formerly beloved of his subjects in short
order becomes a tormented tyrant as Hermione must
stand judgment for the capital offense of adultery. Before then, however, she is prematurely delivered of a
healthy girl—Perdita—in prison. At a critical point in
her trial an officer opens the sealed-up oracle delivered
in sacred Delphos and reads aloud Apollo's pronouncement:

Hermione is chaste, Polixenes blameless, Camillo a true subject, Leontes a jealous tyrant, his
innocent babe truly begotten; and the King shall

live without an heir if that which is lost be not
found. (III.ii.130–33)

Retribution quickly follows: the distraught Mamillius,
having fallen ill, dies; his mother collapses at the news—
apparently dead too.

The rest is an elaborate working-out of the oracle, as
that which has been lost is found. The action includes
a shipwreck on a storm-tossed sea and an infant abandoned on a desolate strand. Years later, a shepherdess—
the image of Flora, goddess of flowers—falls in love
with, and is in turn loved by, a handsome young prince
who happens to be the son of her father's calumniated
friend. In the end a seeming statue of the dead queen
miraculously comes to life. With the aid of tokens—the
mother's mantle, a jewel, preserved letters—the missing
offspring is identified and restored to her natural parents. They for their part are reunited with each other,
as are the estranged kings, and a marriage will seal the
reconciliations. *The Winter's Tale* thus offers the very
stuff of romance.

Shakespeare's materials have an ancient lineage, older
even than the Greek prose romances—Longus's *Daphnis
and Chloe,* Heliodorus's *Theagenes and Chariclea,* and
the others—that enshrined them, and kept drowsy lis-
teners awake from the first centuries of the Christian
era. Such a story, as told by Robert Greene in *Pandosto,*
had lately been making a great impression on readers—
including Shakespeare. Encompassing a long span of
time, two sets of principals (one courtly, the other pastoral), and a broad spectrum of tragic and comic poten-
tialities, it presented the playwright with a considerable
formal challenge: How, amid such diversity and flux,
achieve aesthetic unity?

Shakespeare solves the problem boldly. His vast can-
vas consists of two self-contained, yet intimately cor-
related, panels: the secular theater's equivalent of a
Renaissance painter's hinged altarpiece. The first segment, comprising acts I–III, builds rapidly to a tragic
climax in the public tribunal in Sicily, followed by the

denouement upon the deserts of Bohemia, with the abandoned babe and hungry bear. The second half, of almost equal length, features the lovingly elaborated pastoral of the sheep-shearing feast—at over eight hundred lines one of Shakespeare's longest scenes—and, back in Sicily, a second climax, joyful this time and more spectacular than the first, when the music strikes up and Hermione descends from her pedestal in Paulina's chapel to take Leontes by the hand. With infinite skill the mood is modulated from tragedy to comedy in Act III, scene iii, as a storm breaks with savage clamor, Antigonus cries, "I am gone for ever," and makes his final exit, followed by a bear—one of the most famous stage directions in Shakespeare—leaving the royal infant to be found safe by the Shepherd. "Heavy matters, heavy matters!" he sighs after hearing his clownish son's recital of the catastrophe. "But look thee here, boy. Now bless thyself! Thou mettest with things dying, I with things new-born."

Death and rebirth: such is the work of Time, like Shelley's west wind preserver and destroyer. The two panels of the dramatic diptych are appropriately separated by the familiar allegorical figure of Father Time, who comes on stage as midpoint Chorus to turn his glass, boasting that it is in his power

> To o'erthrow law and in one self-born hour
> To plant and o'erwhelm custom. (IV.i.8–9)

The action demonstrates Time's dual function. Fittingly, he requires a speech of neither more nor fewer than sixteen couplets to survey the passage of sixteen years.

In Leontes's bosom, unlike Othello's, love cannot coexist with *tremor cordis* (fluttering of the heart), but must die and be reborn only after purgation and healing. During the long interval of the king's "saint-like sorrow" Paulina facilitates the regenerative process by remaining at his side—not to soothe his spirit but to keep green recollection of misdeeds past. Her forerunner is found in *King Lear:* like the good Earl of Kent, Paulina courageously refuses to remain silent when a wrathful autocrat unjustly repudiates the woman closest to his affections.

Being, as it is, tragicomedy rather than tragedy, the play offers the welcome presence of the happy mischief maker Autolycus, who early in the fourth act enters singing of seasonal change: Summer has at last arrived, it is a winter's tale no longer. The Folio dramatis personae lists Autolycus as "a rogue." Born, as he tells us, when the planet Mercury—named after the god of thieving—was astrologically in the ascendant, he prides himself upon being "a snapper-up of unconsidered trifles." Autolycus promptly demonstrates his vocation by picking a clown's pocket. He goes on to sing more songs, to peddle ribbons, trinkets, and ballads, and disingenuously to warn the gullible to be wary, for "there are cozeners abroad." Later, attired in court finery, he claims to have once served Prince Florizel, and to reinstate himself in his former master's good graces, he ushers the old Shepherd with his box containing the secret of Perdita's identity aboard the ship that will carry the lovers to Sicily. Thus does a thief and cutpurse contribute to the happy denouement.

The Tempest (c. 1610–11) affords exceptional opportunities for music, dance, costume, and spectacle. Songs, including some of Shakespeare's most exquisite, are numerous: nine in all, more than in any other of his plays. We hear solemn music, soft music, strange music. Pipes and tabors play; nymphs and reapers join in graceful dance. The play abounds in unearthly spirits. They carry in a banquet, dance about it with "gentle actions of salutations" (according to the Folio stage direction), then depart, only to return and dance again, this time "with mocks and mows." To the noise of hunters, spirits in the shape of hounds drive out their prey. Costumes take varied forms. Ariel enters like a water nymph, so visually resplendent as to prompt his master Prospero to admiring exclamation: "Fine apparition!'' Elsewhere, accompanied by lightning and thunder, Ariel appears in the guise of a harpy—the rapacious mythical monster with a woman's face and trunk, and the tail, legs, and talons of a bird—and claps his wings upon a table to make a banquet disappear, before rising into the air to deliver his sermon against the three "men of sin." Misshapen but with his deformities unspecified, Caliban allows free rein to the imagination of producer and actor. How he was imaged on Shakespeare's stage we do not know, but the earliest theatrical tradition (from the eighteenth century) has him covered with a bear skin, or the skin of some other wild beast, and fearsome in long, shaggy hair.

The most spectacular effects take place in the Fourth Act masque. Ceres descends, presumably on a wired throne, to be joined by Juno, after which (we may reasonably speculate) the flight mechanism raises the two goddesses to a position midway between the stage and the playhouse "heavens." Despite masque elements, *The Tempest* is not a masque, but it gave popular audiences a taste of those more removed splendors involving courtly masked revelers: music, dance, poetry, and allegorized spectacle. For some effects, such as free flights, Shakespeare's theater had an advantage over the Banqueting House stage, limited as it was by its shallow proscenium arch.

Despite the spectacle, never had Shakespeare fashioned a simpler, more uncluttered fable, nor one at the same time so richly fraught with mythic resonance. The Renaissance dream of learning was Prospero's dream when he held sway as the admired Duke of Milan. Preoccupied with secret studies, Prospero neglected worldly ends—always a dangerous recourse for a head of state—and entrusted his beloved younger brother, Antonio, with the reins of government while dedicating himself to the betterment of his own mind. But the trappings of power proved insufficient for Antonio, who came to believe he should indeed be duke, and entered into subservient league with Naples—Milan's inveterate enemy—to have rule transferred to him. A bloodless coup followed. In the dead of night, Prospero and his young daughter, Miranda, were hurried aboard a decrepit hulk of a boat—without tackle, sail, or mast—and set adrift. They had only some food and water and Prospero's precious books, supplied by the good Gonzalo. (The malignant potencies of sibling rivalry had more than once occupied Shakespeare—in *As You Like It*, in *Hamlet*, in *King Lear*. The somber tapestry does not, however, exclude brighter strands of regenerative possibility; the wicked brother in *As You Like It* tastes the sweetness of conversion.)

The island on which the refugees set foot, situated as it is somewhere between Tunis and Naples, must be Mediterranean. The word "America" fails to appear in the play, and indeed occurs only once in Shakespeare ("Where America, the Indies?" asks Antipholus of Syracuse, contemplating the rotund geography of the kitchen wench in *The Comedy of Errors);* but Ariel has fetched dew from "the still-vexed Bermoothes," and Trinculo speaks of people in England laying out money to see a dead Indian, an allusion to the exhibition of American Indians, dead or alive, brought home by the explorers. Refreshing breezes from the New World waft through this play written almost at the end of Shakespeare's career.

"Providence divine," as Prospero acknowledges, brought them ashore. These events took place twelve years before *The Tempest* begins. Now "bountiful Fortune" has placed his enemies—deposing duke and confederate king—at his mercy, for they are among the castaways Prospero's tempest has produced. What he does with them furnishes the principal business of the play.

Knowledge is power. No Shakespearean protagonist has better equipped himself for accomplishing his task than this austerely majestic scholar-prince wearing his magic robes and carrying his ceremonial staff. His mind nourished by the occult lore contained in his mysteriously unspecified books, Prospero has struggled to liberate his soul from baser passions, and achieved magical communion with the invisible world. He has freed the delicate spirit Ariel from the cloven pine in which, long years past, he had been imprisoned by the great witch Sycorax for failing to obey her behests. Prospero conjures spirits: Ariel and, through him, the hosts of elvish demi-puppets; he can raise winds and dim the sun, hurl thunderbolts and split (as well as reconstitute) ships, discern future events, render himself invisible, induce sleep, and charm his adversaries into immobility. At his command graves have opened and let forth their sleepers.

In his handbook of Renaissance magic, *De occulta philosophia* (1531), the pious German physician and wizard Henry Cornelius Agrippa postulated a universe divided into three worlds, or spheres: the elemental world of terrestrial nature, the celestial world of the stars and planets, and the super-celestial world in which the highest sanctified magic operates. Through his conjurations Prospero has gained access to all three spheres. As moderns we may fail to appreciate how suspect was the magician's vocation in the Renaissance. Prospero apart, the great magicians of Shakespeare's stage are cautionary examples. Blasphemously persuaded that "a sound magician is a demi-god," Marlowe's Doctor Faustus—the most celebrated case of all—makes his compact with Mephistopheles, and, as time runs out for him, vainly offers to burn his books. Prospero in the end abjures *his* magic, announcing that he will break his staff and drown his book. But no devils hover gleefully on the sidelines, nor does hell mouth gape open for him. In *The City of God*, St. Augustine speaks of "an art which they call either magic, or by the more abominable title necromancy, or the more honorable designation theurgy." Greene's Bacon and Marlowe's Faustus are satanic practitioners of black magic. Prospero's accomplishments are, by contrast, those—to use Agrippa's words—of "an intellect pure and conjoined with the powers of the gods, without which we shall never ascend to the scrutiny of secret things, and to the power of wonderful workings." His way is that of the theurgists revered by the neo-Platonists of the so-called Alexandrian school as ritually initiated holy magicians capable, by their incantations and other ceremonial usages, of exercising control over beneficent spiritual intelligences, high in the scale of goodness, for the working of miraculous ends. Prospero is the virtuoso par excellence of white magic.

Still, despite his superhuman resources, Prospero does not invariably have his way. Witness Caliban. Described in the Folio dramatis personae as "a savage and deformed slave," he is the only native islander "honored / With a human shape." Yet Caliban is not fully human, but, as Prospero indicates, "a born devil"—a variant of the savage man familiar from the literature of exploration and from Elizabethan pageants and masques. Formerly king of the island, Caliban has since Prospero's coming performed a slave's menial practical functions—fetching wood and making fires—for his stern but enlightened European master. The conjunction of overlord and involuntary subject has brought reciprocal benefits and penalties. Caliban has also attempted to violate Miranda, and thus to people the island with Calibans. Nurture cannot alter nature; despite Christian example, Caliban continues to worship his devil god. Inevitably, he rebels against colonizing authority. In a grotesque reprise of the events that drove Prospero from Milan, Caliban prostrates himself before a false new god, revels in illusory freedom, and, red-hot with drink, conspires with two drunken fools to murder his master. In the upshot, pinched sore by Prospero's goblins and dazzled to behold his master once again decked in his ducal finery, Caliban gives signs of having learned his hard lesson. "I'll be wise hereafter," he resolves, "and seek for grace." The devil worshiper has not previously spoken of Christian grace.

Early and late Shakespearean modes meet in *The Tempest*. Sea voyages, storms, and shipwrecks, unspoiled maidens, supernatural interventions, the workings of a beneficent Providence, and happy endings after injustice, loss and the passage of years—these are recurring patterns of Shakespeare's last, tragicomic phase. Structurally, however, *The Tempest* marks a return to the neoclassical discipline of one of the dramatist's first comedies. The play is, after *The Comedy of Errors*, Shakespeare's shortest comedy, and, like it, preserves the unities of time, place, and action. Time assumes an almost mystic import in the play, as all the astrological signs confirm the propriety of the chosen moment (I.ii. 180–84). "What is the time i' th' day?" Prospero asks his ministering spirit in the same scene. Two hours past midday, we learn, with much to be done before six. In the last act, six o'clock—as is clearly avouched—has arrived. It is appropriate that a play in which the particularities of time assume such consequence should contain, in the "Our revels now are ended" speech, Shakespeare's most eloquent evocation—indeed, arguably the most eloquent in world literature—of the transience of earthly glories; indeed, ultimately, of all mortal things.

In four hours—less in the theater—a ship has been wrecked, miraculously without casualties; a young man and young woman have met, fallen in love, and pledged matrimony; a king has given up his son for lost, found him, repented his misdeeds, and begged forgiveness; a magician has freed his spirit servant and recovered his dukedom, and his daughter has discovered how beauteous mankind is. All this, and much more, takes place in *The Tempest*, not to mention the profound philosophical undercurrents of which readers and audiences have for so long been conscious. "O, rejoice," honest old Gonzalo cries in his elated summing up, "beyond a common joy."

In Act I, scene iv, of *Henry VIII*, Cardinal Wolsey—still in his glory as the corruptly rich and arrogant lord chancellor—hosts a lavish supper party at York Place. The guests exchange pleasantries as they gather around the long banqueting table, cheeks flushed with wine. A noble company of masked strangers costumed as shepherds arrives by barge. It is the king and his party. As music sounds, he chooses one of the queen's maids of honor for a partner. Clearly Anne Bullen's beauty instantly entrances him. ''Your grace, / I fear, with dancing is a little heated,'' Wolsey remarks after the measure; and the king replies, ''I fear, too much.'' It is a fateful encounter. Henry will subsequently develop a conscientious scruple that will impel him to dissolve, after an aborted public trial, his marriage with Katherine of Aragon. For his second wife he will take Anne of the thousand days. She will give him—before the play is over—a daughter, Elizabeth, who will become England's greatest queen.

This is the matter of the drama replete with pomp and stage spectacle. In addition to oboes, drum, and trumpet, Wolsey's banquet calls for the discharge of chambers—small cannons used for ceremonial occasions. Calamity resulted when *Henry VIII* had an early performance at the Globe on June 29, 1613. Sir Henry Wotton excitedly described the event three days later in a letter to his nephew, and in so doing reported an alternative title for the play:

> The King's players had a new play, called *All is True*, representing some principal pieces of the reign of Henry VIII, which was set forth with many extraordinary circumstances of pomp and majesty, even to the matting of the stage; the Knights of the Order with their Georges and gaters, the Guards with their embroidered coats, and the like. . . . Now, King Henry making a masque at the Cardinal Wolsey's house, and certain chambers being shot off at his entry, some of the paper, or other stuff, wherewith one of them was stopped, did light on the thatch, where being thought at first but an idle smoke, and their eyes more attentive to the show, it kindled inwardly and ran round like a train, consuming within less than an hour the whole house to the very grounds.

Miraculously there were no fatalities, or even injuries, only a pair of burned breeches. A year later a second

Globe playhouse, rebuilt at company expense on the same site, opened its doors to the public. This time the roof was prudently tiled.

Shakespeare, by then just turned fifty, may well have already reckoned that this was a good time to think seriously of disposing of his share in the King's Men and retiring to the great house he had long since acquired in the town of his birth. John Fletcher was waiting in the wings to take Shakespeare's place as principal dramatist for the troupe. Then in his mid-thirties, Fletcher had already made his mark with stylish plays in varied modes, among them *The Maid's Tragedy* and *A King and No King,* a tragicomedy—both written in collaboration with Francis Beaumont—as well as *The Woman's Prize, or The Tamer Tamed,* a boisterous sequel to *The Taming of the Shrew.* Most authorities now believe that Shakespeare and Fletcher together wrote *Henry VIII.* While there is no corroborating external evidence in the form of a title-page ascription or the like—joint authorship being first suggested by the Victorian scholar James Spedding in 1850—such collaboration between the retiring master and his up-and-coming successor does not inherently strain probability, and a great quantity of stylistic and linguistic evidence has been adduced in support of the hypothesis.

Yet despite stylistic differences from scene to scene, *Henry VIII* in performance leaves a remarkably unified impression. Its subject marks a departure for Shakespeare. If his acting company was now and then summoned by royal command to play before Elizabeth, in his art he mainly left the Tudors well enough alone. To be sure, he salutes their ascendancy at the close of *Richard III* when the Earl of Richmond—the future Henry VII—triumphs over Crookback Richard on Bosworth field, and, comfortably slipping into the royal "we," announces the union of the red rose and the white. But *Richard III* came fairly early in Shakespeare's career, and he did not attempt a full-scale dramatization of a Tudor monarch's reign until a decade after the last had passed from the scene. In Richmond's son he chose a figure that historians, biographers, and other playwrights have found endlessly fascinating.

Little wonder that, after the passage of four centuries, posterity has yet to arrive at any consensus with respect to Henry's character and accomplishment. "Without him the storm of the Reformation would still have burst over England; without him, it might have been far more terrible . . . it was well that she had as her King, in her hour of need, a man, and a man who counted the cost, who faced the risk, and who did with his might whatsoever his hand found to do." So A. F. Pollard concludes his classic biography of Henry VIII. To Charles Dickens, on the other hand, Henry was "a most intolerable ruffian, a disgrace to human nature and a blot of blood and grease upon the history of England." We may with Hamlet say, look here upon this picture and on this. Of course Dickens was no historian, just as Pollard was not an artist. Shakespeare had no such options from which to choose: Writing before revisionist historians called into question the divine-right assumptions of monarchical rule, he and his collaborator (if he had one) were not required to find, much less solve, the riddle of Henry's character. Their mood, as the play's trappings suggest, is celebratory rather than probingly analytic. *Henry VIII* is, uniquely, Shakespeare's festive history.

With *The Two Noble Kinsmen,* performed with great applause at the Blackfriars theater, our survey of Shakespeare's writings comes to a close, for this tragicomedy belongs to 1613, almost certainly the last year of his playwriting career; he had only a few years of life remaining. The morris dance featured in Act III, scene v, makes use of personages who also take part in Francis Beaumont's *Masque of the Inner Temple and Gray's Inn,* presented before King James on February 20, 1613. The masque was a great success, and, accordingly, Shakespeare's troupe—some of whom may have performed in this courtly entertainment—capitalized on its celebrity by incorporating a version of it in a play for the general public soon after. *The Two Noble Kinsmen,* however, did not find a place in the great 1623 Folio—although in the prefatory address "To the Great Variety of Readers" the editors do imply that the collection will include all of Shakespeare's plays—but first saw print in a quarto edition in 1634—almost twenty years after Shakespeare's death—and is described on the title page as the work of "the memorable Worthies of their time; Mr. John Fletcher, and Mr. William Shakespeare Gent." The play was omitted from the 1647 Fletcher folio, although it did appear in the second edition of that collection in 1679. (Fletcher often worked in conjunction with other playwrights.)

The Two Noble Kinsmen belongs far more with Fletcher than with Shakespeare, and has been excluded from many collected editions of Shakespeare. The first sentence of Peter Quennell and Hamish Johnson's *Who's Who in Shakespeare* (1973) states unequivocally that Shakespeare's creative life "had ended before 1613," and that his contribution to *The Two Noble Kinsmen*— if indeed he made one—"is thought to have been relatively small." So much for comprehensiveness. But the tragicomedy appears in the Complete Signet Classic Shakespeare and the Complete Oxford Shakespeare, and will appear in the New Cambridge Shakespeare; scholarly times, as do other times, change. So does performance choice. *The Two Noble Kinsmen* is now beginning to enjoy a belated second stage life. Not known to have been professionally acted from the eighteenth century until its Old Vic revival in 1928, the play was, in 1986, the inaugural choice for the RSC's new intimate house in Stratford-upon-Avon, the Swan Theatre, and on opening night was received with enthusiasm by a large and appreciative audience that included this writer.

In *The Canterbury Tales* Chaucer gave pride of place to the long—over 3,100 lines—and elegantly pictorial Knight's Tale, which itself mainly derived from the much longer *Teseida* of Boccaccio. By Shakespeare's day *The Canterbury Tales,* two centuries or thereabout old, had achieved classic status. Lost plays inspired by the Knight's Tale were staged in 1566 and 1594. Shakespeare knew it early on in his dramatic career, for he used the wedding of Duke Theseus and Hippolyta, Queen of the Amazons—scheduled to take place the night of the next new moon—in *A Midsummer Night's Dream;* Chaucer, at the outset of the tale, had alluded to the couple's wedding feast. Shakespeare's contribution to *The Two Noble Kinsmen,* as far as may be determined by stylistic and linguistic tests, seems to have been after all by no means negligible: He is credited with scenes, in whole or in part, in each of the play's five acts; the style of the Shakespearean passages densely textured, the Fletcherian scenes being more colloquially everyday, as was that playwright's wont. The Epilogue—manifestly by Fletcher—refers to "the tale [e.g., Chaucer's] we have told—/ For 'tis no other" and bids "He that has / Loved a young handsome wench, then, show his face"; for the play *is* a romance.

A spectacular romance. *The Two Noble Kinsmen* opens before a temple. Hymen—the god of marriage— enters *"with a torch burning; a boy in white robe before, singing and strewing flowers; after Hymen, a nymph, encompassed in her tresses* [i.e., with hair loose, betokening her virginity] *bearing a wheaten garland* [symbolic of fertility and peace]; *then Theseus between two other nymphs with wheaten chaplets* [i.e., wreaths] *on their heads; then Hippolyta the bride, led by Pirithous and another holding a garland over her head, her tresses likewise hanging; after her, Emilia holding up her train.* The song that follows celebrates flowers: roses, daisies ("smell-less, yet most quaint"), primrose, marigolds, etc. Flowers are strewn. The entry of three queens in black, with stained veils, interrupts the marriage celebration. The first falls down at the feet of Theseus, the second at the feet of Hippolyta, and the third at the feet of Emilia. The queens beg for the bones of their slain husbands, whom cruel Creon, King of Thebes, will not bury.

War follows. Arcite and Palamon—the two noble

kinsmen of the title (they are cousins and Creon's nephews)—battle heroically, and, wounded and nearly dead,
heal and are imprisoned, supposedly for life. From their
cell on the stage's upper level they look down, and each
in turn spies Emilia, "fresher than May," walking in
her garden below. Both fall irretrievably in love with
the same woman. Spectacular effects and events follow.
Doves flutter, "incense and sweet odors" are wafted,
a rose tree with a single rose ascends, "a sudden twang
of instruments" is heard, "and the rose falls from the
tree." *The Two Noble Kinsmen* is, indeed, as spectacular a play as one could reasonably expect in the intimate confines of the Blackfriars theater. And the Jailor's
Daughter, as she goes mad with necessarily unrequited
love for Palamon, is—as performance has lately demonstrated—one of the play's star turns. *The Two Noble
Kinsmen is* show business. So are all of Shakespeare's
plays. But, at the same time, ever so much more than
show business.

11

Postscript

"He hath much land and fertile . . . ," Hamlet says of the contemptible Osric. " 'Tis a chough"—a bird of the crow family—"but, as I say, spacious in the possession of dirt" (V.ii.88–90). Shortly after writing these lines, their author became himself spacious in the possession of dirt. On May 1, 1601, Shakespeare bought, for £320 in cash, 107 acres of arable land in Old Stratford, a farming area about a mile and a half north of town: a large sum for a large tract. The same month, he also purchased a cottage (perhaps to lodge a servant or gardener) and a quarter acre of land on the south side of Chapel Lane, facing the New Place garden. Three years later, the dramatist laid out £440 for a half interest in the lease of "tithes of corn, grain, blade, and hay" in three nearby hamlets—Old Stratford, Welcombe, and Bishopton—along with the small tithes of the whole of Stratford parish, with certain exceptions honoring former rights. He also agreed to pay rents totaling £22 per annum, and to collect—or have collected—the tithes himself. Shakespeare's portfolio of real estate investments included a London property, the Blackfriars Gatehouse, situated in the desirable Blackfriars district, a stone's throw from his company's winter playhouse. This he bought in 1613. Proximity to the theater would hardly have mattered much, however, if—as may be gathered—Shakespeare had begun to think of retiring from the stage; in making the purchase, he was following the example of his fellow, Richard Burbage, who owned several parcels in the district. To these holdings may be added his father's house in Henley Street. Other townsmen had larger tithe holdings than Shakespeare and were richer. But he had succeeded in restoring his family's decayed fortunes and would pass down to his heirs an entailed estate. He could not have predicted how soon the entire direct line would be extinguished—before the century's end—and that only the art would endure.

"The latter part of his life was spent," according to his early biographer, "as all men of good sense will wish theirs may be, in ease, retirement, and the conversation of his friends. He had the good fortune to gather an estate equal to his occasion, and, in that, to his wish, and is said to have spent some years before his death at his native Stratford." He also had his two daughters. The elder married well. Susanna's husband, John Hall, was a respected Stratford physician who gained (we are told) "great fame for his skill, far and near." They had one child, Elizabeth; she married twice and died childless in 1670. The other daughter, Judith, did not marry until 1616, when she was thirty-one; her husband, Thomas Quiney, was the ne'er-do-well son of an upstanding Stratford citizen. Before marrying, he had had an affair with a Stratford woman, Margaret Wheeler. Just a month after the wedding she died in childbirth, and the infant with her. For this delinquency Quiney was hailed before the ecclesiastical court, but let off with a small fine. A vintner, he set up shop at The Cage in the town center. The Quineys had three children, all born after Shakespeare's death.

On January, either in 1615 or 1616, while still "in perfect health and memory," the dramatist drew up his last will and testament. In March 1616, after Judith's wedding, he summoned his attorney to make revisions dictated, it seems, by the Margaret Wheeler scandal. By now he was dying; a feeble hand held the pen that validated the three sheets of the will. To Judith he left money—with strings attached—and his silver-gilt bowl. The bulk of the estate, including the Great House of New Place, the double house in Henley Street, the gatehouse in Blackfriars, and all the rest of his "goods, chattels, leases, plate, jewels, and household stuff,'' after his debts and legacies had been paid, and his funeral expenses discharged, was bequeathed to the Halls. All the goods, that is, except the second-best bed. This went to the widow. It is the only mention of Anne in the will, and in an interlineation at that. What are we to make of this bequest? Its significance, despite endless debate, can only be guessed, but possibly the bed carried rich matrimonial associations, the best bed being reserved for guests at New Place; an heirloom, it would naturally pass to the legal heir. Custom entitled the widow to her portion, a life interest of one third of her husband's land and possibly also of his chattels. There was no need for further testamentary specification. In his will Shakespeare remembered Stratford locals, and he did not forget the town poor. Nor did he overlook his long-standing fellows, friends of his days with the King's Men, for he left sums for memorial rings for Burbage, Heminges, and Condell. The last two, very tangibly, would not forget him either.

Presumably one or more of the surviving adult members of Shakespeare's family commissioned the white marble monument, with a limestone bust, in Holy Trinity, executed by Gheerart Janssen, a Southwark stonemason of Dutch origin whose shop stood not far from the Globe. The half-length effigy—one of only two authenticated likenesses—represents the poet as a plump Stratford burgher in the act of composition, a quill in his right hand and a sheet of paper under the left.

The monument must have existed by 1623, for it is mentioned in one of the commendatory poems published that year in the First Folio collection of Shakespeare's plays that his ''pious fellows,'' Heminges and Condell, issued. They dedicated the large and expensive volume, for which the Jonson folio of 1616 furnished a precedent, to two noble brethren, the earls of Pembroke and Montgomery, noting that their lordships had ''been pleased to think these trifles something, heretofore; and have prosecuted both them, and their author living, with so much favor.'' The title page features the familiar

Droeshout engraving, the second authoritative representation. In their epistle "To the Great Variety of Readers," the first editors praise (with pardonable exaggeration) the happy facility of their friend and fellow: "His mind and hand went together, and what he thought, he uttered with that easiness, that we have scarce received from him a blot in his papers." From study of the text we know that Shakespeare, like other authors, did in fact revise. There follows Jonson's celebrated eulogy of the Sweet Swan of Avon, the monument without a tomb, the artist who was not of an age but for all time. Some half of the plays in the Folio, including some of the best loved (among them *Twelfth Night*, *Julius Caesar*, and *Macbeth*) had not before seen print; their creator's satisfaction must have lain not in seeing them through the press but in performance on the living stage. Posterity would ask for more.

Shakespeare's old colleagues speak with self-effacing affection about their departed colleague. Theirs has been clearly a labor of love, "without"—they attest— "ambition either of self-profit or fame; only to keep the memory of so worthy a friend and fellow alive, as was our Shakespeare." Greene excepted, none of his contemporaries seems to have uttered, publicly at least, a harsh word about Shakespeare, although we could wish the scattered testimonials were ampler and more numerous. On October 25, 1598, Richard Quiney, twice elected bailiff of Stratford, had written to his "loving good friend and countryman Mr. Wm. Shakespeare," requesting a loan of £30 (in those days no inconsiderable sum) upon good security; evidently Shakespeare was considered a solid enough citizen to be worth so approaching. In 1605 the actor Augustine Phillips remembered Shakespeare in his will with a thirty-shilling piece in gold. When not under encomiastic obligations, Jonson in his commonplace book confessed he loved the man and honored his memory this side of idolatry. Other poets refer to "good Will," to Shakespeare as generous "in mind and mood," and to "friendly Shakespeare's tragedies." More than half a century after the dramatist's death, Aubrey noted in his jottings: "He was a handsome, well-shaped man: very good company, and of a very ready and pleasant smooth wit."

Let Shakespeare's first biographer, himself a poet and playwright, have the last word. Nicholas Rowe thus sums up his subject: "Besides the advantages of his wit, he was in himself a good-natured man, of great sweetness in his manners, and a most agreeable companion; so that it is no wonder if with so many good qualities he made himself acquainted with the best conversations of those times." He would be remembered as Gentle Will Shakespeare: a fitting designation for the innate gentleman who was not gently born.

Reading List

Biography

The author himself has written extensively on Shakespeare's life. In *Shakespeare's Lives* (Oxford, 1970; rev. 1990) he chronicled the search for information, the discovery of the Shakespeare records, and the evolution of Shakespearean biography from the beginnings to the present day. This book was followed by *William Shakespeare: A Documentary Life* (Oxford, 1975), containing numerous photographic facsimiles individually commented upon, and by *William Shakespeare: A Compact Documentary Life* (Oxford, 1977; rev. 1987), furnishing the essential information—*sans* most of the facsimiles—in a more economical format. This volume was followed by *William Shakespeare: Records and Images* (London/New York, 1981), containing, in addition to exposition, numerous additional facsimiles. He has also contributed chapters on the life of Shakespeare to *A New Companion to Shakespeare Studies*, ed. Kenneth Muir and Schoenbaum (Cambridge, 1971) and *The Cambridge Companion to Shakespeare Studies*, ed. Stanley Wells (Cambridge, 1986). Always a vigorous articulator of his views, A. L. Rowse has produced a number of books on Shakespeare's life, of which the first, *William Shakespeare: A Biography* (London, 1963), although in some ways superseded by the author's subsequent polemics, remains the fullest and most useful. Mark Eccles, *Shakespeare in Warwickshire* (Madison, Wis., 1961), is a slender volume which repays consultation for the wealth of reliably presented factual information.

217

E. A. J. Honigmann's *Shakespeare: the 'lost years'*
(Manchester, 1985) is more stimulating and also more
controversial.

Shakespeare's Language

The state of the English language in Shakespeare's day
and his deployment of English grammar, idioms, vocabulary, etc., are most conveniently surveyed by Karl J.
Holzknecht, ''Shakespeare's English,'' *Backgrounds
of Shakespeare's Plays* (New York, 1950), pp. 186–
219. Still useful is Stuart Robertson, *The Development
of Modern English* (2nd printing, with additions and
revisions; New York, 1946). More recent work includes, among others, James H. Sledd, *A Short Introduction to English Grammar* (Chicago, 1959) and
Thomas Pyles and John Algeo, *Problems in the Origin
and Development of the English Language* (2nd ed;
New York, 1972).

Shakespeare's Predecessors, Contemporaries, and Successors

In a series of major historical surveys of dramatic history, E. K. Chambers (later Sir Edmund) assembled a
vast corpus of English dramatic history: *The Mediaeval
Stage* (Oxford, 1903), *The Elizabethan Stage* (4 vols.;
Oxford, 1923), and *William Shakespeare: A Study of
Facts and Problems* (2 vols.; Oxford, 1930). Never mind
that the legitimate terminus for a history of the early
English stage is 1642, when the theaters were shut down
until the Restoration of the monarchy in 1660; Chambers carries on until 1616—the year of Shakespeare's
death—even though players and playwrights carried on
for decades after the master's demise. Fortunately, a
splendidly equipped historian was found in G. E. Bent-
ley to continue the account in *The Jacobean and Car-
oline Stage*, which requires seven volumes to chronicle,
with inevitable overlaps with Chambers, some twenty-

five years of dramatic history (Oxford, 1941–68). F. P.
Wilson did not live to complete his volume on the drama
for the Oxford History of English Literature, but his
segment, *The English Drama, 1485–1585* (1969) was
edited and seen through the press by G. K. Hunter,
who has promised to continue the story until 1660. Pe-
destrian in style and sensibility but conveniently economical and level-headed is Thomas Marc Parrott and
Robert Hunter Ball, *A Short View of Elizabethan Drama*
(New York, 1943). Two extensive series of editions of
individual plays, the Revels Plays (London; subsequently Manchester), of which Clifford Leech was General Editor from 1958 until his death in 1971,
responsibilities then assumed by F. David Hoeniger; and
the more numerous, if less elaborate, editions in the
Regents Renaissance Drama Series (Lincoln, Neb.), of
which Cyrus Hoy was General Editor from the outset
in 1963, perform an invaluable service for students.

Playhouses and Stages

The most useful and up-to-date guide is Andrew Gurr,
The Shakespearean Stage 1524–1642 (2nd ed,; Cambridge, 1980). Chapters on the subject by Richard Hosley, "The Playhouses and the Stage," and Daniel
Seltzer, "The Actors and Staging," are to be found in
the *New Companion*, pp. 15–31, 35–54, and by Peter
Thomson, "Playhouse and players in the time of Shakespeare," in the *Cambridge Companion*, pp. 67–83, as
well as by Hosley in "The playhouses," in *The Revels
History of Drama in English* (London, 1975), vol. III,
1576–1613.

In 1916—midway through the Great War—the Clar-
endon Press published, in a sumptuous edition to mark
the tercentenary of Shakespeare's death, *Shakespeare's
England: An Account of the Life and Manners of His
Age*. The work had been long in preparation: Sir Walter
Raleigh had sketched the first plan for the contents in
1909; Sir Sidney Lee and C. T. Onions would serve as

General Editors. *Shakespeare's England* consists of chapters by many hands: on the age, on religion, the army and navy, voyages and land travel, education and scholarship, the fine arts, heraldry, costume, the homes, London and the life of the town, authors, patrons, booksellers, printers, and the stationers' trade, rogues and vagabonds, ballads and broadsides; not to mention Shakespeare's English and a number of other topics: God's plenty. Needless to say, this compilation—now almost three quarters of a century old—no longer has an air of the first freshness. But in its own day it no doubt helped keep the home fires burning during the mayhem and privations of war. And these volumes bring together a wealth of information which has never in their aggregate been superseded and which may still be consulted with pleasure and enlightenment.

Criticism

A concise, selective, and engaging survey is Arthur M. Eastman, *A Short History of Shakespeare Criticism* (New York, 1968). Chapters reviewing critical history are M. A. Shaaber, "Shakespeare Criticism: Dryden to Bradley" and Stanley Wells, "Shakespeare Criticism Since Bradley," in the *New Companion*, pp. 239–48, 249–61; and, in the *Cambridge Companion*, by Harry Levin, "Critical Approaches to Shakespeare from 1660 to 1904," and "Twentieth-Century Shakespeare Criticism: (a) Lawrence Danson, The Comedies, (b) Kenneth Muir, The Tragedies, (c) Edward Berry, The Histories," in the *Cambridge Companion*, pp. 213–29, 230–56. In addition, original critical essays and annual surveys of the year's work in criticism may be found in *Shakespeare Survey* (an annual publication sponsored by Cambridge University Press) and *Shakespeare Quarterly*, sponsored by the Folger Shakespeare Library in Washington, D.C.

Addenda

Glynne Wickham's worthy survey of the development of dramatic art in Christian Europe during the Middle Ages, *The Medieval Theatre* (3rd ed.; Cambridge, 1987), inadvertently failed to be included in the Reading List. Ms. Margaret Tocci helpfully furnished an additional pair of eyes when I had to go over page proofs on short notice.